La Cucina Siciliana di Gangivecchio

Gangivecchio's Sicilian Kitchen

La Cucina Siciliana di Gangivecchio

Gangivecchio's Sicilian Kitchen

Wanda and Giovanna Tornabene
with Michele Evans

Photographs by Michele Evans

Alfred A. Knopf   *New York*   1996

THIS IS A BORZOI BOOK
PUBLISHED BY ALFRED A. KNOPF, INC.

http://www.randomhouse.com/

Library of Congress Cataloging-in-Publication Data
Tornabene, Wanda.
La cucina siciliana di Gangivecchio = Gangivecchio's Sicilian
kitchen / Wanda and Giovanna Tornabene with Michele Evans.
—1st ed.
p.   cm.
Includes index.
ISBN 0-679-42510-1
1. Cookery, Italian—Sicilian style.   I. Tornabene, Giovanna.
II. Evans, Michele.   III. Title.
TX723.2.S55T67   1995
641.5945'8—dc20   96-4119
CIP

Manufactured in the United States of America

First Edition

for Enzo

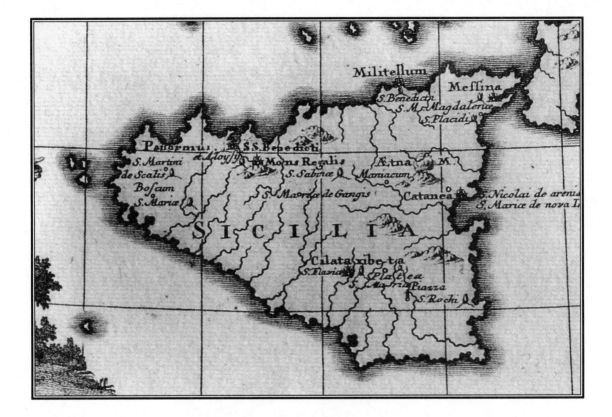

$\mathcal{C}$ontenuto

(Contents)

Full-color photographs follow pages 12, 108, 172, 236, and 268.

$\mathcal{P}$remessa

(Foreword)

$\mathcal{W}$riting about Italian food always appealed to me tremendously, but, aside from passion, there was never solid justification to do so—until, in the fall of 1992, I had the unique opportunity to work with Wanda and Giovanna Tornabene, a mother and daughter who live in the remote interior mountains of Sicily in a restored fourteenth-century Benedictine monastery where they operate an extraordinary restaurant. If I had any reservations about this undertaking, they vanished at my first meeting with the Tornabenes in New York when Giovanna told me, "For this book, we will let our hearts talk." They kept that promise.

Wanda, the charming matriarch of the family, is diminutive, with short blond hair and a winning smile. A dynamic personality, she also possesses a fiery temper and an enthusiasm for life that is contagious. I came to regard her as a spirited heroine, a Sicilian Karen Blixen—proud, courageous, enterprising, stubborn, wise, nature loving, and wonderfully eccentric, witty, and fun.

Green-eyed Giovanna, also blond and petite with a radiant smile, is extremely bright and genial with a keen sense of humor. Fiercely loyal and somewhat shy, she prefers to remain quietly in the background. Her refrain is, "Mamma is the star. I am the happy stage manager in our production of life."

Wanda and Giovanna spent the fall and winter accumulating and working on their recipes. I arrived in Sicily the following May to live and work with them for a month—the first of four such visits. At the time, Wanda spoke no English and my Italian consisted only of kitchen, food, restaurant, and shopping vocabulary, so throughout our collaboration, Giovanna was the consummate translator, with ever enthusiastic responses to Wanda's "*Che dice?*" or my "What did she say?"

Just reaching Gangivecchio, in the northeast inland Madonie Mountains, roughly halfway between Palermo and Taormina, is a rather daunting, if fascinating two-hour pilgrimage. It's necessary to follow a network of small roads that turn and climb and dip through breathtaking views over expansive valleys—a dramatic geography of extremes dotted with shepherds with their flocks of sheep, grazing cattle, isolated farms, and stone house ruins. In the spring vast patches of green pastures, rose-purple sulla, yellow ginestra, and red poppy fields carpet the landscape. In the fall the panorama is transformed into a sepia canvas. Eventually, across an enormous valley, the startling sight of the ancient town of Gangi appears. Its buildings completely cover the cloche-shaped slopes of Monte Marone like a gigantic, intricately carved piece of ivory.

From Gangi, it's only a short distance to Gangivecchio, where I had my first meal in Wanda and Giovanna's magical restaurant. It began with creamy black olive and tuna pâtés on grilled bread (*crostini*) and anchovy fritters as antipasti, followed by two pastas: one with a red sauce—a sumptuous blend of eggplant and tomatoes; then one with a green sauce—an unusual five-nut-based pesto that became one of my favorite Gangivecchio dishes. A buttery-textured, intense-flavored veal *involtini* stuffed with bread crumbs and cheese came served with slightly bitter-tasting fresh wild greens and spicy stewed and sautéed potatoes. Desserts were the best-imaginable cannoli and Wanda's splendid *sofficini,* light-as-air, square little pastries filled with lemon pastry cream.

That meal, I soon discovered, was typical of the Tornabenes' singular style of delicious Sicilian cooking, whether in the restaurant or their home dining room—straightforward, well balanced, and extremely flavorful. Individual dishes are wondrous blends of foods and textures, such as fragrant pasta with cauliflower, pine nuts, raisins, and saffron; *anelletti al forno,* a luscious baked timbale of pasta with veal and vegetables; and other remarkable offerings, like a two-inch-thick slab of swordfish roasted on bay leaves with an oregano-and-bread-crumb topping, drizzled with lemon juice and olive oil.

The Tornabenes' is a flexible, robust cuisine, created in an alliance with nature, but one that is uncomplicated and easy to translate into the American kitchen. It is a universally appealing Sicilian version of regional comfort food.

Beyond the recipes themselves, I was introduced to the Madonie's incredible ferla mushrooms, one of the world's greatest and least-known species, as well as *estratto,* a pungent concentrated paste extract of tomatoes. The Tornabenes' exuberant, basic old-fashioned cooking also taught me sensible techniques and practices, such as using Parmesan cheese rinds—normally discarded as useless—in sauces, soups, and ragus, to impart a subtle flavoring. I quickly came to appreciate the rewards of their inherently fundamental cooking style. Wanda's *spezzatino di vitello,* a veal stew made only with olive oil, onion, veal, tomato paste, water, and vegetable bouillon cubes, sugar, salt and pepper, plus a little flour as a thickener, is a masterpiece of simplicity with a distinct, bold flavor.

Throughout our work sessions Wanda and Giovanna also continued to cook for and run their restaurant, so I was able to sample a little—sometimes a lot—of everything. Wanda feels most comfortable cooking in her home kitchen, but for guests in the restaurant she works in a sizable contemporary kitchen.

Although sensible portions are served in the restaurant (seconds are always available), informal meals are a leisurely paced, generous succession of dishes. At least four forks rest next to your plate at the table at Gangivecchio. The mere sight of this quartet of forks elicits contented sighs of anticipation from diners, especially the restaurant's loyal Sicilian followers.

With the passage of time I became more immersed in the Tornabenes' lives, got better acquainted with their staff, their family and friends, and their beloved animals. During my four extended stays at Gangivecchio, I consumed hundreds of outstanding dishes and meals with Wanda and Giovanna in their restaurant, and when there were no guests, we ate in their home dining room or at Tenuta Gangivecchio, the restaurant in the small *albergo* that is adjacent to the abbey and is run by Wanda's son, Paolo, and his wife, Betty. All the Tornabenes are superb cooks and dine together every night.

After dinner on quiet evenings, Wanda and Giovanna regaled me with family stories, amusing or haunting, of past and present days at Gangivecchio. They brought out old family photograph albums and antique, exquisitely beaded gowns and mother-of-pearl and lace fans that Wanda's mother-in-law, Giovanna, had once worn to elegant balls in Palermo's grand palazzi. On breaks from our daily work, Giovanna showed me the abbey's sixteenth-century frescoes, and the wine and olive oil presses. Ultimately, we explored every inch of the abbey and grounds: the private family chapel and the main church; secret passageways; glassless round-windowed attics atop the restaurant, where only pigeons and other birds live; the gardens, orchards, and the stables—even the animal cemetery.

Thanks to the Tornabenes, Gangivecchio was a place I came to know intimately and where I felt completely at home. This chance assignment (for which I am eternally indebted to Esther Newberg, my agent) has been an illuminating privilege, an unforgettable, joyous chapter of my life. Beyond the immeasurable pleasures of Wanda and Giovanna's friendship and engaging days at Gangivecchio, foremost in my recollections are the heady aromas and earthy flavors of food—bowls of steaming pasta laced with sauces of fennel and lamb, creamy fresh fava beans or sardines; plates of velvety mushroom and pumpkin risottos; chickens roasting with onions and rosemary; bubbling, herb-infused succulent veal and sausage ragus; and the sweet smells of ricotta, watermelon, and wild berry tarts baking in ovens. These are but a few exhilarating food memories from the wealth of dishes in this collection that I now re-create in our own kitchen.

After reading this enchanting, candid portrait and trying the Tornabenes' recipes, I think these two amazing women will have the same effect on you that they had on me—they will enrich not only your dining habits but your life as well.

—*Michele Evans*

I Miei Ringraziamenti Come una Favola

(My Acknowledgments Are a Little Tale)

Now that this book is done, with the exception of these words, I'm sitting in the second-floor living room at Gangivecchio in my favorite chair gazing out the balcony doors. But what I'm looking at is not the usual view, not the ancient pine trees. What I see are the images of personal memories. Although these vivid images come to me in a flash, like a movie passing before my eyes, in reality they occurred over two years, took many miles of travel, and involved family as well as old and new friends in my life. They make up the story of how this book became a reality. To my daughter, Giovanna, and me, it is a little fairy tale.

The story begins when Peter Gethers, a writer and editor from New York, arrived with his friend Janis Donnaud for their second lunch, four days after their first, at our restaurant at Gangivecchio in the late spring of 1992. Peter, satiated with spectacular Greek temples, Norman cathedrals and palazzi, Baroque museums and Roman mosiacs during their brief tour of Sicily, returned here hungry for the simpler pleasures of my *casareccia con la frutta secca* (pasta with a nut pesto sauce) and *sofficini* (small pastries filled with lemon-flavored cream). After their meal, a pleasant, long conversation, and a tour of our fourteenth-century home, Peter asked Giovanna and me if we would consider writing a cookbook for Americans about our Sicilian food. This was a great compliment, but flattered as we were, we thought he was simply being kind. After he and Janis left, we put the book idea totally out of our minds. When Peter called several weeks later, inquiring when we could come to New York to sign a contract and find a co-author, we were, all at once, astonished, elated, and terrified. I would not be honest if I didn't admit that, initially, I was strongly opposed to writing this book, adamantly refusing to give away our family recipes. It's true, Giovanna's enthusiasm and persuasive arguments in favor of the project began to wear me down. But the ultimate reason I finally agreed to embark on this extraordinary adventure was that Peter Gethers, a tall, bearded, mysterious young American man, traveled to Gangivecchio—and everywhere else, I later learned—not only with his companion, Janis, but with Norton, his handsome little cat. Such a man as this, I decided, could be trusted in life.

With butterflies in our stomachs, Giovanna and I soon found ourselves on a plane flying to New York for our first trip to the United States. Packed in our bags in the giant belly below us were my late mother-in-law's one-hundred-year-old *mattarello* (rolling pin), a plastic bag of *estratto* (Sicily's rich concentrated tomato paste), a fresh Gangivecchio caciocavallo cheese, tiny envelopes of vanilla crystals, and a few other foods—practical culinary amulets of travel. Also with us was Lucia Regalbuto, our young maid and kitchen assistant, who was leaving Sicily for the first time ever, and our good friend Princess Giuseppina di Salvo De Gregorio, who, exhausted from the pressures of managing her vineyards and related businesses here in Sicily, appreciated an excuse to get away, especially to return to New York. She had told us not to worry about anything. "New York is a fantastic city. I know it well and I will show you everything." This turned out to be true, except that we got lost on our first subway ride and ended up in a strange city called Queens. We were mesmerized by everything we saw in New York—from Ellis Island, the Statue of Liberty, the great museums, and colossal buildings to terrific restaurants, shops and stores, and an enchanting Broadway musical, a fantasy called *Cats*. So far, we have seen it twice.

These surprising, exciting developments were all happening because Mary Taylor Simeti, an American-born food historian and author of several books, who has lived in Sicily for over thirty years, had written a generous article about Gangivecchio and our restaurant that had appeared in *The New York Times* the previous spring. As a result of having read the article, Peter, Janis, and Norton came the long distance to sample our food, and believe me, hidden away in the interior Madonie Mountains, we are not easy to find. So to Mary, we are more than a little appreciative.

To Peter Gethers, for liking our food so much, proposing the book idea, having faith in us, and for his editorial wisdom and many kindnesses, including many splendid dinners and his company on a daylong tour of New York's outstanding food shops and markets, Giovanna and I can only express our sincerest, heartfelt gratitude. We would like to acknowledge Judith Jones for allowing us to become Knopf authors and Amy Scheibe for her expert editing on the recipes. And we warmly thank Janis Donnaud for being supportive through this whole endeavor.

On that first trip to New York we cooked a dinner for a dozen members of our new publishing family. We thank Kathleen Moloney and Dominick Abel for welcoming two Sicilian strangers into their home and abandoning their kitchen to us for that dinner party.

From the time we met our co-author, Michele Evans, in New York over lunch, our collaboration has been a joy. Beyond her love of food and culinary skills, she listened well. Michele has interpreted Giovanna's own English translation of our story—our history, lives, and environment, and, most important, our recipes—with sensitivity. She also tested and adapted our recipes in her American kitchen. And we will never forget her superb work photographing the pictures in this book, capturing for us, through her eyes, the exact beauty of our little world and our food.

I can still see Giovanna and Michele in their small office off the dining room, writing at their desks or at the computer monster. And I can hear their voices talking, talking, talking. I hear Giovanna call to me, "Mamma, she wants to know exactly how much sugar you add to the *cassata,* or to this or that." More measuring. More weighing. More questions. More talking.

During the times we worked together here at Gangivecchio, Giovanna and I cooked our recipes for Michele so she could see the methods we use and taste the way the food must taste, but we also had to cook for our restaurant and operate it on the usual schedule. Michele followed us everywhere like a magnet—listening, watching, photographing, writing, and tasting—a peculiar sensation for us, since we are normally very private people. But because Michele is Michele, she became our *ombra* (shadow of sunshine).

To further understand our Sicilian food firsthand, we took her to the countryside home of Gaetano and Anna Mazzola, a family of shepherds near Gangi, to observe the cheesemaking process. Francesco and Pietro Lo Giudice welcomed Michele into their excellent bakery in Gangi for an inspection. Santo Castagna, the owner of a pasta mill in Petralia Sottana, showed her, step by step, his factory's pasta operation. Our dear friend Vincenzo Mollica hosted an old-fashioned breadmaking day with a tremendous meal at his home in the Madonie Mountains—Elisa D'Arpa was the master breadmaker and cook, along with her sister, Maria D'Arpa, and a dozen other Madonie food enthusiasts. Giuseppina di Salvo gave a grand tour of her vineyards and fruit orchards, and served us some of her wines at a traditional Sicilian lunch. Several other friends prepared special meals and dishes, while others shared interesting ideas or recipes with us: Gina Degano and Antonio Pucci, Ginevra Carapezza, Francesca Orestano, Peter Goodliffe, Annamaria Bellina, Cetta Teresi, Caterina Mollica, Bruna and Franco Loiacono, Pino and Oriana Varia, Santina and Luciano Consolo, Lisa Briguglio, Lina

Alberti, Tanino Raimondi, and Maria-Angela Ucelli. To all of these kind, generous friends and artisans above, *mille grazie*.

Over the course of two years we worked many months together in Sicily, in New York, and in St. Thomas in the United States Virgin Islands, where Michele and her husband, Tully Plesser, live. Going to the Caribbean was a wonderful, unforeseen adventure, even in the fantasy of this fairy tale. In our wildest dreams Giovanna and I never imagined we would be visiting a beautiful tropical island in such a distant world.

In St. Thomas, as at Gangivecchio, we wrote, cooked, and worked together. We solved such problems as finding a good ricotta substitute for our fresh sheep's ricotta and calculating the difference between our powdered vanilla and liquid vanilla extract. How strange it was for us Sicilians to smell Gangivecchio's recipes simmering on the stove in a West Indian kitchen. On this small island we cooked with excellent-quality fresh herbs and vegetables, including splendid West Indian pumpkin, very similar in flavor to our own, and found all the foods we needed for our testing, which surprised and delighted us. In Sicily we introduced *nespole* and *zucchine di quaranta giorni* (medlars and long forty-day green squash) to Michele. In St. Thomas she acquainted us with the exotic flavors of papaya and soursop. Food is a great world ambassador.

With much affection we thank Tully for being such a gracious host and sharing his wife with us, especially during the long periods he and Michele were separated when she was here with us in Sicily.

Finally, we would like to thank: Gita Mehta for her graciousness and warmth, and for opening up her home to us; Sonny Mehta for opening up his entire *company* to us; Virginia Tan for making the book so lovely and so much like Gangivecchio; and Carol Devine Carson for giving us the most beautiful jacket in the world.

So, now as I sit here in Gangivecchio, with my dog, Puffo, on my knees and Perlina, my cat, sleeping by the fire, I have to say that even *they* were collaborators in this effort, just for the look of love in their eyes and their companionship.

I hear Peppe Bevacqua, our houseman, moving about in the kitchen at his work—a sound that always comforts me. He was a valuable participant in our project, as were Giovanni Salerno, our cheesemaker and farmhand; Lucia Regalbuto, our maid and kitchen assistant who has since gone on to other things, and Lucia Guarcello, whom we call Lucia Due, who took over the first Lucia's duties in our home and restaurant.

Indispensable to me in this project and in life is my beloved daughter,

Giovanna. Without her, this book would simply not exist. Because of her command of the English language, we were able to meet Peter Gethers in the first place, and through her translation efforts we were able to communicate and work with Michele. I am the proud mother of a London-educated, sophisticated daughter with a sharp intellect and a great knowledge and sense of Sicilian history. Giovanna has been as cheerful and tireless a worker in writing and producing this book as she is in all areas of our restaurant business and in our family life. I am a mother blessed.

My son, Paolo, and his wife, Betty, perhaps skeptical at first, have both been encouraging supporters, generous with their time, making significant contributions to this book. I can never forget the expression on Paolo's face at the airport in Palermo when Giovanna, Betty, and I left for our second trip to New York and our first journey to the Virgin Islands. My strong Sicilian son had a look on his face of total abandonment—the three women in his life were leaving him for alien destinations. He, of course, had to stay behind to run his hotel and look after our restaurant. When we returned, his face, powerful again, shone with delight and love—but also with relief that the hard work would again be shared by all of us.

Thanking my family is an odd thing for me. So, as this little tale comes to an end, I only add thanks for the fortunate life I chose and which you all have given me at Gangivecchio.

I did not describe to you the chair I am sitting in as I write, because it is too ugly for words, but, like a happy, comforting memory, I refuse to let it go. To be honest, I am relieved that this book is finally finished and that the hard work is done. It is already a great pleasure remembering our delicious adventures from my faded, cozy throne in our ancient Sicilian home.

—*Wanda Tornabene*

La Cucina Siciliana di Gangivecchio

Gangivecchio's Sicilian Kitchen

Introduzioni

(Introductions)

A Proposito di Ricette e Cucina di Gangivecchio e Siciliana

(About the Recipes and Kitchens of Gangivecchio and Sicily)

It has always been my intention to pass my recipe collection on to my children, Giovanna and Paolo, one day. It is a time-honored tradition in the Tornabene family, like it is in many other Sicilian homes. The two women who preceded me as head of this household at Gangivecchio, my mother-in-law, Giovanna, and her mother-in-law, Giulia, kept a little exercise book containing their handwritten recipes. I still have that book, old and full of charm, and for many years I have continued the tradition by writing recipes and comments of my own in the last pages of this book. Fragile and soiled now, from age and constant referral, it is, to me, a treasure. No one outside the family, until now, has ever been allowed to read the secrets kept within its pages.

When fate decided that I share our family recipes with a larger audience, it was with great love that I entrusted them to paper. Love, not just in offering the right ingredients and amounts for good results but also of the memories connected with each dish: of dear voices, silent now forever, voices that taught me how to cook, voices demanding something special for lunch or dinner.

Giovanna and I have added little anecdotes to many of the recipes in this book, a mirror of our family and daily lives, then and now, at Gangivecchio. Within the chapters and recipes we've also provided plenty of information about our style of Sicilian cooking and our thoughts about food—some ideas haven't changed for generations. We like to think we are modern women, but we resist tampering with what works. We remain devoted to tradition. My daughter-in-law, Betty, is trying to move us into the 1990s, and, I must say, she has succeeded where healthful salads are concerned. In cooking, it is always important to listen to the advice of others. After all, that is how I learned to cook.

Our book is about Gangivecchio's practical country cooking made with the food that is our heritage. In our circumstances, living on a farm in Sicily's mountainous, rugged interior, our cuisine has been, by necessity, dictated by the land. We cook and eat mainly what we grow and produce at home, in a culinary communion with nature and the earth. Our orchards are filled with cherry, mulberry, pear, fig, and apple trees. We also have the bountiful harvest from almond, hazelnut, olive, and pine trees. Our gardens produce tomatoes, eggplants, peppers, onions, green beans, cauliflower, spinach, broccoli, arugula, and many other vegetables, plus a multitude of herbs. Gangivecchio's walkways are bordered with ancient bay laurel trees and rosemary bushes; the fruit of our cow's milk brings us caciocavallo cheese; our chickens give us eggs. Greens and fantastic ferla mushrooms grow wild in our fields. We like to say that to produce our dinners, we just pick what is outside.

The variety in Sicily's cuisine is based on economic circumstances, the geography and climate of specific regions of the island, and, perhaps most important, history.

No other country in the world has suffered as many defeats by such a varied mixture of cultures as Sicily. Each culture—from the Greeks, Romans, and Arabs to the French and Spanish—has left behind its own imprint on our eating habits. Although all these defeats are painful reminders in our history, in the end, we have been the beneficiary. We have the Greeks to thank for bringing olives, grapes, honey, and fava beans. The Romans, who followed, introduced precious wheat and other grains. The Arabs made the most remarkable contributions, strongly influencing our cuisine by advanced agricultural techniques, like irrigation, as well as introducing us to eggplants, citrus and other fruits, spices, nuts, rice, and sugarcane. We Sicilians have the Arabs to thank for our love of all things sweet, from sweet-and-sour dishes and sauces to candies like *torrone* (almond brittle) and our rich desserts and *gelati*. The Spanish, via South America, contributed numerous valuable foods, especially tomatoes and peppers. And in the nineteenth century the French baronial cooking that came into favor with the Sicilian aristocracy became our most complex, rich, and elegant style of cooking. We might say that the only ingredients added by the Sicilian people were the passion to eat and the talent for combining all these lovely foods into one of the world's most distinctive cuisines. Giovanna says that "we are the saucepan of the Mediterranean."

Each region of Sicily prefers its own specialties. We in the Madonie most admire our hearty pastas, meat ragus, veal or pork *involtini*, fresh vegetables like wild mushrooms, wild asparagus and greens, fava beans, and delectable fruits. We also love our wonderful country breads made from the best durum wheat possible. I can't imagine any better-quality cheeses made from sheep's and cow's milk than the ones that are produced right here. The Madonie's favorite desserts—exquisite fresh fig tarts and ricotta cakes—are supreme in their simplicity. Our recipes are our personal legacy and our own interpretations of classic Sicilian dishes, such as *pasta con le sarde, caponata, arancine, salsa picchio pacchio, involtini,* and *panelle.*

However, there are no recipes in this book for dishes that Americans might consider synonymous with Sicilian cooking. You will not find couscous, *cassata alla Siciliana,* or *pasta reale,* because we cook none of these. Couscous is a well-known and wonderful Arabian-inspired dish, best sampled where it originated, in the western area of Sicily, especially in the city of Trapani. Couscous requires not only the special knowledge of how to make it, passed down through generations, but also special equipment and the patience of a saint. We once had a friend from Trapani, who is a very good and dedicated cook, staying with us for the weekend, so she prepared seafood couscous for the restaurant at Gangivecchio. It took forever to make. And after it was served, we heard some of our Madonie guests whispering, "Do they think we are chickens?" Of course, they wanted, demanded, and received pasta.

Another Arabian inspiration, *cassata alla Siciliana,* made with cake, sweetened ricotta cream, almond paste, and candied fruits, also requires a long, tedious preparation. For us it is much easier—and better—to buy one of these glorious cakes from any number of our excellent *pasticcerie.* We prefer spending our time on dishes we are experts at preparing, such as sweetened fresh ricotta-filled cannoli.

We also don't make *pasta reale.* These delicate almond-paste jewels are artfully fashioned into hand-decorated and hand-painted miniature confections that are exact replicas of everything from fruit, vegetables, and flowers to buttons, pencils, and boxes. The nuns in convents used to excel at this speciality and still do to a lesser degree, but now there are talented artisans in every major city in Sicily who create these delicacies. When you come to Sicily, you should seek out and sample all these excellent foods, but you will not find them here at Gangivecchio.

Added to the complex equation of defining our cuisine is the reality that every Sicilian wife and mother has her own variation and style of cooking at home. No two tomato sauces are exactly the same. We are a country of five million people, and I know of no Sicilian household without *salsa di pomodoro* on the stove.

As a whole, Sicilian cooking is really a wonderfully healthy, true Mediterranean cuisine. We consume enormous amounts of vegetables and legumes, herbs, fruits, nuts, pasta, and cheeses. Our diet is supplemented by bread, olive oil, and occasionally fish and meat. While it is true that we Sicilians love sweets and foods that are fried, we normally eat these delicious foods in small or moderate amounts.

To me, apart from good natural instincts, practical knowledge, and experience, a good kitchen is created from the joy of satisfying others. How can you talk about cooking without talking about eating? I can think of no greater happiness than serving a good meal to family, friends, and guests. In Sicily, meals are never, ever hurried; they are relaxed interludes to be savored along with the further nourishment of good conversation and laughter.

At Gangivecchio, cooking is an occupation we practice daily, to enjoy ourselves in our home dining room and for the public to appreciate in our restaurant in the countryside. Our simple rules are that all food should be as fresh as possible and that it be respected, thoughtfully prepared, and never wasted.

I believe that cooking is an entirely individual matter. Like regulating the temperature of the water you bathe in or choosing clothes to wear, you must be comfortable and suit yourself. We are a proud family of cooks—Giovanna, Paolo, Betty, and I—but each of us is in charge of our own spoon.

If our collection of recipes does find a place on your cookbook shelf, my greatest wish is that you will find it useful. Nothing could be more gratifying to me than knowing it is in your kitchen, stained with the evidence of good use.

—Wanda Tornabene

Abbandonarsi ai Ricordi: Mia Madre, La Cucina e Gangivecchio

(Reminiscences: My Mother, the Kitchen, and Gangivecchio)

This book is a tangible reward for my mother's nearly fifty years of devoted work at Gangivecchio, and it is she I would like to speak of first. My mother taught me to love our home, Gangivecchio, and to fight to preserve it like she has always done. We possess it, but it possesses us, too.

Mamma introduced me to the kitchen quite late in life. Because of this—and my laziness—she pushed me very hard. For example, when some dish I was uncomfortable cooking had to be prepared right away for three dozen people expected for lunch at the restaurant, she would suddenly develop a monstrous headache, vanish into her bedroom, and close the door. Once the task was successfully accomplished—by me—she would suddenly appear, having made a remarkable recovery. I saw through her clever strategy, but how could I not admire her wisdom and be amused? And the happy result has been my own slowly formed love affair with the kitchen. A love affair that, like a solid friendship, grows stronger with each passing day.

My mother and I complement each other in our work together. Mamma's primary concern, as always, is the alchemy of the ingredients. I've been at her side at the restaurant for eighteen years now—she remains the poetry while I've become the prose. My duties, apart from cooking, are business administration and handling the reservation book. I do most of the food shopping (only Mamma selects the meat), deal with the staff, and see to the table settings, choosing plants and flowers or any other special decorations at Gangivecchio. My titles include that of chief hostess, welcoming visitors of every nationality. I can recite Gangivecchio's history in several languages in my sleep.

To help Mamma now, running our restaurant and cooking just as she has done for so many years, is not only my job but one of life's sweetest pleasures. There are countless large and small joys between us, from orchestrating a beautiful wedding dinner for 175 people to seeing her eyes light up when I surprise her by bringing home her favorite gelato, *nocciola*.

Oh, I won't deny that she is still the stern boss of Gangivecchio—Paolo, Betty, and I, along with our household and restaurant staff and farmworkers, can only discreetly help as she barks orders that can be heard for miles. But before we decided to do this book, age had been sneaking up on my mother. Her afternoon naps, which she has taken every day of her life, had become longer, the sleep deeper.

When we began to think seriously about going ahead with this project, I saw my mother revitalized. First there were the long discussions into the early morning hours about divulging the family's and the restaurant's secret recipes. Then came the debate about the two of us having no time to write a book. When we began talking about actually going to New York, I could see that Mamma was walking with a new, purposeful pace. Her siestas shortened, and she began admonishing Peppe for not peeling the artichokes right and criticizing Lucia for not properly ironing her blouses. We were all very happy to see her back to her old self again. A bit of personal recognition is good medicine for all of us.

Now, it is I who am an old woman of forty-five with a young mother of twenty, who spends her nights inventing new recipes, writing poems, studying English, and planning another trip to the United States to see Boston, Washington, and Los Angeles and visit the Wild West. Every day there is something new; then, all of a sudden, she will press my hand and say, "I am almost sure the Americans will love my *sofficini dolci*."

From the first day of our project—"*il libro*," as Mamma and I have always referred to it—it has been a demanding undertaking. Finding calm periods for discussion and writing *il libro* has not been easy, particularly from early spring to the fall, our busiest seasons. At times, when Mamma would see me approaching her with a notebook and pen, she would announce firmly, "For you, I am invisible." But whenever we did find quiet moments, she would talk until I could no longer hold the pen. On her own, she, too, filled many pages.

During Michele's four delightful visits here, our trips to New York and the Virgin Islands, where she lives, we worked seven days a week, and in between there was continual communication—correspondence, telephone meetings, and faxes. Michele and I eventually came to call the latter invention "Saint Fax," for without this instant assistance we could not have completed our work in only two years. There is no saint for the Italian mail.

Throughout these pages, in words and photographs, we are able to share a place that we think is unique in the world, a place destiny honored us with by selecting us as guardians.

It is a great gift to be able to live where you can breathe the ancient history of your family and country in every corner. But it is also comforting, from these fourteenth-century walls, to hear the clicking sounds of my word processor and printer in my office. Within the antique walls of our kitchen we are now also relieved to have modern ranges and refrigerators and telephones. (We have telephones everywhere, even one that travels with us.) Gangivecchio's feet may be implanted on a piece of land that saw the Greeks and Romans, but its alert Sicilian head is wide-awake today and looking forward to the future.

In this introduction I know I should talk about the recipes, but I honestly believe they will speak for themselves. Our recipes are the instruments of a harmonious choir of joy and health that represents every table we have ever set.

I hope that those who cook our recipes from so far away will feel they are joining a melodious chorus of aromas and flavors born of love in the heart of Sicily.

It is my great pleasure to welcome you to Gangivecchio.

—*Giovanna Tornabene*

_L_a Storia dell'Abbazia di Gangivecchio

(The History of Gangivecchio's Abbey)

Once upon a time, on the exact site where Gangivecchio stands today, there was a pre-Greek village called Engio, believed to have been established by the Cretans by 1200 B.C. We say "once upon a time" because precise origins of ancient villages in Sicily are debatable.

It is difficult to be exact when your history includes, just from 500 B.C., occupation and invasions by Carthaginians, Greeks, Romans, Arabians, Normans, Angevin French, and Aragon conquerers.

From the thirteenth century we can trace Gangivecchio's history with more certainty. It is generally accepted that the fate of the town of Engio, which, after Roman domination, was called Engyon, was sealed when anarchy erupted following the Sicilian Vespers revolt that began in Palermo in 1282 against French Angevin rule of Sicily. After the Vespers' bloodbath (over two thousand French were killed), the crown of Sicily passed briefly to James of Aragon, then back to his brother, the more powerful Frederick II. Of course, James, who'd allied with the Pope, wanted the throne back, so fierce battles between the brothers commenced. Engyon chose to fight on the side of the loser, James. As punishment to the residents of Engyon for this rebellion against the king and their appointed feudal lord, the Count of Geraci and master of Engyon (Enrico Ventimiglia), Frederick II razed the town in 1299. Only the small chapel of the Church of St. Mary of the Annunciation remained.

After a valiant but lost battle, the surviving residents of Engyon escaped to nomadic refuge in the nearby hillsides in the Madonie—our north central mountain range.

In 1300 a beneficent, perhaps uneasy, Count Ventimiglia granted the former inhabitants of Engyon authorization to build homes and establish a new town on Mount Marone, a strategic, elevated location about two miles west of the valley where Engyon had once stood. They called the new town Gangi, a name that evolved linguistically from the name of their original village.

In 1363 Benedictine monks obtained permission to build a priory around the Church of St. Mary of the Annunciation in the destroyed former village, which came to be known as Gangivecchio (meaning old Gangi). A descendant of Count Ventimiglia's donated about 1,600 acres of adjacent land to the order.

In Sicily, as in all of Europe, the monks brought civilization's lights to the remotest of places. The religious communities were established as cultural and economic centers, providing spiritual and practical education and agricultural assistance to the local citizenry. They introduced such up-to-date farming methods as irrigation for crops, produced wine, and helped develop a local economy based on bartered farm products.

The Benedictine monks who came to Gangivecchio found themselves in a place where the people, nearly all illiterate, were struggling to survive with their primitive farming techniques. The monks had their work cut out for them not only as teachers, but also with the stupendous task of renovating the church and building an abbey from nothing. Able and tenacious workers, the monks constructed a fortresslike three-story monastery, a square structure with four wings (the church took up the entire northern side) surrounding a large central courtyard. Eventually the flourishing small priory became an enviable community. In 1413 it was elevated to the high rank of "abbey."

The Abbazia di Gangivecchio continued its influence on Gangi and the immediate region for more than two hundred years, gradually reducing activities and the maintenance of its structures until 1653, when it was abandoned, leaving only a single member of the order as guardian and revenue collector. After his death the abbey stood empty and crumbling for more than one hundred years.

In 1770 a wealthy local

squire, Francesco Bongiorno, who lived in a magnificent palazzo high atop Gangi (currently beautifully restored and the seat of our local government), seeking a location for a summer residence, discovered the ruins of Gangivecchio. He obtained a perpetual lease from the church and set about the extensive, expensive renovation of the dilapidated former abbey. It was during this period that the graceful exterior freestanding wall and fountain with four putti-faced water-spouts, fed by a crystal-clear natural spring, and the columned entranceway were added—or perhaps reconstructed. Attractive family living quarters were created in the second story of the east wing. He installed beautiful, colorful ceramic tile floors and wood-framed windows and doors with little wrought-iron balconies. No doubt, Bongiorno furnished it handsomely.

The church sold Gangivecchio to Bongiorno in 1778. In 1783 the estate was designated a barony by King Ferdinand IV. A two-headed eagle became Gangivecchio's imperial coat of arms in honor of the Bourbon king's Austrian wife, Maria Carolina. Today Gangivecchio's emblem is displayed in a sculpture over the main doors and in frescoes painted on the walls inside the entranceway. The twin-headed eagle with outstretched wings also shines under glaze on the sides of enormous old ceramic pots that are now ours.

Bongiorno built a small family chapel, Our Lady of the Stair, in 1793 on the ground floor of the south wing. In the same wing of the building, also on the ground floor, is the former abbey's ancient refectory dining room, where fading frescoes painted on vaulted ceilings signed by Pietro Billio, dated 1577, remain.

In 1828, with the death of Francesco Bongiorno's son, and only surviving heir, ownership of the property reverted to the church. Gangivecchio sat empty and decaying again.

After several years of complicated, frustrating negotiations, my great-grandfather, Vincenzo Tornabene, bought the former abbey in 1856. That was just four years before Garibaldi and his "Thousand," the Red Shirts, came ashore near Marsala, on Sicily's western coast, to conquer the then ruling Bourbon troops. A year later, in 1861, under Garibaldi's leadership, Sicilians elected by plebiscite to unite with the new Kingdom of Italy in a movement known as the Risorgimento.

Meantime, great-grandfather Vincenzo had begun his own warriorlike efforts on behalf of the Tornabene dynasty high in the Madonie Mountains at our beloved Gangivecchio.

Mariano Tornabene, c. 1840

Granny Giovanna's father,
Pietro Randazzo, c. 1878

Sixteen-year-old Giovanna Randazzo, third from left, in college at Palermo, 1902

Giovanna and Mariano Tornabene
on their honeymoon, in 1911

Vincenzo Tornabene in 1912,
at six months

Wanda and Enzo hunting
at Gangivecchio, 1949

Gangivecchio e la Famiglia Tornabene

(Gangivecchio and the Tornabene Family)

If family history is correct, and we like to believe it is, the ancient ancestors of the Tornabene family were Tuscan, some of whom relocated to Catania at the end of the fifteenth century. In the late seventeenth century the second son of a lower branch of the family tree resettled in Gangi in the Madonie region of Sicily. We do not know his first name or why he came.

In the Sicily of that time, ownership of land was fundamental to the prestige and richness of noble families that expanded and strengthened their heritage through marriage. As you will see, the various future barons Tornabene had propensities for marrying well in the Sicily of the time.

Our most intimate knowledge of the family begins in the early nineteenth century, in 1820, when Mariano Tornabene married Angela Parlato, a wealthy woman from Petralia Sottana, a neighboring village. They were blessed with four children; their first was my great-grandfather Vincenzo. By a strange coincidence, he was born in April 1828 in the same month of the same year of the death of the last Bongiorno, the previous and only other known private owner of Gangivecchio.

When Mariano and Angela's only son, Vincenzo, took control of Gangivecchio in 1856, he transformed it from a summer home to a working farm. He planted wheat and almond, hazelnut, and olive orchards with 500 trees each; he reestablished a vineyard, eventually produced wines, precious olive oil, and vinegar, and set about refurbishing the long-neglected abbey. For twenty-nine years a reclusive Vincenzo Tornabene lived what must have been an extraordinarily desolate life here on 1600 acres in Gangivecchio's restored abbey as its sole inhabitant, with the exception of household and farm help. Perhaps he was content. Perhaps he would have remained here in his peculiarly un-Sicilian solitary confinement for the rest of his life if destiny had not interfered.

On a May evening in 1884, a terrifying event occurred that altered Vincenzo's life and decided mine. Returning to Gangivecchio from Gangi on horseback, my great-grandfather grew weary of containing his spirited white stallion. At one point along the trail he asked the farmhand accompanying him to switch horses, so he could ride the quieter brown horse the rest of the way home in peace. Later on, in the darkness, from behind the ruin of an old stone house, a shot rang out aimed directly at the rider of the white horse—the bullet clearly intended for Vincenzo. Fortunately, the gunman was a poor shot; the farmer sustained only a minor wound, and Vincenzo escaped injury. My great-grandfather never learned who was behind this frightening murder attempt, but he surely began reflecting on mortality and the dangerous circumstances of a rich man living alone in a remote, private wilderness.

Deeply troubled over the shooting incident, he tried calming his nerves by the diversion of a few leisure months of travel. During this chance but fortuitous journey, he met and fell in love with a twenty-year-old woman from Bologna, thirty-seven years his junior, named Giulia Colombari. She had, it seemed, a pretty face atop a fat little body, a cheerful personality, as well as a willful, fearless constitution. In an old yellowing photograph that now hangs on the wall, stopped in time with my great-grandfather, Vincenzo, Giulia watches me every day.

Vincenzo married Giulia two months after their first meeting and brought her back to the beautiful but isolated and harsh environment of Gangivecchio, so foreign and unlike her own cosmopolitan home. From the day of her arrival Giulia ran her husband's kingdom with vigorous, iron-fisted control.

With the help of the Bolognese cook that she brought with her, Giulia began successfully combining two contrasting gastronomic traditions—her native, rich Emilia cooking with her newly acquired and expanding knowledge of natural, hearty Sicilian cuisine—quickly mastering the latter to please her new husband.

Giulia soon gave birth to their only child, a son, Mariano. For the first time in the Tornabene history at Gangivecchio, a lively family household was born. Giulia enjoyed the company of others, so she busied herself entertaining and giving elaborate lunches and dinner parties, which became legendary in the minor way of out-of-the-way places in the world.

Giulia and Vincenzo's life ran a happy, normal course, scanning years of the changing seasons, holy day celebrations, long winters in Palermo, and joyful returns in the spring to the countryside at Gangivecchio, in the constant presence of family and friends. Their son, Mariano, my grandfather, inherited Giulia's beautiful maternal face, but neither the strength nor fighting spirit both his parents had.

Mariano married a charming young blond woman, Giovanna Randazzo, from a prominent Palermo family. For her, regrettably, it was not an entirely happy union. This extremely beautiful and sophisticated lady never came to fully appreciate country life. She always preferred the more cultivated atmosphere and social world of Palermo. Nevertheless, my grandmother Giovanna lived her adult life true to her marriage vows, as a good wife and devoted mother. She had one son, Vincenzo, my father, and was forbidden to have another child to prevent the inheritance from scattering.

When the old man Vincenzo died, a dashing but frivolous Mariano became the boss of Gangivecchio. Although the inheritance had not been scattered, Mariano soon began squandering it by selling pieces of Gangivecchio's land to pay for his enormous appetite for personal possessions and pleasures. He had great style, but no taste for work of any kind. I have a vague memory of my tall, impressive grandfather, who for all his life looked timid only in the presence of his refined wife. In photographs we see a sadness in her eyes.

To forget her personal sorrows, Giovanna started a happy gastronomic association with her widowed mother-in-law, Giulia. Good food replenished disenchantment of the heart.

Together the Tornabene women began writing down their recipes in an exercise book. Giulia, the northern Italian woman, had great influence: Parmigiano-Reggiano cheese was now ever present on the table, and butter was often substituted for the olive oil used in the Sicilian kitchen. Giovanna, thoroughly Sicilian and a gifted cook, melded the ingredients into a distinct cuisine that became Gangivecchio's own special legacy. Every kitchen in Sicily has an original cuisine created by its own family members—the reason there can never be strict rules in Sicilian cooking.

My father met my mother, Wanda Di Paola (pronounced Vanda), in 1948 at a dinner party at a mutual friend's home in Mondello, a small seaside fishing village a few miles outside Palermo. Located between Monte Pellegrino and Monte Gallo, Mondello has a long sandy curve of beach, surrounded by elegant villas resting on the coastline and climbing up into the hillsides. Today it's a popular resort area with lots of hotels, restaurants, and shops. We still have an apartment in a cool, breezy residential area there. In the summer Palermo turns into a steaming inferno. Throughout history, those who could afford it have always retreated from the city's heat to the seashore or mountainside.

When my parents met, they were both recovering from unhappy love stories. Mamma's first impression of Vincenzo Tornabene, called Enzo by his family and friends, was that he was very nice but quite an old man—she was twenty-one and he was thirty-six. However, a serious relationship developed.

My mother has told me many times that when she first saw Gangivecchio she had a powerful emotional reaction—a mystical premonition that she would live the rest of her life in this great ancient place, and for the privilege, she would endure hardships and make sacrifices. She made a vow that if she did marry Enzo Tornabene, she would devote herself to him and to Gangivecchio with all her might.

Enzo and Wanda's love blossomed, and Mamma eventually began her life with my father at Gangivecchio, still unable to forget the mysterious omen. We Sicilians are superstitious by nature—witchcraft is still practiced here.

My parents moved into the house with Papa's parents, Giovanna and Mariano. Mamma became very close to Granny Giovanna (who gave me her name), soon loving her like a mother. They lived happily together for twenty years. It was Granny Giovanna who introduced Mamma to the art of cooking. Giovanna found an eager pupil in her daughter-in-law, and it didn't take long for an affectionate cooking competition to begin. Friends began praising the newest member of the family for her culinary skills, saying that all the Tornabene women were excellent cooks.

My younger brother Paolo and I, two years apart in age, had a wonderful childhood living in the natural wonderland of Gangivecchio. When it came time for our education, Mamma traveled back and forth with us to and from Palermo, where we went to school during the week while living in Mondello. Papa had to remain at Gangivecchio most of the time to run the farm.

On weekends we joined Papa, along with friends and other family members. Over delicious meals in the evening, Paolo and I listened silently to hunting stories, legends, history, politics, and gossip with big ears. We grew up mainly with adults, but what a lot we learned. Summers were spent at Gangivecchio. We missed the excitement of Palermo and the sea and beach at Mondello, but life was full of adventure for us here. The enormous hazelnut, almond, and olive groves were transformed into a jungle wilderness. We explored every inch of the farm and abbey, played with the animals, learned to ride horses, and dug for buried treasure. Secrets weren't easily kept from us. Exhausted from curiosity, we were always hungry, and of course, we ate very well.

When Paolo was nine, he was given his first gun and taught to hunt by Papa and his friends. I was only allowed to follow behind and carry the game— woman's work.

In the presence of such good cooks as my granny and mamma, it was hard for me to approach the kitchen in our house. I have always loved food, so when I was very young, I longed to cook. But something always went wrong with what I tried, even something as simple as frying two eggs—the yolks would break, the whites would burn. I finally gave up and left the pleasures of the kitchen to the skilled older ladies of the house.

These years, for the most part, were idyllic, consistent, and carefree. I imagined all other children in the world lived exactly the same way we did. But when children grow into adults the world changes.

As a young woman, for a decade I lived far away from Gangivecchio, first studying in London, then working as a travel representative at an agency in Palermo. I traveled throughout Europe and Africa and, frankly, forgot all about cooking. But not about food. There is still nothing I would prefer to do than eat out in a good restaurant.

I am quite sure that when my brother, Paolo, was a boy he never thought of himself as a countryman, let alone an innkeeper or cook—certainly not at Gangivecchio, although it was my father's fondest wish. Like me, he had chosen an independent, different way of life. Paolo went to university in Palermo and studied architecture. He also played a part in faculty politics, but suddenly, when he was just three credits short of a degree, he chose, on his own, to return to Gangivecchio to live his life. He bought cows and horses and started working with Papa on the farm with great enthusiasm.

I, too, left my comfortable life in Palermo and moved back to Gangivecchio permanently. This ancient place had silently touched both our hearts, just like it had touched Mamma's so long ago. Back in the Madonie, I opened an antiques business.

Granny Giovanna wasn't with us anymore, so little by little I began helping my mother in the kitchen. I can honestly say that I started my new career by rising from the very lowest rank. Today nobody smiles anymore when I prepare a sauce or a cake, and even my brother, my worst critic, sometimes says "*brava*" to me. A few of the recipes that are in this book come from my mind.

The story of Gangivecchio, during my lifetime, is divided into two parts: before the restaurant—when life was wonderful until economic troubles developed in the early seventies; and after the restaurant—when all our lives were altered so dramatically.

Il Ristorante—
Salvare Capra e Cavoli

(The Restaurant—Saving the Goat and the Cabbage)

At the end of 1976 the road from the neighboring town of Gangi to Gangivecchio was completed. It's only a distance of three and a half kilometers—about two miles—but the route is precarious, with various turns snaking up and down steep hills. The old road was a nightmare, a terrible bumpy passage. This good thoroughfare greatly improved our lives in terms of mobility, and provided easier access for people coming to visit us. Life at Gangivecchio has always been very sociable, so our friends were as grateful as we were to finally have a proper road. One of these good friends is Father Calogero, a frequent visitor who lives in Petralia Soprana, another village nearby in the Madonie. About two years after the road had opened, he came for dinner one evening. There was nothing unusual about this, but the discussion on that particular night changed our lives forever, so I remember the conversation very well.

Mamma: "We live in a wonderful place on this earth with a beautiful road, but we have the same old money problems. How can we possibly survive?"

Father Calogero: "Listen to me, Wanda. You are a superb cook, and it's something you love to do. You could open a restaurant, and your children can help you. *Fare soldi e salvare capra e cavoli* [You'll make money and save the goat and the cabbage]."

Mamma considered the suggestion a moment, then replied, "This is an exciting idea. Perhaps it could work."

Papa: "Are you crazy? How can we ask people to pay to come into our home? My ancestors will turn over in their graves!"

Mamma: "If we don't do this, they will turn over for other reasons."

After Father Calogero left, a big argument followed. Papa was against the idea entirely. Aside from being embarrassed at the prospect of selling food at Gangivecchio, which is how he viewed opening up a restaurant here, he reasoned that none of us knew anything about running a place of business and were destined to fail. Anyway, he wanted to know, who would come? Mamma, always a loyal fighter for Gangivecchio, persevered. The only thing he and Mamma did agree upon that night was that some kind of battle had to be waged to save Gangivecchio. If we didn't make a move quickly, it would have to be sold.

At the time, the agricultural economy that supported Gangivecchio had been steadily weakening. With every passing day it became more difficult to pay increasing expenses and taxes. I can remember many long discussions around the table about money. I saw worried expressions on my parents' faces. Mamma's eyes often glazed over with tears, and, therefore, mine did, too. She kept repeating, "What are we going to do?"

Although Papa was an educated man of solid character, his only working experience and skills were in farming. He responded to the crisis passively, with resignation, as if fate would make the judgment for us. He had inherited this unfortunate trait from his late father, Mariano. But Mariano, a dilettante accustomed to living well and working as little as possible, had always solved any money troubles by simply selling off Gangivecchio land. By 1978 the property had dwindled in size from the original 1600 acres to a mere 140.

Mamma adamantly refused to sell one more meter of Gangivecchio, remembering the strange omen she felt on her first visit and her promise of a lifetime of devotion. Instead of land, my parents had already resorted to selling a few treasured pieces of furniture—irreplaceable family heirlooms. The situation was desperate.

After Father Calogero's visit, Mamma sat down at the dining-room table and began devising a simple plan. Aside from cooking for the family and friends, we had no experience in running a restaurant. Papa had certainly been right about that, but to her, there was nothing unusual or difficult about cooking a meal for twenty people or more. And, as Father Calogero had so kindly pointed out, cooking was not only something Mamma did well, she enjoyed it.

Mamma decided to locate the restaurant in our first dining room, which has a private entrance. Guests would enter Gangivecchio's courtyard, climb the stairs, and be led through a short hallway directly into the restaurant.

Our home is a square, divided into four wings, containing about forty rooms that surround a large central courtyard. We live on the second floor of the east wing in fourteen rooms. Our living quarters are structured like a typical nineteenth-century Sicilian house, with rooms following one after the other in succession in a layout that is called *rappresentanza*. For every large room, which has a window facing outside, there is an attached smaller room, each with a window facing the courtyard. The small and large rooms run parallel to each other from one side of the house to the other. At the extreme southern end there is an open-air outdoor terrace, followed by two dining rooms, a kitchen, a living room, a library, and, to the northern side of the house, a series of large and small bedrooms with one large bathroom at the end. There is no privacy whatsoever, unless you retreat into one of the small bedrooms and lock yourself inside.

By 1978 our kitchen, which faces the courtyard and has its own private entrance from a little balcony off the outside staircase, had been divided into two parts—the modern side with a gas range, and the old side with three built-in wood-burning stovetops that were seldom used anymore. Mamma planned to transform this portion of the kitchen into a work area, so there would be plenty of space for food preparation for the restaurant, located only a few steps away through the other connecting dining room.

We would serve the traditional Sicilian food that everyone loved, using as much of our own seasonal products as possible—wild greens, mushrooms, vegetables, and herbs from the garden, fruits and nuts from the trees, and our own cheeses and pressed olive oil. The major expenditures were going to be buying meat and wine, but customers would, of course, be paying for the wine they drank. Our own natural spring would provide the water. Only a set menu would be offered, because Mamma said she couldn't plan efficiently or economically if she had to cook separate special dishes.

The menu would consist of an antipasti of grilled breads with olive pâtés, wild green fritters and other delicious dishes like caponata, and two kinds of pastas—one with a red sauce based on tomatoes and one with a green sauce featuring fresh herbs, vegetables, and nuts. Meat would be served with fresh vegetables followed by *panzerotti* (little pillows of fried dough stuffed with ham). For dessert there would be cakes and tarts with ricotta and seasonal fruit and a changing variety of Mamma's excellent recipes but, always, extra little plates of sweet *sofficini*. No one would ever leave Gangivecchio hungry, and we hoped our guests would be pleased with their meals and want to return.

To make things simpler, we would charge a fixed price. I appreciated that because, although I care about the bills, I'm not very strong with the numbers, and I had been appointed—and still remain—in charge of the money transactions. Mamma also insisted that lunches would be served precisely at 1:30 p.m. and dinners at 8:30 p.m.

We knew we would have to keep a book for reservations in order to be able to organize the food shopping, preparation, and the setting-up of the dining room each day.

Mamma's plans concluded with a list of inexpensive items we needed to buy in Gangi: tables and chairs (we started out with five tables), tablecloths and napkins, dishes, cutlery, and glasses.

These plans, the list, and Mamma's courage, endless energy, and big cooking talent were the ingredients in our recipe for opening up Gangivecchio's restaurant. Paolo and I, in our late twenties, and his girlfriend and my boyfriend at the time, were enlisted to help. Like parsley, we were everywhere. We painted the dining-room walls white, moved our furniture out and set up the tables and chairs, food-shopped, and ran errands. We were enthusiastic supporters and helpers, and had a great time through it all. As jolly as we appeared, Paolo and I were actually terrified. Terrified of the bleak consequences should the enterprise fail.

Papa stayed out of the way, ignoring us, tending to his own tasks—looking after his horses, the orchards, and olive oil production—shrugging or shaking his head in disbelief as he observed the comedy of activity. But he never said anything to stop us. Mamma, the commanding officer, issued orders and stayed busy in the dining room and kitchen. Peppe Bevacqua, our farmhand, was brought in to help. He was very willing—the work inside was much easier than in the fields. Mamma said he showed great promise in the kitchen.

We spread the word around Gangi that a restaurant at Gangivecchio was about to open. News travels very quickly here. Mamma had a reputation as a fine cook, and those who had never been inside Gangivecchio were very curious to see it. So, soon the phone started ringing.

Before we opened, we were already fully booked for the first week. Everything at our little restaurant ran smoothly enough for the first two days. Everyone loved Mamma's food, and we all rejoiced until early on the morning of the third day when local authorities arrived and closed our doors. We hadn't known that a license was required to operate a restaurant. After banishing the dogs and cats from the kitchen, we got our license, which Mamma proudly framed, and we continued operating our restaurant with amazing success. Soon we were balancing the books.

Mamma's willingness to take a risk and her fortitude had saved Gangivecchio. She was a formidable opponent, even against fate. Papa eventually grew to accept the idea and became an engaging proprietor, greeting guests and taking an interest in the restaurant while he continued running the farm.

We do not wish to suggest that our little enterprise was without problems or that it ran as perfectly—with the exception of the brief forced closing—as those first days. It is one thing to cook for a large number of visitors for a few days in a row, and quite another to do this day after day. While the principle is the same, other factors enter the equation. A large party of guests ring up an hour before dinner—customers that we don't want to turn away but simply don't have enough food on hand to feed. Guests have always been unpredictable. One might have an allergy to some basic food but neglect to tell us about it in advance. Others demand something not on our set menu—spaghetti with only tomato sauce, when all our tomato sauce has been used to make a meat-based sauce for the penne with the last bit of spaghetti in the stomachs of our sleeping cats.

So we soon learned about stocking the pantry with plenty of extra foods and pacing our work—preparing sauces and desserts and anything we could ahead of time. There were still disasters. At first we didn't have large enough pots and pans to cook all the food, so we had to cook small amounts in each of four pots or pans. Naturally, sauces and pastas weren't always hot at the same time. Mamma remembers so well the day long ago when we forgot to pick up the bread at the baker's. Paolo was sent begging to our neighbors for as many loaves as he could find. She also recalls the night of the great theft. When we first opened the restaurant, Mamma displayed some of her beautiful inherited family possessions on a small side table in the dining room to make it attractive—crystal vases and bowls, figurines, and silver pieces, like tiny boxes, salvers, teapots, creamers, pitchers, and spoons. After dinner one evening, we entered the dining room and saw that everything she'd carefully arranged on the table had disappeared. Luckily, Mamma knew the name of the man who had made the reservation for the special dinner party that night. She called him immediately and left his ear stinging. All the items were eventually returned, except for one small silver spoon. From then on, Mamma put bowls of fruit and plants and vases of fresh flowers on the little table and locked her treasures away.

There have been embarrassing incidents where guests have come to the aid of our pride. Like the day a man found a hair in his pasta—it can happen—and summoned the waitress. He said, "Lucia, if this hair is Signora Tornabene's, I will eat it. Otherwise, take it away." "Expect the unexpected" became our motto.

By 1980 we had more requests for reservations than space to handle them. So we used the money we had saved to enclose an enormous second-floor covered terrace on the western side of Gangivecchio. We included an adjoining good-sized room with a fireplace in it off the northern end of the terrace as part of the renovation for our new restaurant.

The wall-to-wall windows in the main dining room have expansive, sunny views stretching from a vine-covered arbor directly below to the vast hazelnut, almond, and olive groves and out for miles beyond to rolling Sicilian valleys and hillsides.

Our dining room is a simple, country place, with white walls and wood-beamed ceilings. The tables are covered with yellow tablecloths topped with little vases of flowers. We decorated the restaurant, the hallways, and staircases leading to it with plants and pictures and ancient farm equipment like hand plows, rakes, and milk cans, colorful Sicilian ceramic pitchers and immense platters, and kitchen equipment, like my great-grandmother's old meat grinder and *maidda* (wooden bread tray). Don't worry, the meat grinder is nailed to a table, and the *maidda* is firmly attached to the wall. Anyway, we are always adding something and don't concern ourselves about the new things.

Our lives became very busy and hectic, but it was fun and we felt safer now that we were solvent, and we were content until the worst tragedy of our lives occurred: Papa died suddenly in 1984. In her profound grief it fell to Mamma to look after the whole of Gangivecchio. She has been in charge ever since.

But that is not the end of our history.

Eventually we converted a series of the former monks' rooms in the long hall leading to the restaurant into a brand-new kitchen with an eight-burner gas range, a large refrigerator unit and dishwasher, several sizable sinks, and plenty of counter and storage space. As you can imagine, this beautiful new kitchen simplified our work tremendously. We have saved one of these newly remodeled rooms as a space to hold cooking classes, which we will get around to starting one of these days.

Throughout the year Sunday lunch is our busiest meal of the week. In Sicily, it's traditional for families to gather together over a meal at midday every Sunday. Since the women look after their children and cook all week long, they welcome the opportunity to dine out, especially since extended Sicilian families tend to be very large. We can accommodate up to 150 people now, but normally serve between 75 and 100 guests for Sunday's lunch. During the week we serve lunch from two to as many people who want to dine. And we serve dinner by special request every day except Sunday and Monday.

Paolo and his wife, Betty, opened a nine-room *albergo* next door on the property where they operate their own restaurant, Tenuta Gangivecchio. They are both wonderful cooks, so we've included many of their recipes.

With all the unexpected changes and events in our lives, kind and cruel, writing this book has made Mamma the happiest I've seen her in years. And who knows what the future will bring, although I hope it will be even more happiness.

$\mathcal{P}$rima di Cucinare

(Before Cooking)

L'ATTREZZATURA DI CUCINA
(Cooking Equipment)

At Gangivecchio, we are primarily concerned with the basics when it comes to cooking equipment. I already know that Mamma's most cherished culinary possession is her mother-in-law's hundred-year-old *mattarello* (rolling pin), which she uses for making fresh pasta and pastry. Although priceless to her, it is an ordinary large wooden rolling pin with two easy-to-grasp red handles.

I approached Mamma at the wrong moment in the kitchen to ask what other items she would like to suggest for a list of indispensable cooking equipment. Lucia, our main kitchen worker, had called in sick and fifty people were coming for lunch, so Mamma said, "The most important kitchen equipment are hands . . . as many as you can find." While stirring a big pot of *salsa di pomodoro* with one hand, she swept her free arm around the kitchen in a wide gesture and told me to just look around at everything there and in the pantry and write it down. Then, like a shopping list, she named an inventory of items: Lots of wooden spoons, good knives, bowls, pots and pans, baking sheets, mold rings, and cake pans—of all sizes. A rolling pin and a double-wheeled pastry cutter—with one straight-edged wheel and one serrated-edged wheel—a scale, meat pounder, spatulas, cheese and vegetable graters, strainers, colanders, a food mill for producing purées, and also a fine-mesh sieve. The *mezzaluna* (single- or double-bladed half-moon–shaped cutter) is a terrific instrument for chopping herbs and other ingredients, like capers, anchovies, and currants. You can work with a *mezzaluna* on a flat wooden cutting board or in a curved wooden bowl that fits or is larger than the blade or blades of the *mezzaluna*. A big wooden chopping block and slab of marble for making pasta and pastry are other essentials. "Say we don't use anything fancy, but I suppose you should mention the grinder wizard"—by that she meant our food processor, a wonderful invention that Mamma refuses to touch. Although she knows how much work and time it saves us, she considers it a terrifying machine. As a cook, I couldn't work without it now. I use the processor to purée olive and tuna pâtés, to grind our five-nut pesto sauce, and to process many, many other things. We also recommend a hand-turned pasta machine, which Mamma won't use either.

GLI INGREDIENTI CHE USIAMO NELLA NOSTRA CUCINA
(Ingredients That We Use in Our Kitchen)

We would like to offer some general comments and information about several foods and ingredients that we use regularly in our home and restaurant kitchens at Gangivecchio. And there are a few other select foods, fundamental to our cooking, that you might be curious about. These ingredients and special foods are located in the following list or are featured in separate information boxes throughout the book.

Among the foods profiled in boxes are our unique ferla mushrooms, superb Sicilian capers, fava beans, eggplant, pasta, anchovies, and Parmesan cheese rinds; the latter are never thrown away. Bread, very sacred in Sicily and all of Italy, is never wasted either; we use it to the very last crumb. We like to sprinkle toasted bread crumbs onto some of our pasta dishes.

In another special box we write about our caciocavallo cheese, made from cow's milk at Gangivecchio, as well as how a local shepherd's wife makes *tuma,* ricotta, *primo sale,* and pecorino cheeses from sheep's milk. American commercial ricotta is very unlike Sicily's own superior, creamy sheep's ricotta. There are some American sources for fresh ricotta, but too few to say that it is readily available. We have created a method using regular commercially produced ricotta that best duplicates our own (page 39).

We have also written about Sicily's fantastic outdoor markets: our local market in Gangi, including a description of the boisterous oldtime animal fair (page 169), Palermo's fabulous food bazaar, La Vucciria (page 202), and the gardens of Gangivecchio (page 219).

When we first began organizing our recipes, we worried that many of our ingredients wouldn't be available in America or have the same taste and quality as the products Sicilians normally use. That, of course, was before we'd ever been to the United States. We were astonished to find first-rate equivalents for the majority of our foods; some foods and products, like beef and butter, we actually liked better than the Sicilian counterparts. Navel and Valencia oranges are also superb. In New York, we sampled products from greengrocers and outdoor farmers' markets, supermarkets, and Italian butcher shops—all excellent sources for produce, quality fish and seafood, veal and pork products. Since Italian specialty stores and other markets import many Italian products, such as anchovies, olives, and pecorino and Parmigiano-Reggiano cheeses, duplicating our recipes, for the most part, should present no problem.

If you do not live in a large city, have an Italian grocer nearby, or your local markets don't carry some of the products we use, may we suggest asking the proprietors to order these items for you. Michele tells us that this is common practice in America and that most local store owners will try to be as accommodating as possible. But, for example, if you still can't get specific herbs like fresh rosemary, or vegetables such as tomatoes or arugula, order some seeds and plant your own. Herbs are easy to cultivate in small gardens or pots placed in windows with southern exposure. Arugula planted in boxes in sunny windows grows like a weed.

Unfortunately, there are some foods that we use that are not easily found in America, like wild fennel and greens, bitter almonds, cardoons, and long forty-day green squash. We either give substitutes within individual recipes or don't include recipes using these foods.

ACCIUGHE *(Anchovies)*   Refer to information box on page 214.

ALLORO *(Bay leaves)*   We use aromatic bay laurel leaves to flavor soups, stews, sauces, and meat and fish *involtini*. Our *alloro* are picked fresh from ancient evergreen trees that line pathways at Gangivecchio. Each of the hundreds of laurel branches sprout many fragrant leaves. The branches grow so mightily that every year Peppe must cut them back drastically.

Use fresh bay leaves whenever possible, but if you can find only dry ones, buy only whole leaves that still have a nice green color and bend without breaking.

AMIDO *(Cornstarch)*   We use wheat starch, but have substituted regular cornstarch in our recipes. The amount had to be slightly increased.

BURRO *(Butter)*   We use only sweet butter.

CAPPERI *(Capers)*   Refer to information box on page 43–4.

CARCIOFI *(Artichokes)*   Refer to information box on page 58.

DADI *(Bouillon cubes)*   Canned broths don't exist in Sicily, so it is traditional for us to flavor soups, stews, and sauces with bouillon cubes—usually vegetable or beef, sometimes chicken.

For certain soups and risottos we must prepare fresh stock or broth. In our recipes we give directions for which we use—bouillon cubes or homemade stock—but homemade stock or canned broth can always be substituted for the bouillon cubes.

When using bouillon cubes, remember that they are already flavored with salt, so add salt sparingly and taste as you cook, particularly near the end of cooking time.

ERBE *(Herbs)*

> *Basilico, Origano, Prezzemolo, Salvia, Menta, Rosmarino e Timo*
> (Basil, Oregano, Parsley, Sage, Mint, Rosemary, and Thyme)

The above herbs are the ones we use most often at Gangivecchio. Each has a beautiful, distinct aromatic bouquet with which most everyone is familiar. You may be surprised to see how much mint we use in our recipes, including pasta dishes and sauces. Of course, we always prefer fresh herbs to the dried variety, with one exception—oregano, which we like only dried. Read about *origano* on page 252.

Flat-leaf parsley, which Americans call Italian parsley, is the one we like best, because it has a more pronounced earthy-green flavor. We think of the curly variety only as a garnish, but it has a good flavor, too. We normally keep both on hand. If Italian parsley isn't available, by all means use the curly kind.

ESTRATTO *(Concentrated sun-dried tomato paste extract)*   Refer to *pomodori* in this listing on page 29. The recipe for this fantastic food is on page 94.

FARINA *(Flour)*   The flour we use for bread calls for semolina. For all other uses, including sauces, homemade pasta, and desserts, we use unbleached all-purpose flour similar to our "00" flour.

Chick-pea flour is used to make *panelle,* delicious Sicilian chick-pea fritters. Chick-pea flour isn't easy to find, so we have listed some sources where it can be found in the United States at the end of the *panelle* recipe on page 48.

Fave *(Fava beans)* Refer to the information box on page 24.

Funghi di Ferla *(Ferla mushrooms)* Read about this rare, delicious mushroom on page 234.

Formaggio *(Cheese)* For information on cow's milk caciocavallo, and for information on sheep's milk *tuma, primo sale,* pecorino, and ricotta as well, refer to the information box on page 178. The instructions for draining and weighting ricotta, which is a necessary procedure for duplicating our recipes and requires one or two days' advance preparation, is on page 39. Our suggestions for using Parmesan cheese rinds are on page 82.

Parmigiano Reggiano, the great hard grana cheese, is referred to as Parmesan throughout the book.

Lievito *(Yeast)* At Gangivecchio, we use fresh yeast, but for the recipes here we have substituted active dry yeast granules.

Melanzane *(Eggplant)* Eggplants are one of Sicily's most respected vegetables. You will find a lot of recipes including eggplant in this book. Refer to information box on page 51.

Melograne *(Pomegranates)* Refer to the information box on page 251.

Mollica *(Bread crumbs)* Refer to the information box on page 121.

Frutta Seca *(Nuts)* At Gangivecchio, we cultivate almonds *(mandorle)*, hazelnuts *(nocciole)*, walnuts *(noci)*, and pine nuts *(pinoli)*. See the separate box for information about pine nuts on page 103. We utilize our wonderful nuts in almost all categories of food, including sauces, stuffings, pastas, and desserts. Pistachio nuts are very popular in Sicily, too, especially in desserts and *gelati.* We should add that we use only the natural pistachios, not those strange ones that have been dyed red. All these nuts are easily found in America.

We also want to mention that we have two kinds of almonds—regular and bitter almonds. When raw, the bitter almonds are unpleasant-tasting, but they are powerfully flavored and a source for Amaretto liqueur and are used in a few desserts. Bitter almonds can't be found in the United States, so we use only normal almonds in our recipes.

Olio d'Oliva Extra Vergine *(Extra-virgin olive oil)* Refer to information box on page 67.

Olio Santo *(Hot oil)* Refer to information box on page 76.

Olive *(Olives)* Sicily is a land of olives and many are exported to America, especially the big green ones. We also recommend using Gaeta olives, from an area near Naples, or from other Mediterranean countries, including Greece. The olives are cured or packed in vinegar, brine, or oil. We do not recommend using canned California olives, especially the black ones.

Pane *(Bread)* Read about an old-fashioned breadmaking day in the Madonie Mountains on page 259. The recipe for the bread begins on page 263. For information on bread crumbs, turn to page 121.

Pancetta *(Italian bacon)* Refer to information box on page 80.

Pasta Read all about our national dish, pasta, beginning on page 91, our method of cooking dried pasta on page 100, and our local pasta mill on page 130.

Pinoli *(Pine nuts)* Refer to information box on page 103.

Pomodori *(Tomatoes)* At Gangivecchio, we grow cherry tomatoes, Roma, and San Marzano varieties, but any juicy ripe tomato is good to use, as long as they are full-flavored and ripen on the vine.

We include instructions for reconstituting sun-dried tomatoes (page 68) and how to make our famous *estratto* (concentrated tomato paste extract) on page 94. *Estratto* is almost impossible to find in the United States, so you might want to try preparing this sun-dried tomato paste extract during the hot sunny days of summer.

We use a good amount of tomato paste at Gangivecchio. For home use it is best to use the kind that comes in little tubes, which is more convenient to use in small amounts than the canned variety. When only a few tablespoons are required, all you have to do is recap the tube and store in the refrigerator until you need it again.

Salsa di pomodoro (fresh tomato sauce) is indispensable in Sicilian cooking. We use it in many of our pastas, ragus, and in our egg, vegetable, and antipasti dishes. The easy recipe is on page 93.

Prosciutto *(Ham)* Our ham is *crudo* (raw) or *cotto* (cooked). Air-dried prosciutto is *crudo,* and *cotto* is cooked ham—usually boiled—which we use often, but any good unsmoked cooked ham will do.

RISO *(Rice)*   In Sicily, rice is used mainly for our *arancine* (rice croquettes) and risotto. Arborio, Vialone Nano, or Carnaroli, short-grained rices, are types of rice required for both these wonderful dishes. But there is a rice war raging in our household between my brother, Paolo, and his wife, Betty, and my mother. Read about rice and this battle beginning on page 141.

SALE *(Salt)*   Enormous salt flats exist at the town of Trapani on Sicily's west coast. This salt is unavailable in America, so all the recipes in this book were tested with fine sea salt imported from Europe, but regular table salt can also be used.

SARDE *(Sardines)*   Refer to information box on page 207.

SPEZIE *(Spices)*   The spices we utilize most in our recipes are black pepper (*pepe nero*), cinnamon (*cannella*), nutmeg (*noce moscata*), saffron (*zafferano*), cloves (*chiodi di garofano*), and ground hot pepper (peperoncino or cayenne pepper). These are all commonly known and readily available in the United States.

In Sicily, it is not traditional to use cayenne pepper, but you will see it in a number of our recipes, because we use it at Gangivecchio.

STRUTTO *(Lard)*   Refer to information box on page 38.

UOVA *(Eggs)*   We use large eggs throughout this book. Fresh farm eggs are always superior, if you can find a source for them.

When baking, eggs should be at room temperature.

VANIGLIA *(Vanilla)*   In Sicily, we use powdered vanilla crystals or vanilla sugar. Vanilla extract has been substituted in our recipes with very good results.

ZAFFERANO *(Saffron)*   We value saffron highly as an ingredient in Sicilian cooking in pasta, rice, and vegetable dishes. But its most renowned use is as a vital flavoring element in Pasta con le Sarde (page 124).

Nutrirsi di cibi prelibati è trasformare una necessità in estasi.
(To nourish ourselves with delicious food turns necessity into ecstasy.)

—*Wanda Tornabene*

Antipasti

(Antipasto)

(Apart from the over three dozen recipes in this chapter, there are many other dishes that can be considered excellent antipasti in the *verdure* section, beginning on page 216.)

Cuddura Patedda *(Fried Dough with Tomato, Anchovy, and Onion Topping)*
• Calzoncini con Prosciutto *(Fried Dough Stuffed with Ham)* • Strutto *(Lard)* •
Ricotta • Panzerotti con Ricotta *(Fried Dough Stuffed with Ricotta)*
• Polpette di Melanzane *(Fried and Braised Eggplant Balls)* •
Polpette di Baccalà *(Salt Cod Balls)* • Polpette di Sarde *(Sardine Balls)*
• Capperi *(Capers)* • Caponata *(Sweet and Sour Eggplant Stew)* •
Caponata di Verdure *(Green Vegetable Stew)* • Cazzilli o Crocchè di Patate
(Sicilian Potato Croquettes) • Crocchè di Latte *(Milk Croquettes)*
• Panelle *(Chick-pea Fritters)* • Arancinette *(Miniature Rice Ball Croquettes)* •
Involtini di Melanzane al Forno *(Baked Eggplant Rolls Stuffed with Frittata Strips)*
• Melanzane *(Eggplant)* • Frittata della Mamma *(Baked Omelet Lasagne)* •
La Pizza di Cipolla di Bruna *(Bruna's Onion Pizza)* • Frittelle di Fiori di Zucca
(Zucchini Flower Fritters) • Frittelle di Verdure *(Green Vegetable Fritters)*
• Bruschetta Classica *(Grilled Bread with Garlic and Olive Oil)* • Bruschetta
con Pomodori *(Grilled Bread with Tomatoes)* • Torta Rustica di Ricotta *(Ricotta
and Ham Tart)* • Carciofi *(Artichokes)* • Sformato di Carciofi *(Artichoke Tart)*
• Carciofini Fritti *(Small Breaded and Fried Artichoke Hearts)* •
Carciofi Ripieni *(Artichokes Stuffed with Garlic and Seasoned Bread Crumbs)*
• Pomodori Ripieni di Risotto *(Tomatoes Stuffed with Rice)* • Melanzane
Ripiene *(Baby Eggplants Stuffed with Mint and Caciocavallo)* • Peperoni Ripieni
(Baked Yellow and Red Peppers) • Gnocchi di Ricotta di Paolo *(Paolo's Poached
Lemon-flavored Ricotta Gnocchi with Sage Butter)*
Formaggio all'Argentiera *(Silversmith's Cheese)* • Crêpes con Ricotta e Salsa di

Finocchietto di Betty *(Betty's Crêpes with Ricotta and Fennel Sauce)* •
Patè di Olive Bianche *(Green Olive Pâté)* • Patè di Olive Nere *(Black Olive Pâté)*
• Patè di Tonno *(Tuna Pâté)* • Le Olive Bianche Consate *(Green Olives with
Herbs)* • Olio d'Oliva Extra Vergine *(Extra-virgin Olive Oil)* •
I Pomodorini Consati di Giovanna *(Giovanna's Preserved Sun-dried Tomatoes with
Basil, Garlic, and Parmesan Cheese)* • Tonno Sott' Olio *(Preserved or
Homemade Tuna Fish)* • Funghi Sott' Olio *(Preserved Mushrooms)* •
Melanzane Sott' Aceto di Peppe *(Peppe's Preserved Pickled Eggplant)*

Antipasti as part of a meal in Sicily is a relatively new concept to us. Throughout history, the people, especially here in the mountain countryside, have always worked long, hard hours during the day tending their gardens or crops in the fields or caring for their animals, particularly sheep. So when it came time for a meal, they wanted to sit down and eat—eat pasta, not nibble. Stimulating the palate wasn't necessary. To be honest, it still isn't. When we are just the family, we never have antipasti before dinner. We still want to get right to the spaghetti.

But if we have company or are entertaining, along with an *aperitivo,* we normally serve a small choice of light foods, such as herbed olives or cubes of our caciocavallo and pecorino cheeses or mortadella. At the restaurant, meals begin with a plate of *antipasti rustici* for each guest. These antipasti normally consist of a changing variety of three offerings, which might be *panelle* (chick-pea fritters), *cuddura patedda* (puffy pieces of fried dough with a tomato, anchovy, and onion topping), grilled eggplant, *frittelle* (fritters) of batter-coated zucchini blossoms, or a green or black olive or tuna pâté on grilled bread slices. The selection is based on what seasonal foods are in the garden or what is available to us at the market. When our figs at Gangivecchio ripen, we serve this luscious fruit with thin slices of prosciutto.

For special occasions and holidays more substantial fare is required. These more elaborate dishes range from aromatic *involtini di melanzane al forno* (baked eggplant rolls stuffed with thin strips of frittata) and *arancinette* (miniature versions of Sicily's famous stuffed rice croquettes) to *sformato di carciofi* (a savory artichoke tart). Most of the recipes included in this chapter can be served as appetizers, as a little snack or antipasti, or as an individual first course as the prelude to a meal; many others can be served as side dishes or light meals. You will notice that a large number of our antipasti are made with vegetables. We Sicilians are a people who live from the land and love vegetables, historically true to our wholesome Mediterranean diet.

Nowadays it has become traditional for restaurants throughout Sicily to offer diners an expansive antipasti table. One of our favorites is served at an excellent, unpretentious, indoor/outdoor seafood restaurant called Cambusa (meaning "ship's galley" in Italian), in the Piazza Marina in Old Palermo, a short distance from the port. Our friends Pino and Oriana Varia have been the owners for six years, and they serve the freshest fish and seafood imaginable. Oriana is the gregarious, superb cook, and Pino, her husband, is the jolly welcoming captain in charge. He never stops moving. Customers at Cambusa must call several days in advance. Most are Sicilian regulars who want to sit down, place their pasta and fish course orders, then begin the meal with Oriana's tempting, freshly prepared antipasti. She serves more than a dozen dishes, like stuffed zucchini and tomatoes, sweet and sour pumpkin, marinated onions, roasted peppers, and stuffed sardines.

When Pino and Oriana come to rest and relax in the country and dine at Gangivecchio, what do you think we talk about? Always antipasti and fish and seafood recipes, of course. After the meal, delicious gossip follows, like a second dessert.

Cuddura Patedda

(Fried Dough with Tomato,
Anchovy, and Onion Topping)

DOUGH

2 packages active dry yeast
4 cups all-purpose flour
1 teaspoon salt
3 tablespoons lard, melted and
    cooled, or olive oil
Sunflower or vegetable oil, for
    frying

TOPPING

½ cup olive oil
4 medium onions, thinly sliced
3 large fresh, ripe tomatoes,
    peeled, seeded, and minced
    (or 3 cups canned Italian
    plum tomatoes, finely
    chopped)
4 anchovy fillets, finely chopped
½ teaspoon sugar
Salt and freshly ground pepper
Freshly grated pecorino or
    Parmesan cheese

*H*ere is the recipe for one of Mamma's most enchanting antipasti, called Cuddura Patedda. Small, rectangular pieces of dough are fried and puff up into airy-light, crisp pillows that are topped with a savory mixture of tomatoes, anchovies, onion, and pecorino cheese.

Serves 8

Combine the yeast with ½ cup of warm water in a bowl. Let rest for 10 minutes so the yeast dissolves.

Put the flour into a large bowl with the salt. Make a well in the center of the flour and pour in the dissolved yeast-and-water mixture, plus 1 cup of cool water and the melted lard or olive oil. With a wooden spoon, work the ingredients until they form a dough, adding a little more water, as needed. Turn the dough onto a lightly floured work surface and knead it for about 10 minutes, until silky smooth.

Put the dough into a large, lightly floured bowl and turn it so that the entire surface of the dough is lightly coated with flour. Cover with a dishcloth and let the dough rest in a warm area of your kitchen until it has doubled in size, about 1½ hours, depending on the warmth of the room.

Meanwhile, prepare the topping. Heat the olive oil with 1 tablespoon of water, add the onions, and cook over low heat until the onions are tender, about 15 minutes. Add the tomatoes, anchovies, sugar, and salt (add sparingly, remembering that anchovies are salty) and pepper to taste. Simmer for about 15 minutes over low heat, stirring often. Turn off the heat and transfer the mixture to a bowl. Let cool to room temperature.

When the dough has doubled in size, punch it down and knead it for 1 minute. On a lightly floured work surface, roll out the dough into a large rectangle, about ¼ inch thick. Cut the dough in 2 × 4-inch rectangles.

Heat 2 inches of sunflower or vegetable oil in a deep-sided frying pan until the oil is hot but not smoking. Cook the pieces of dough in batches, turning once, until golden brown on each side. As the dough pieces cook, drain them on paper towels.

Meanwhile, reheat the tomato topping and stir well.

Arrange the fried dough pieces on a warm serving platter.

Spoon about 2 tablespoonfuls of the mixture over the top of each piece of dough. Sprinkle with pecorino or Parmesan cheese and serve immediately.

Calzoncini con Prosciutto

(Fried Dough Stuffed with Ham)

his version of fried dough contains a ham stuffing. *Calzoncini* means "little trousers" in Italian.

Prepare the dough. When it has doubled in size, punch it down and knead it for 1 minute on a lightly floured surface.

Divide the dough into 3 equal portions. Roll each into a 36-inch-long piece, about 4 to 5 inches wide and ¹⁄₁₆ inch thick. This is most easily accomplished using the widest opening of a manual pasta machine, but a rolling pin can be used. We suggest rolling, stuffing, and cutting 1 strip of dough at a time. It uses less space.

For each strip of dough, put rounded teaspoonfuls of minced ham 1 inch from one edge of a lengthwise side of the dough, spacing the ham about 2 inches apart. Fold the dough in half lengthwise, covering the ham-filled portion to the edge, as if you were folding a sheet of paper. Press the outer edges of the dough together, then press the dough down between each of the ham-filled portions lightly with your fingers. Using a 3-inch-round serrated biscuit-cutter, cut little individual crescent shapes around each ham-stuffed portion of the dough, leaving the folded-over edge uncut. The dough will have one straight side (where it was folded over) and a curved serrated shape.

Put the stuffed *calzoncini* on a lightly floured baking sheet, uncovered, and let them double in size, about 30 minutes.

DOUGH

Same as in preceding recipe for Cuddura Patedda

1 pound boiled ham, thinly sliced and minced
Sunflower or vegetable oil, for deep-frying

Strutto
(Lard)

Using lard—pure animal fat—is frowned upon nowadays in American cooking, and we appreciate this. All over the world today, fat has become the chief enemy of the diet. We know we must eat only a little. But, unless specific health problems strictly forbid it, how can we, for example, give up butter entirely? It's too delicious and too important an ingredient in cooking.

The small number of dishes that we normally cook at Gangivecchio that contain or are cooked in lard today are few—*cuddura patedda, panzerotti, calzoncini,* cannoli, *sofficini,* and various other pastries. Cooking with lard makes an enormous difference in the lightness and crispness of pastry, as well as the taste. We used to fry many foods in lard. For this book we suggest frying only the pastry shells for cannoli in hot lard—Mamma won't budge on this practice. She says, "I have lived a very long time and have eaten foods made with, and fried in, lard all my life. If you don't cook my recipe for cannoli in lard, they won't be *my* cannoli." Even so, she compromised and has given ingredients you can use instead of lard.

If you want to avoid lard as an ingredient in certain recipes, substitute olive oil. Do not use Crisco—we tried this in America and found the taste quite peculiar, even when frying foods. For deep-frying, substitute sunflower or other seed or vegetable oil for the lard.

If you do wish to use lard, you will have a difficult time finding it in American supermarkets today. Buy fresh pork fat from your butcher. Perhaps you'll need to order it in advance, and you may also be forced to buy a larger amount than you actually need. Don't worry, it freezes very well. Anyway, buying more will save you another trip to the butcher next time you need lard.

Before using fresh fat, it must be rendered. Cut the lard into little cubes and render it in a heavy-bottomed, deep-sided frying pan over very low heat. The lard turns into a clear liquid. Discard the pieces of cracklings and filter the clear, hot liquid fat through several layers of cheesecloth into a crock or heatproof glass container. When it cools, the rendered lard will congeal. Cover the container and freeze the lard until needed.

Heat 3 inches of sunflower or vegetable oil in a deep-sided frying pan until the oil is hot but not smoking. Cook the *calzoncini* a few at a time, in batches, until golden brown all over. It takes only a few minutes. Drain the *calzoncini* on paper towels as they are cooked. Serve immediately.

Ricotta

To best duplicate sumptuous Sicilian sheep's milk ricotta from the American commercially made cow's milk product, it is necessary to drain out the excess liquid by straining it over a bowl with a weight on top for one or two nights—two are best. The ricotta won't taste exactly like our fresh creamy sheep's ricotta, but depending on the product, it is usually quite an acceptable substitute in texture and consistency. Read more about ricotta and other Sicilian cheeses on page 178.

There are a few sources for fresh sheep's ricotta in the United States. If you are fortunate enough to live nearby, use fresh sheep's ricotta in our recipes.

1–3 pounds ricotta (whatever amount required in recipe)

Line a large plastic strainer with three layers of cheesecloth and place over a bowl. The bottom of the strainer should rest at least 1 inch from the bottom of the bowl, so the liquid that drains out of the ricotta can collect freely there. Spoon the ricotta into the lined strainer. Put a small saucer on top of the ricotta. Rest a 16- or 28-ounce can of some ingredient like tomatoes on the saucer. Cover the can and cheese in the bowl loosely with plastic wrap and refrigerate overnight. Up to ½ cup liquid will drain out of the ricotta when it is strained in this method. We have found that the procedure works best if left for two days. If you have time to leave it for two days, remove the can and saucer and stir the ricotta at the end of the first day. Discard any drained liquid in the bowl. Replace the ricotta in the strainer over the bowl, and the saucer and can, cover, and refrigerate the cheese overnight again.

Panzerotti con Ricotta

*(Fried Dough Stuffed
with Ricotta)*

DOUGH

3¾ cups all-purpose flour
¼ teaspoon salt
⅓ cup lard, melted and cooled,
    or olive oil

FILLING

2 cups drained ricotta (see
    instructions on page 39—
    must be prepared one to two
    days in advance)
Salt and freshly ground pepper
Sunflower or vegetable oil, for
    deep-frying

Combine the flour and salt in a large bowl. Make a well in the center of the flour, then add the lard or olive oil and about 1 cup of lukewarm water. Stir with a wooden spoon until a dough is formed, adding a little extra water as needed. Knead the dough on a lightly floured work surface for 10 minutes. Let rest for 10 minutes.

Meanwhile, season the ricotta to taste with salt and pepper.

Divide the dough into 3 equal portions. Roll each into a 35-inch-long piece, about 4 to 5 inches wide and 1/16 inch thick. This is most easily accomplished by using the widest opening of a manual pasta machine, but a rolling pin can be used. We suggest rolling, stuffing, and cutting 1 strip of dough at a time. It uses less space.

For each strip of dough, put rounded teaspoonfuls of ricotta 1 inch from one edge of a lengthwise side of the dough, spacing the ricotta about 2 inches apart. Fold the dough in half lengthwise, covering the ricotta-filled portion to the edge, as if you were folding a sheet of paper. Press the end edges of the dough together, then press down the dough between each of the ricotta-filled portion with your fingers. With a serrated pastry cutter, cut around the ricotta, making 2-inch squares. Place the *panzerotti* on a lightly floured baking sheet, uncovered. Make the remaining *panzerotti*. They can rest for up to 1 hour.

Heat 3 inches of sunflower or vegetable oil in a deep-sided frying pan until the oil is hot but not smoking. Fry the *panzerotti* a few at a time, in batches, until golden brown all over. Drain on paper towels as they are cooked. Serve immediately.

Polpette di Melanzane

Serves 6 to 8

(Fried and Braised Eggplant Balls)

Bring 4 quarts of water to a rolling boil in a large pot. Add the eggplant pieces and return to a boil. Reduce the heat and simmer until tender, about 10 minutes.

Drain the eggplant pieces well in a colander and squeeze out the excess liquid by placing the eggplant, a few pieces at a time, in a clean dish towel and twisting it over the sink.

With your fingers, shred the meat of the eggplant into little pieces and chop it fine.

Put the eggplant into a bowl with 1 of the eggs, the grated pecorino or Parmesan cheese, mint, currants, pine nuts, and bread crumbs. Mix thoroughly. Season to taste with salt and pepper. The mixture should be quite moist but not wet. Add a little more bread crumbs, if necessary.

Beat the 2 remaining eggs in a shallow bowl. Shape the eggplant mixture into balls about 1¼ inch in diameter. Coat each ball with egg and then roll in bread crumbs. Let the breaded eggplant balls rest for 10 minutes on a large plate or platter.

Heat about 3 inches of sunflower or vegetable oil in a deep-sided frying pan until the oil is hot but not smoking. Fry the eggplant balls, in batches, until golden brown all over. Drain on paper towels as they are cooked.

Transfer the eggplant balls to a large saucepan and add the tomato sauce. Over medium-low heat, simmer for 30 minutes and occasionally stir very gently. Taste for seasoning.

Serve at room temperature.

4 medium eggplants, peeled and cut in half lengthwise
3 large eggs
½ cup freshly grated pecorino or Parmesan cheese
2 tablespoons freshly chopped mint leaves
⅓ cup currants, soaked in warm water for 10 minutes, drained, and chopped
⅓ cup chopped pine nuts
¾ cup fresh bread crumbs, or as needed, plus extra for breading
Salt and freshly ground pepper
Sunflower or vegetable oil, for deep-frying
1 quart fresh tomato sauce (Salsa di Pomodoro, page 93)

Polpette di Baccalà

(Salt Cod Balls)

2 pounds salt cod (must be
    soaked overnight)
2 large eggs
¼ cup currants, soaked in warm
    water for 10 minutes,
    drained, patted dry, and
    chopped
2 tablespoons finely chopped
    pine nuts
⅓ cup fresh Italian parsley,
    finely chopped
1 garlic clove, minced
1 small onion, minced
Salt and freshly ground pepper
1¼ cups fresh bread crumbs
Flour
Sunflower or vegetable oil, for
    frying
1 lemon, cut into 4 wedges and
    seeded

Sicilians in the Madonie Mountains have an affinity for salt cod, because until the last few years, no fresh fish or seafood was available to us. It is true that when you are denied a particular food, it becomes something you long to have. Everyone in our household loves Mamma's little salt cod balls.

Serves 4

Soak the salt cod, immersed in cool water, overnight in the refrigerator, covered well—two nights are even better. Change the water four times at 3-hour intervals during day hours.

Drain the salt cod well and pat it dry, pressing out excess water. Clean thoroughly, removing any skin and bones.

Finely chop the salt cod and put it into a bowl with the eggs, currants, pine nuts, parsley, garlic, onion, salt and pepper to taste, and the bread crumbs, and mix well.

Form the mixture into little egg shapes and coat with flour.

Heat ½ inch of sunflower or vegetable oil in a large frying pan until the oil is hot but not smoking. Cook the salt-cod eggs until golden brown all over and serve immediately with lemon wedges.

Polpette di Sarde

(Sardine Balls)

2½ cups cleaned, boned,
    skinned and deheaded fresh
    sardines, finely chopped
    (Thawed frozen sardines can
    also be used. Read about sar-
    dines in the information box
    on page 207.)

*Serves 6 as an appetizer or 4 as a main course
or for 4 with 1 pound of spaghetti*

Combine the ingredients from the sardines through the grated cheese in a large bowl and mix well. Add a little hot water if the mixture isn't moist enough. Season to taste with salt and pepper. Shape into eighteen 1¼-inch balls and let rest.

Put the tomato sauce, onion, and sugar into a wide, deep saucepan or frying pan and bring to a boil. Immediately reduce the heat to a simmer and add the sardine balls. Simmer for 30 minutes and occasionally stir gently. Discard the onion. Serve cold as an appetizer or at room temperature as a main course. This dish, heated, is also excellent sauce for spaghetti.

*C*apperi
(Capers)

Capers are the unopened flower buds of the caper bush found throughout the Mediterranean. When allowed to bloom, the flower is a tiny delicate spray of white and lilac. Long ago, capers grew wild in chinks of stone walls at Gangivecchio.

Sicilian capers are highly esteemed. They come from Pantelleria, an arid, remote volcanic island about sixty miles southeast of Trapani, near the coast of Tunisia. Pantelleria is famous for two things—capers and Moscato di Pantelleria, an amber-colored, delicious, smooth, sweet dessert wine. This ancient, windy island has a very inhospitable, rocky geography. To cultivate the grapes and capers, walls had to be built as protection from the harsh winds.

Our capers are larger than the nonpareil French variety, and in Sicily they are normally packed in sea salt rather than vinegar brine. This method of preservation helps retain their pungent flavor, which we think is the best in the world.

Capers play a distinctive role in our cuisine. They are a crucial flavor ingredient in producing the exceptional taste of our ca-

1 large egg
1 cup fresh bread crumbs
¼ cup olive oil
2 tablespoons currants, soaked in warm water for 10 minutes, well drained, and chopped
2 tablespoons chopped pine nuts
1 tablespoon freshly chopped mint leaves
1 tablespoon grated caciocavallo, pecorino, or Parmesan cheese
Salt and freshly ground pepper
3 cups fresh tomato sauce (Salsa di Pomodoro, page 93)
1 medium onion, peeled and left whole
1 teaspoon sugar

ponata. We also like to marry capers with olive oil and lemon juice for flavoring fish, and we add them to countless pasta sauces.

Sicilian capers packed in salt in small jars or plastic bags are available in the United States in Italian food shops, and they are worth seeking for more authentic-tasting dishes. Before using them, rinse the salt off briefly under cool running water, drain, and gently pat them dry. Do not squeeze or flatten them. If you can't find imported Sicilian capers packed in salt, substitute other varieties that are preserved in vinegar brine.

When capers are patted dry and fried in hot oil, the buds open up into crisp little flowers, producing a delightful, crunchy garnish.

Caponata

(Sweet and Sour Eggplant Stew)

Olive oil
3 large eggplants, with stem ends removed, cut into 1-inch cubes
1 large onion, chopped
3 cups fresh tomato sauce (Salsa di Pomodoro, page 93)
¾ cup pitted green olives, Sicilian, if possible

*N*owadays caponata is known throughout the world as a savory eggplant stew. In Sicily, we use it as an important part of an antipasti selection or as a side dish, best served cold. Since it keeps well for several days in the refrigerator, improving in flavor every hour it marinates, we make a big amount to enjoy for as long as it lasts.

Makes about 1½ quarts

Heat ½ inch of olive oil in a large frying pan and cook the eggplant, in batches, until golden brown. Drain the cooked eggplant on paper towels. Add extra oil to the pan, as needed.

In a large, heavy-bottomed saucepan, heat ½ cup olive oil and cook the onion for 5 minutes, stirring often. Add the remaining ingredients and the drained eggplant. Combine gently but thoroughly, and simmer over low heat for 30 minutes. Taste for seasoning. The caponata should have a pleasant sweet-and-sour flavor.

Transfer the caponata to a large bowl and let cool. Serve at room temperature or cover and refrigerate overnight and serve cold.

½ cup capers
1 cup thinly sliced hearts of celery including 2 tablespoons chopped leaves
5 anchovy fillets, finely chopped
½ cup red wine vinegar, or to taste
1 tablespoon sugar, or to taste
Salt and freshly ground pepper

Caponata di Verdure

(Green Vegetable Stew)

*W*e prepare a large amount of this green caponata in the Madonie Mountain countryside when friends come to dinner, especially on Easter or Christmas. All green vegetables are used in the dish, unlike the classic caponata in which eggplant and olives are featured.

Serves 10 to 12

Boil all the vegetables separately in lightly salted water until just cooked. Drain the vegetables well, squeezing extra water out of the chard, spinach, broccoli, and chicory, then coarsely chop.

Heat the olive oil with the garlic in a large frying pan and cook for 5 minutes over medium heat, stirring often. Add the vegetables, season to taste with salt and pepper, mix well, and let simmer for 15 minutes. Taste again for seasoning. Sprinkle a little vinegar to taste over the top and toss again.

Transfer to a large, round platter and arrange in a high, round dome shape. Sprinkle the top with bread crumbs and capers. Arrange the anchovy fillets across the top of the caponata and sprinkle with pine nuts. Garnish the platter with lemon slices. Serve cool.

1½ pounds Swiss chard, cleaned
1½ pounds spinach, cleaned
1½ pounds broccoli, cleaned
1½ pounds chicory, cleaned
½ cup celery, thinly sliced
1 cup olive oil
5 garlic cloves, thinly sliced
Salt and freshly ground pepper
Red wine vinegar
½ cup toasted bread crumbs (page 121)
1 tablespoon capers
8 canned anchovy fillets
2 tablespoons pine nuts
1 lemon, seeded and very thinly sliced

Cazzilli o Crocchè di Patate

(Sicilian Potato Croquettes)

3 pounds boiling potatoes
    (mature ones are best)
⅓ cup fresh parsley, very finely
    chopped
Salt and freshly ground pepper
4 large egg whites
Dried bread crumbs
Sunflower or vegetable oil, for
    deep-frying

The Sicilian dialect word *cazzilli* (little penises) was humorously given to these tasty fried potato croquettes because they are formed into little rod shapes. Whenever we shop in Palermo's old market, La Vucciria, we can never resist a midmorning snack of hot, crisp *cazzilli* that are sold at a fry shop there. *Cazzilli* are just one of the many typical street foods sold in roadside *friggitoria* in Palermo and surrounding areas.

At Gangivecchio, we cook batches of *cazzilli* to serve as hot appetizers or as a side dish. They must be eaten piping hot, but *cazzilli* can be prepared a day in advance, so serving them to company is easy—you simply bread and fry them at the last minute. They taste better when eaten with the fingers.

Serves 6 to 8

Cook the potatoes in their skins in lightly salted, boiling water until very well done. Drain and cool for 3 hours.

Peel the potatoes and force them through the blade of a food mill over a large bowl. Add the parsley and salt and pepper to taste. Mix with a wooden spoon until well blended.

With your hands, form little rod-shaped croquettes 2½ inches long and 1 inch wide with about 2 rounded tablespoons of the potato mixture. Press each croquette together well. As the croquettes are shaped, put them onto a baking sheet lined with aluminum foil. Cover with foil and refrigerate overnight. The *cazzilli* can be cooked immediately, but they have a better flavor if cooked the next day; they are also less likely to break apart during cooking.

When ready to prepare the croquettes (if refrigerated overnight, bring them back to room temperature), completely coat each croquette with egg white, then gently roll in bread crumbs. Be sure each one is thoroughly coated, or else the croquette will crack and break apart during cooking.

Heat 3 inches of sunflower or vegetable oil in a deep-sided frying pan until the oil is hot but not smoking. Lower each croquette into the hot oil with a slotted spoon. Cook in batches of 6 or 7.

Sometimes the croquettes will sink to the bottom of the pan. After a few seconds, move them very gently around with the spoon. Soon they will float to the top. Roll them over and over and cook until golden brown—this takes only a few minutes. Drain on paper towels and continue cooking the remainder, in batches, in the same manner. Sprinkle lightly with salt and serve immediately.

Crocchè di Latte

(Milk Croquettes)

𝒩ormally served as an appetizer, these cheese-flavored béchamel croquettes also go very well with meat dishes, especially roasts.

Makes about 2 dozen croquettes to serve 6 to 8

Prepare the hard béchamel sauce and stir in the Parmesan cheese. Cool the sauce completely. Cover and refrigerate the sauce at least 1 hour before preparing the croquettes.

Shape 1 rounded tablespoonful of the cold béchamel into a barrel or oval shape. Coat the shaped béchamel with egg white and then completely cover with bread crumbs. Place the croquette on a baking sheet and prepare the rest in the same manner.

Heat 3 inches of sunflower or vegetable oil in a deep-sided frying pan. When the oil is hot but not smoking, fry the croquettes a few at a time, in batches, gently lowering them into the oil with a slotted spoon. Gently turn the croquettes until golden brown all over. Drain the cooked croquettes on paper towels as they are cooked. Season lightly with salt and serve immediately.

3 cups hard béchamel sauce
    (Salsa Besciamella Sostenuta,
    page 96)
3 tablespoons freshly grated
    Parmesan cheese
3 large egg whites
Dried bread crumbs
Sunflower or vegetable oil, for
    deep-frying
Salt

Panelle

(Chick-pea Fritters)

3 cups chick-pea flour*
5 cups water
½ teaspoon salt
⅓ cup fresh Italian parsley, very
    finely chopped
Freshly ground pepper
Sunflower or vegetable oil, for
    deep-frying
Soft bread rolls (optional)
Salt

   *Chick-pea flour is difficult to find
in the United States, although many
health-food shops stock it. Two mail-
order sources are: Walnut Acres, Penns
Creek, PA 17862 (800-433-3998), and
King Arthur Flour, Rt. #2, P.O. Box 56,
Norwich, VT 05055 (802-649-3881). It
is also available at Dean & DeLuca, 560
Broadway (at Prince Street), New York,
NY (212-431-1691) or (800-221-7714).

*P*anelle—small, flat, fried chick-pea fritters—are one of Palermo's most popular street foods sold in *friggitoria* (fry shops) all over the city. The first step in preparing *panelle* is the same as that of northern Italy's polenta, except chick-pea flour is used in place of cornmeal. The chick-pea flour is combined with water, salt, pepper, and a little parsley, and is constantly stirred over heat in a saucepan for about 15 minutes. Here the similarity ends.

Panelle's smooth, sticky batterlike mixture is then poured onto an oiled surface, flattened very thin, and cooled. The mixture hardens quickly and is normally cut into about 4 × 3-inch rectangles, deep-fried, and placed inside soft plain buns or bread rolls and handed to customers to eat while standing—Sicilian fast food. *Panelle* are not, however, a fast food for the cook, and they are only good eaten hot. Cooled or reheated, they become rubbery. They are delicious hot appetizers served with or without the bread.

Depending on the size and shape, makes 24 to 36 panelle
to serve 8 to 12

Lightly oil a large area of marble or another nonporous surface near the stove and have ready a lightly oiled rolling pin.

    Put the chick-pea flour into a large, heavy-bottomed saucepan. Off the heat, slowly add the water, stirring constantly with a wooden spoon to prevent lumps. It's okay if a few lumps stubbornly form. Over medium-high heat, stir in the salt, parsley, and pepper. Stir the mixture constantly for about 15 minutes, until the mixture has thickened and begins to roll off the sides and bottom of the pan. You must regulate the heat between medium-high, medium, and low during cooking time in order to keep the mixture bubbling and to avoid scorching the pan. During the end of cooking time, taste for salt, adding more, if desired.

    When the desired consistency is reached, immediately turn the hot mixture onto the oiled surface. Without delay, flatten the mixture evenly with the oiled rolling pin to slightly less than a ¼-inch thickness. Let cool. It can be left for up to 1 hour.

Cut the dough into 4 × 3-inch pieces, small squares, ovals, triangles, circles, sticks, or any shape you wish.

Heat 2 inches of sunflower or vegetable oil in a deep-sided frying pan until the oil is hot but not smoking. Cook the *panelle* a few at a time in batches until golden brown on each side. They will puff up slightly. Use 1 or 2 spatulas to turn the *panelle*—a fork or metal tongs will tear or make indentations in them. Drain the *panelle* on paper towels as they are cooked. Sprinkle lightly with salt the instant they come out of the pan. Serve immediately, inside the bread rolls or on plates, while still nice and hot.

NOTE: This recipe is easily cut in half to serve 4 to 6.

Arancinette

(Miniature Rice Ball Croquettes)

Sicily's famous fried stuffed rice croquettes make an excellent appetizer. The recipe is the same as that given for large-sized *arancine* on page 145. (The recipe can easily be cut in half.) When served as an antipasto, we shape the cooked saffron rice—see Il Mio Risotto, page 143, for the recipe—into little balls about the size of a walnut. The stuffing we use is simply a small piece of mozzarella, about a ½-inch cube. Sometimes we don't use a stuffing at all.

Involtini di Melanzane al Forno

(Baked Eggplant Rolls Stuffed with Frittata Strips)

Vegetable oil
3 medium eggplants, with stem
    ends removed, cut length-
    wise into ⅓-inch-thick slices
4 large eggs
⅓ cup freshly grated pecorino
    or Parmesan cheese, plus
    extra to sprinkle on top
⅓ cup freshly chopped Italian
    parsley
Salt and freshly ground pepper
2 cups fresh tomato sauce (Salsa
    di Pomodoro, page 93)
1 tablespoon butter

*M*amma's lovely baked eggplant-and-cheese-flavored frittata rolls are superb as an antipasto, vegetable side dish, or a light
meal served with a green salad.

Serves 6

Heat ½ inch of vegetable oil in a large frying pan, and fry the eggplant slices a few at a time, in batches, until lightly browned on
each side. Drain the cooked eggplant slices on paper towels, adding
more oil as needed.

To make the frittata (an Italian flat, open-faced omelet), whisk
the eggs together in a bowl with the pecorino or Parmesan cheese and
parsley, and season lightly with salt and pepper. Heat 2 tablespoons
of oil in a large, nonstick frying pan with curved sides. Pour in the
egg mixture and cook, swirling the eggs around in a circle, tilting the
pan until the eggs are set and a light gold color on the bottom.

Over the sink, invert the frittata onto the lid of the pan or onto
a plate or platter larger than the diameter of the pan, and slide the
frittata back into the pan. Cook for a minute or two until lightly
golden on the bottom side. Transfer the frittata to a cutting board
and cut into 1½-inch strips. Cut each of the strips in half, crosswise.

Preheat the oven to 350°F.

Place a piece of frittata in the center of each eggplant slice—a
few of the eggplant slices will need 2 shorter pieces of frittata. Roll
the eggplant and frittata up from one end to the other and place,
seam side down, in a lightly greased, shallow baking dish. Prepare
the remaining rolls in the same manner. The rolls should be placed
side by side, touching each other, in rows. Spoon the sauce over the
top and dot it with the butter. Sprinkle lightly with additional
freshly grated Parmesan cheese. Bake in the preheated oven for 30
minutes. Let rest 5 minutes before serving.

$\mathcal{M}$elanzane

(Eggplant)

Eggplant is the second-most-popular vegetable in Sicily, preceded only by the tomato. If my son, Paolo, had to choose his last meal, it would be spaghetti with fried eggplant—sometimes called *pasta alla Norma.*

Of the hundreds of *melanzane* recipes we have in Sicily, the most well known, apart from spaghetti with eggplant, are caponata, an aromatic sweet-and-sour stewed mixture, and *melanzane alla parmigiana*—layers of fried eggplant topped with tomato sauce, fresh basil, and Parmesan cheese, and baked.

Among cooks, there is always the debate over whether to salt, weigh down, and drain slices or pieces of eggplant before cooking them. This procedure is said to extract any bitter flavor. We have never found fresh, firm eggplant bitter, so we do not recommend this method. We also rarely peel off one of the eggplant's greatest assets, its delicious, smooth skin, which adds an appealing, contrasting texture and taste to any dish.

In Sicily, eggplants range in color from a streaked pale violet and white to deep purple, and they range in size from small, round, or elongated to large oblong shapes. We prefer round eggplants for their sweetness, but any shape and color can be used unless a specific type or configuration is needed in an individual recipe. The least recommended are the extra-large sizes, because the larger the eggplant, the bigger the seeds.

Frittata della Mamma

(Baked Omelet Lasagne)

Serves 4

12 large eggs
3 tablespoons freshly grated
    pecorino or Parmesan cheese
    plus extra to sprinkle on top
⅓ cup freshly chopped Italian
    parsley
Salt and freshly ground pepper
Olive oil
1½ cups fresh tomato sauce
    (Salsa di Pomodori, page 93)
1 tablespoon freshly chopped
    basil, plus sprig of basil for
    garnish
1½ tablespoons sweet butter

Combine the eggs, pecorino or Parmesan cheese, and parsley in a bowl and season lightly with salt and pepper.

Heat a little olive oil in a large, nonstick frying pan with curved sides and ladle in about ½ cup of the egg mixture. Cook the frittata over medium-high heat, tilting the pan in a circle and letting the egg mixture run over the pan until it sets. Invert the frittata onto a flat lid, slide it back into the pan, and cook over medium-low heat for about 30 seconds. Transfer to a large plate and make 3 more frittatas in the same manner, adding a little olive oil as needed. Preheat the oven to 300°F.

Cut each frittata into thin ¼-inch strips (like tagliatelle).

Grease a shallow, oval baking dish or pan with olive oil. Arrange one third of the frittata strips over the bottom of the dish. Spoon ½ cup of the tomato sauce over the top and sprinkle lightly with the additional freshly grated Parmesan cheese and 1 teaspoon of the chopped basil. Repeat, making two more layers in the same manner. Dot the top of the casserole with butter.

Bake in the preheated oven for about 30 minutes. Let rest 30 minutes before serving and garnish with the sprig of basil.

La Pizza di Cipolla di Bruna

(Bruna's Onion Pizza)

DOUGH

1 package active dry yeast
½ teaspoon salt
2½ cups all-purpose flour, and as
    needed to knead the dough
Olive oil

*A*lthough Bruna, my daughter-in-law's mother, is from Calabria, this is a typical pizza from Apulia, where her husband was born. The pizza has a very beautiful design—a pie-shaped dough bottom that is topped with a sweet-and-sour mixture of onions, anchovies, currants, green olives, and tomatoes. An island of flattened dough, sprinkled with sugar, floats in the center of the filling. It's a fantastic dish served as a first course or light meal. —w.t.

Serves 6

Put ¾ cup of hot water (about 105° to 110°F) in a small bowl with the yeast. Stir the mixture and let it rest for 10 minutes.

Meanwhile, combine the salt and flour in a large bowl. Make a hole in the center and pour in the yeast mixture. Stir with a wooden spoon until a dough forms. Knead the dough on a lightly floured board or work surface until silky smooth.

Put a little olive oil on your hands and lightly coat the dough. Let it double in size in a clean bowl, covered with a dish towel, and set in a warm area of your kitchen.

Meanwhile, prepare the topping. Heat the olive oil with the onions in a large frying pan over medium-low heat until golden, stirring often. This will take about 20 minutes. Add a little extra oil, if needed—the mixture should be moist but not wet. Season the onions lightly with salt.

Stir in the olives, anchovies, currants, tomatoes, and sugar, and season lightly with pepper. Taste for the amount of sugar you like, although the filling should be only lightly sweetened. When you are satisfied with the seasoning, set the topping mixture aside.

When the dough has doubled in size, punch it down with your fists and preheat the oven to 400°F.

Lightly grease a shallow, round baking dish about 10 to 12 inches in diameter. Reserve a small amount of the dough, about the size of a small orange, and set it aside.

Roll the dough into a circle large enough to cover the bottom and come up over the side of the baking dish—12 to 14 inches. Fit the dough into the pan and spread the topping evenly over the dough. Now bring the edges of the dough up over the dough, making a little ruffled collar directly over the topping, about 1 inch from the edge of the pan.

Roll out the reserved piece of dough into a circle about 10 inches in diameter. With the tines of a fork, prick all over and place this piece of dough over the center of the pizza. The dough should almost touch the edges of the dough collar. Brush the exposed collar and the center piece of dough lightly with olive oil. Now generously sprinkle sugar on the center piece.

Bake in the preheated oven until golden on top, about 20 minutes. Serve warm or at room temperature.

FILLING

⅓ cup olive oil
2¼ pounds yellow onions, thinly sliced
Salt
¾ cup chopped green olives, Sicilian, if possible
5 anchovy fillets, chopped
⅓ cup currants
2 medium tomatoes, peeled, seeded, chopped, and well drained
1 teaspoon sugar, or as desired, plus extra for the top
Freshly ground pepper

Frittelle di Fiori di Zucca

(Zucchini Flower Fritters)

BATTER

2 teaspoons active dry yeast

2¼ cups warm water (about 105°F)

2 cups plus 2 tablespoons all-purpose flour

Salt and freshly ground pepper

1 tablespoon olive oil

24 large or 36 small zucchini flowers

Sunflower or vegetable oil, for deep-frying

With absolute confidence I can boast that my Frittelle di Fiori di Zucca are the best in the world. The delicate flowers inside the fritters take on a golden, creamy consistency, while the outside is light and crunchy. One of the secrets is the sunny flavor that the soil of Gangivecchio bestows on the blossoms. The other secret is in the batter mixture.

Many other vegetables and foods can be batter-coated and fried in the same way with fine results. The suggestions follow the recipe. —W.T.

Serves 8

Sprinkle the yeast over ½ cup of the warm water in a small bowl and stir with a fork. After 10 minutes, stir the mixture with a fork again. The yeast should have dissolved.

Pour the mixture into a large bowl, add the remaining 1¾ cups of water, and mix well. With a fork, stir in the flour ¼ cup at a time. No lumps should remain in the batter. Season lightly with salt and pepper and whisk in the olive oil.

Cover the bowl and let it rest in a warm place for about 1 hour. When bubbles form on the surface of the batter, it is ready. Stir well again.

Heat 3 inches of sunflower or vegetable oil in a deep-sided frying pan until the oil is hot but not smoking. Place the batter and zucchini flowers next to the stove. Dip a flower into the batter, completely coating it, and shake off any extra dripping batter. Gently release into the hot oil. Continue cooking the fritters in the same manner, in batches, about 4 to 6 at a time, depending on the size of the flowers. (At Gangivecchio, ours are huge.) As the batter cooks, it will puff up and more than double in size.

When the fritters are immersed in the oil, some will sink and stick slightly to the bottom of the pan. With a slotted spoon or long, wooden-handled wire strainer (two are even better), coax the fritters off the bottom of the pan. They normally release willingly. Little balls of batter will fall off the fritters and cook separately.

Skim these tiny bits out of the pan as this occurs. When the pieces cool, eat them—the cook's reward.

Turn the fritters until golden and crisp all over. They cook very quickly.

When done, drain the fritters on paper towels. Then sprinkle lightly with salt and serve immediately.

VARIATIONS: Many other vegetables can be coated with the batter and cooked in the same manner, like slices or florets of zucchini, artichoke hearts, cauliflower, broccoli, bell peppers, or whole mushrooms. The artichoke hearts, cauliflower, and broccoli must be parboiled and drained before being dipped into the batter and fried. Eggplant can be fried, drained, and dipped in the batter and fried, too. Butterfly and boil some large shrimp, just until they turn white. Drain and cool completely. Dip the shrimp in the batter and fry until golden brown.

Herbs, such as sage leaves or sprigs of parsley, can also be batter-dipped and fried.

Frittelle di Verdure

(Green Vegetable Fritters)

Serves 8 to 10

1 recipe for batter on page 54
1 pound Swiss chard or spinach,
    cooked, well drained,
    cooled, and finely chopped
Olive oil
Salt and freshly ground pepper

Prepare the batter and let rest for about 1 hour, until bubbles rise to the surface. Stir in the Swiss chard or spinach.

Heat ½ inch of olive oil in a large frying pan until the oil is hot but not smoking. Spoon rounded tablespoonfuls of the batter into the oil a few at a time in batches. Cook the fritters until golden brown all over. These are slightly flat fritters. Drain on paper towels. Season to taste with salt and pepper, and serve immediately.

VARIATION: For Frittelle di Acciughe (Anchovy Fritters), prepare the batter and let it rise. Stir in 8 finely chopped anchovy fillets and follow the same cooking directions given above.

Bruschetta Classica

(Grilled Bread with Garlic and Olive Oil)

Twelve ½-inch-thick slices Italian country bread
2 garlic cloves, peeled and halved lengthwise
Best-quality olive oil
Dried oregano

*W*e think that recipes for *bruschetta,* a well-loved antipasto, must exist in most Italian cookbooks, but since we serve it often at home and in our restaurant at Gangivecchio, we include our versions—the classic, with garlic and olive oil, and *bruschetta* with a seasoned tomato topping. We also very much like Funghi Sott' Olio (Preserved Mushrooms, page 70), Melanzane Sott' Aceto di Peppe (Peppe's Preserved Pickled Eggplant, page 71), and Il Nuovo Pesto di Rucola di Paolo (Paolo's New Arugula Pesto Sauce, page 104) as *bruschetta* toppings.

Serves 6

Grill or toast the bread slices under a broiler on both sides. On one side of each slice of toast, rub garlic over the surface and brush with olive oil. Sprinkle with oregano and serve immediately.

Bruschetta con Pomodori

(Grilled Bread with Tomatoes)

½ cup best-quality olive oil
6 small ripe, firm tomatoes, halved and diced, with seeds and liquid squeezed out
2 garlic cloves, minced
6 basil leaves, freshly chopped
Salt and freshly ground pepper
Twelve ½-inch-thick slices Italian country bread

Serves 6

Combine the ingredients from the olive oil through the basil leaves in a bowl and season to taste with salt and pepper. Let rest for 30 minutes.

Grill or toast the bread slices under the broiler on both sides.

Toss the tomato mixture again, and spoon it over the grilled bread in equal amounts. Serve immediately.

Torta Rustica di Ricotta

(Ricotta and Ham Tart)

Serves 8

Butter the bottom and sides of a 9-inch springform pan and lightly coat with flour.

Roll out two thirds of the pastry into a 10½-inch circle that is ¼ inch thick. Fit the pastry into the baking pan, gently pressing the edges of the pastry up against the sides.

Combine the filling ingredients through the parsley together well in a large bowl, adding salt and pepper to taste.

Spoon the filling into the pastry and smooth the top evenly with the back of a spoon.

Form the remaining dough into several ⅓-inch-thick ropes by rolling them on a lightly floured work surface. Beginning at the center, place one of the strips from one side of the tart to the other and press the ends of the strips into the dough at the opposite sides of the pan. Continue placing these strips at even intervals across one side of the tart and then the other. To make a lattice (*griglia*) design across the top of the tart, turn the cake one-quarter turn and repeat, placing the little strips of dough across the top of the tart, starting in the center and pressing the ends of the pastry together at each side of the pan. If you have any dough left, roll it into tiny balls and place them inside the lattice design.

Bake on the middle rack of the oven on a baking sheet. Turn oven on to 350°F and cook for about 45 minutes, until golden brown.

½ recipe Pasta Frolla Piccante (page 275)
Butter and flour, for coating pan

RICOTTA FILLING

3 cups well-drained ricotta (see instructions on page 39—must be prepared one to two days in advance)
½ cup diced boiled or other cooked ham
½ cup diced provolone
1 tablespoon butter, melted
3 tablespoons freshly chopped parsley
Salt and freshly ground pepper

Carciofi

(Artichokes)

When spring arrives in Sicily, we have in our local market in Gangi an abundance of superb, delicate artichokes, sometimes sold right from the back of a truck. They come with long, prickly stems attached. To us, they are beautiful bouquets of spring, even though they must be handled with gloves until the thorny stems are removed.

In artichoke season we prepare many of Mamma's artichoke recipes for our guests in the restaurant, and for ourselves, too—especially Sformato di Carciofi (page 59), her wonderful artichoke tart. We also stuff and fry artichokes. One of our favorite dishes is Risotto con Carciofi (Risotto with Artichokes, page 153).

Along the road from here to Palermo, there are vast fields filled with rows and rows of this noble vegetable. We have heard that there is a restaurant in the area in the village of Cerda whose menu features artichoke dishes when they are in season. We must go one day.

Sicilian artichokes are smaller than the American globe variety. Ours are small to medium-sized, and the pointy leaves are green with a purple tinge. Similar varieties can be found in America, but if you can't locate these, the medium-sized globes are fine.

TO CLEAN ARTICHOKES: First you must fill half a large bowl with cool water, add the juice of 1 seeded lemon, then drop in the lemon halves.

To prepare the artichokes, cut all but 1 inch off the stem ends and about 1 inch off the tough tops—how much depends on the size of the artichoke. Remove the inedible outer leaves by pulling them downward. Trim away the top end's prickly little leaves and the fuzzy choke center. Also, evenly trim the uneven sides of the artichokes, but take care not to cut away too much of the delicious heart. Peel off the skin of the stem ends. As the artichokes are cleaned, drop them into the lemon water. This prevents the artichokes from turning brown. When ready to use the artichokes, drain and pat them dry.

Sformato di Carciofi

(Artichoke Tart)

Serves 8

First, prepare the Pasta Frolla. Form into a ball, cover, and refrigerate until needed.

Clean the artichokes and chop into small pieces. Put into a saucepan with the olive oil and onion, and season to taste with salt and pepper. Barely cover with water and bring to a boil. Reduce the heat to medium and cook for 15 minutes, or until the artichokes are very tender.

Drain the artichokes and onion and transfer to a bowl. Mix in the parsley and set aside.

Prepare the béchamel sauce. Fold the artichokes into the sauce and taste for seasoning.

Preheat the oven to 350°F.

Grease a 9-inch springform tart pan with olive oil and lightly coat with flour.

Roll out two thirds of the pastry into a 10½-inch circle that is ¼ inch thick. Fit the dough into the center of the pan, pressing evenly halfway up the sides.

Turn the filling into the pastry shell and smooth the top across evenly.

Take small pieces of the remaining dough and roll them into little ropes about ⅓ inch thick. Place these ropes across the top of the artichoke filling in 5 or 6 rows about 1 inch apart, pressing the ends into the edge of the tart's dough. Make more little ropes with the remaining dough. Turn the tart one-quarter turn. Place the ropes on top of the other ropes in the same manner, forming a lattice design. If you have any leftover, make tiny balls and fit them in between the ropes on top of the filling.

Bake the tart on a baking sheet in the preheated oven for about 45 minutes, or until golden brown.

Remove the cooked tart and let it cool. It's best served at room temperature.

½ recipe Pasta Frolla Piccante (page 275)
Olive oil, for coating the pan
Flour, for coating pan

FILLING

10 medium artichokes, cleaned (page 58), or 2 cups frozen (thawed) artichoke hearts
½ cup olive oil
1 small onion, finely chopped
Salt and freshly ground pepper
¼ cup freshly chopped Italian parsley
2 cups béchamel sauce (Salsa Besciamella Morbida, page 96)

Carciofini Fritti

(Small Breaded and Fried Artichoke Hearts)

3 large eggs
Salt
16 small artichokes, cleaned
(page 58) and quartered, or
two 10-ounce packages
frozen artichoke hearts,
thawed, well drained and
patted dry (pieces left as cut,
usually halved)
Dried bread crumbs
Sunflower or vegetable oil, for
deep-frying
Freshly ground pepper
1 lemon, cut into 6 wedges and
seeded

*F*ried artichokes are excellent when served as a first course or a side dish with veal or chicken. We recommend serving red wine with artichokes because the artichokes sweeten the flavor of the wine.

Serves 4 to 6

Break the eggs into a shallow bowl and season with salt. Dip the artichoke pieces into the eggs. Shake off any excess and coat with bread crumbs. Let rest.

Heat 2 inches of sunflower or vegetable oil in a deep-sided frying pan until the oil is hot but not smoking. Fry the breaded artichokes a few pieces at a time, in batches, until golden brown. As they are cooked, drain on paper towels and sprinkle lightly with salt and pepper to taste.

Serve immediately with the lemon wedges.

Carciofi Ripieni

*(Artichokes Stuffed with
Garlic and Seasoned Bread
Crumbs)*

12 large fresh artichokes,
cleaned, with stems removed
(page 58)
6 garlic cloves, peeled and cut in
half
Lemon
Olive oil
Salt

Serves 6

Inside the top of each artichoke, place half a garlic clove.

Combine the filling ingredients; the filling should be moist but not wet. Press the stuffing in equal amounts into the center of each artichoke.

Transfer the stuffed artichokes to a saucepan just large enough to hold them comfortably; they should be gently touching each other. Pour a little olive oil into the side of the pan and drizzle lightly over the tops. Next, pour cold water into the side of the pan until the water rises 1 inch up the sides of the artichokes. Cover the pan and slowly bring to a boil. Immediately reduce the heat and simmer for 20 minutes, or until tender. The tops should separate slightly.

Transfer the artichokes to a serving platter and cool. Serve at room temperature.

NOTE: The artichokes can be covered and refrigerated for up to two days. To serve after refrigeration, bring them to room temperature.

FILLING

2 cups dried bread crumbs
1 tablespoon freshly chopped
   Italian parsley
1 tablespoon freshly grated
   pecorino or Parmesan cheese
½ teaspoon salt
Freshly grated pepper
⅓ cup olive oil, or as needed

Pomodori Ripieni di Risotto

(Tomatoes Stuffed with Rice)

Serves 6 to 8

Preheat the oven to 350°F.
   Prepare the risotto. When done, stir in the parsley and cool to room temperature.
   Fill the tomatoes with equal amounts of the risotto. Flatten the top with the back of a knife. Replace the tops of the tomatoes.
   Place side by side in a generously oiled, shallow baking dish, and cook in the preheated oven for 30 minutes.
   Cool 10 minutes before serving, or serve at room temperature.

½ recipe for Il Mio Risotto
   (page 143)
½ cup freshly chopped Italian
   parsley
11 medium-sized ripe, firm
   tomatoes (cut about ½ inch
   off tops and save the lids)
Olive oil

Melanzane Ripiene

(Baby Eggplants Stuffed with Mint and Caciocavallo)

Serves 6 to 8

Cut 1-inch-deep incisions on a diagonal on one lengthwise side of each eggplant, making little pockets.
   Combine the garlic, mint, and cheese together well in a small bowl. Stuff equal amounts of the mixture into the little pockets.
   Pour enough olive oil into a large frying pan to just coat the bottom, and heat until the oil is hot but not smoking. Fry the eggplants, in batches, until the skins begin to wrinkle.
   Meanwhile, heat the tomato sauce in another large frying pan

12 baby eggplants, 4–5 inches
   long and a little over 1 inch
   thick, with stem ends cut off
2 garlic cloves, minced
12 fresh mint sprigs
1 cup caciocavallo, pecorino, or
   Parmesan cheese, finely diced

Melanzane Ripiene *(cont.)*
Olive oil
2 cups fresh tomato sauce (Salsa
   di Pomodoro, page 93)
2 teaspoons sugar
Salt and freshly ground pepper

with the sugar, and season to taste with salt and pepper. Stir in 1 cup of water.

Transfer the cooked eggplants to the sauce and spoon it over the eggplants.

Simmer over medium heat for about 10 minutes. Turn the eggplants and cook for 5 minutes more. Serve hot or at room temperature.

Peperoni Ripieni

(Baked Yellow and Red Peppers)

Serves 8

4 each, yellow and red bell peppers (select peppers that are
   as equal in size as possible)
¾ cup fresh bread crumbs
¾ cup diced caciocavallo or provolone cheese
¾ cup grated pecorino or
   Parmesan cheese
1 large egg yolk
1 medium onion, finely
   chopped
2 medium tomatoes, peeled,
   seeded, and chopped
⅓ cup currants
⅓ cup pine nuts
Olive oil
Salt and freshly ground pepper

Preheat the oven to 350°F.

Cut off the tops of the stem ends of the peppers and reserve. Be sure to remove the white membrane and the seeds from inside.

Combine the ingredients from the bread crumbs through the pine nuts in a large bowl. Add enough olive oil for a light, moist consistency and season with salt and pepper.

Fill the peppers with equal amounts of the stuffing and replace the tops.

Put the peppers into a shallow baking dish just large enough to hold the sides comfortably, with the tops pressing against the edge of the pan. Drizzle lightly with olive oil. Cook for about 30 minutes, or until the skins begin to brown and wrinkle. Serve hot, at room temperature, or cold.

Gnocchi di Ricotta di Paolo

Serves 4

(Paolo's Poached Lemon-flavored Ricotta Gnocchi with Sage Butter)

Mix the ricotta, bread crumbs, lemon zest, egg, and Scotch together in a bowl. Add more bread crumbs, if necessary—the mixture should be fairly firm, but light and moist. Shape into 8 ovals about 3 inches long and 1 inch thick. Let rest for 10 minutes.

Bring 3 inches of lightly salted water to a rolling boil in a large, deep-sided frying pan. Gently lower the gnocchi into the boiling water with a slotted spoon. Gently roll each over with a wooden spoon to cook evenly. After about 5 minutes, when the gnocchi float, they are done. Drain on paper towels.

Meanwhile, melt the butter and stir in the sage leaves, keeping the heat very low.

Arrange 2 gnocchi on each of 4 first-course plates. Spoon equal amounts of the sage butter over the tops and sprinkle with Parmesan cheese. Serve immediately.

1 pound ricotta (see instructions on page 39—must be prepared one to two days in advance)
½ cup dried bread crumbs, or as needed
Finely grated zest of 1 lemon
1 large egg
1 teaspoon Scotch whisky
Salt
½ cup sweet butter
4 sage leaves, freshly chopped
Freshly grated Parmesan cheese

Formaggio all'Argentiera

(Silversmith's Cheese)

*I*n this typical Sicilian cheese dish, popular in Palermo, flour isn't normally used to coat the cheese. But we like the color it produces, and it also helps prevent the cheese from running.

Serves 8 as a first course or 4 as a main course

Cut the cheese into 6 slices or wedges about ½ inch thick. Press flour onto both sides of the cheese, shake off any extra, and let rest.

Heat the olive oil in a large, nonstick frying pan. Add the garlic cloves and push them around in the pan for a few seconds, then move the garlic to the edges of the pan. Add the cheese and cook over medium-high heat. Immediately sprinkle lightly with the vinegar and cook for 2 minutes. Turn the cheese pieces and sprinkle each with oregano and pepper. Cook for about 2 minutes more. Serve immediately with the pan juices spooned over the top. Discard the garlic cloves. Pass the bread.

2 pounds caciocavallo or provolone cheese
Flour
3 tablespoons olive oil
3 garlic cloves, peeled
White wine vinegar
1 teaspoon dried oregano
Freshly ground pepper
Italian bread slices

Crêpes con Ricotta e Salsa di Finocchietto di Betty

(Betty's Crêpes with Ricotta and Fennel Sauce)

CRÊPE BATTER

1 cup all-purpose flour
2 cups cool milk
2 large eggs
Salt
1 teaspoon olive oil
Butter

FILLING

3 cups ricotta (see instructions
    on page 39—must be pre-
    pared one to two days in
    advance)
½ cup freshly grated Parmesan
    cheese
Few grates of nutmeg
Salt and freshly ground pepper

SALSA DI FINOCCHIETTO

½ pound dark green fennel
    tops, chopped (use white
    bulb for another purpose)
3 tablespoons sweet butter
3 tablespoons all-purpose flour
2 cups hot chicken or vegetable
    broth, homemade or canned
Salt and freshly ground pepper
Freshly grated Parmesan cheese

*D*uring the Christmas holidays there is nonstop cooking both at our main restaurant in Gangivecchio and at Tenuta Gangivecchio, Paolo and Betty's hotel restaurant, for family, friends, and hotel guests. These holiday feasts have developed into little cooking contests between my mother and her daughter-in-law, like the two generations before them. Betty invented this beautiful crêpe recipe for last year's Christmas dinner.

Serves 6

To make the crêpe batter, combine the flour, milk, and eggs in a bowl with a whisk. Season lightly with salt. If any little lumps of flour do not dissolve, strain the mixture. Cover the batter and let it rest at room temperature for 1 hour.

Stir the batter well. Heat 1 teaspoon of butter in a nonstick 7-inch crêpe or omelet pan until hot. Take care not to let the butter burn. Add a scant ¼ cup of the batter to the pan and swirl it around in a circular motion to just cover the bottom. Cook until lightly browned. Carefully turn the crêpe with a spatula and brown lightly on the other side. Transfer to a plate and continue making 11 more crêpes, adding 1 teaspoon of butter at a time, as needed, and stacking the crêpes when cooked.

Preheat the oven to 300°F.

For the filling, put the ricotta, Parmesan cheese, and nutmeg in a bowl and mix thoroughly. Season to taste with salt and pepper.

Lightly butter an au gratin or shallow baking dish, about 9 × 16 inches, and set aside.

Spread equal amounts of the ricotta filling across each crêpe and roll up, placing them side by side in the baking dish, seam side down. Let rest.

For the Salsa di Finocchietto, add the chopped dark green fennel tops to 3 cups of boiling water. Cook over high heat for 10 minutes. Transfer the fennel to the bowl of a food processor with only 2 tablespoons of the cooking water. Purée the fennel well and set aside.

Heat the butter in a saucepan and whisk in the flour. Cook over medium heat for about 1 minute, stirring constantly. Little by little, whisk in the hot chicken or vegetable broth, stirring constantly. When the sauce has thickened, season to taste with salt and pepper and blend in the fennel purée. Cover the pan and let rest off the heat.

Bake the crêpes in the preheated oven for 10 minutes. Reheat the sauce for 2 minutes, then spoon over the top of the crêpes. Sprinkle lightly with Parmesan cheese and serve immediately.

Patè di Olive Bianche

(Green Olive Pâté)

*G*reen and black olive pâtés are very popular antipasti in Sicily. Here is a very *gustoso* (tasty) spicy green olive pâté; a milder black olive pâté recipe follows.

Makes 2½ dozen crostini

3 cups pitted green olives, Sicilian, if possible
5 large garlic cloves
⅓ cup fresh Italian parsley, coarsely chopped
10 large basil leaves
8 fennel seeds
1 tablespoon freshly chopped mint leaves
Pinch of cayenne pepper
Olive oil
Thirty ⅓-inch-thick slices Italian country bread

Put all the ingredients through the cayenne pepper into the bowl of a food processor. Turn it on and pour olive oil through the opening in the lid in a thin, steady stream until the mixture becomes a thick but spreadable consistency. The pâté can be used immediately or covered and refrigerated for up to two days. Bring the pâté to room temperature before using it.

Grill or toast the bread slices under the broiler on both sides.

Serve the pâté in a small bowl on a platter with the grilled bread and a small spreading knife, or spread equal amounts on the bread.

Patè di Olive Nere

(Black Olive Pâté)

3 cups pitted black olives,
    Gaeta, if possible
4 garlic cloves
Salt and freshly ground pepper
Olive oil
Thirty ⅓-inch-thick slices Ital-
    ian country bread

*I*n Sicily, black olive pâté is called "caviar" of the poor people, but everyone is rich when eating black olive pâté.

Makes 2½ dozen crostini

Put the black olives and garlic into the bowl of a food processor. Season to taste with salt and pepper. Turn the processor on and, through the opening, add olive oil in a thin, steady stream until the mixture becomes a thick but spreadable consistency. The pâté can be used immediately or covered and refrigerated for up to two days. Bring to room temperature before using it.

Grill or toast the bread slices under the broiler on both sides.

Serve the pâté in a bowl on a platter with the grilled bread and a small spreading knife, or spread equal amounts on the bread.

Patè di Tonno

(Tuna Pâté)

1 medium onion, coarsely
    chopped
¾ cup chopped celery, with
    leaves
Grated zest of 1 small lemon
Freshly squeezed juice of 1
    lemon, seeded
Three 6⅛-ounce cans white
    meat tuna fish
2 tablespoons Cognac
2 tablespoons milk
Twenty ½-inch-thick slices Ital-
    ian country bread

Makes 20 crostini

Put all the ingredients, except the bread, into the bowl of a food processor and purée. The consistency should be thick but spreadable.

Transfer to a bowl, cover, and refrigerate for at least 1 hour, or until you're ready to use it. The pâté will keep in the refrigerator for two days.

Grill or toast the bread slices under a broiler on both sides. Serve the pâté in a bowl on a platter with the toasted bread and a small spreading knife, or spread in equal amounts on the bread.

Le Olive Bianche Consate

(Green Olives with Herbs)

e serve this simple but aromatic olive dish at home when we have company. The herb-flavored olive mixture is prepared in the morning. When guests arrive, we've only to open a chilled bottle of white wine. White wine goes very well with the dish because it helps cancel out the salty taste of the olives.

Serves 6 to 8

Put all the ingredients in a bowl. Toss well, cover, and leave at room temperature for several hours. Toss a few times during the day.

Toss again just before serving. We eat the olives by hand, but you can serve them with toothpicks or on small plates.

3 cups pitted green olives, Sicilian, if possible
⅓ cup best-quality olive oil
¼ cup red wine vinegar
¼ cup fresh Italian parsley, very finely chopped
½ teaspoon dried oregano, or to taste
Pinch of hot pepper flakes or cayenne pepper (optional)

Olio d'Oliva Extra Vergine

(Extra-virgin Olive Oil)

In our recipes we use only cold-pressed extra-virgin olive oil with a full-bodied, fragrant olive flavor. In Sicily, we produce a stupendous amount of excellent olive oil, much of which is exported in drums and bottled elsewhere. One of Sicily's highest-quality brands is Barbera, but its label on a bottle means an elevated price.

At Gangivecchio, for years we used to produce wonderful olive oil, but the press has been silent since my father's death. Now we send our olive harvest to a local press. We keep half the production of the oil and give the other half to the processor.

I Pomodorini Consati di Giovanna

(Giovanna's Preserved Sun-dried Tomatoes with Basil, Garlic, and Parmesan Cheese)

½ pound loose sun-dried tomatoes
Best-quality extra-virgin olive oil
4 garlic cloves, cut into slivers
12 small fresh basil leaves
Dried oregano
Salt
Freshly grated Parmesan cheese

*I*t is much more economical to buy loose sun-dried tomatoes and reconstitute them yourself than to buy them already preserved in oil. After sun-dried tomatoes are reconstituted, they can be used immediately in recipes or they can be preserved by covering them with good-quality olive oil. There are many ways of flavoring the sun-dried tomatoes with various ingredients, herbs, and spices. A combination of rosemary, thyme, and oregano imparts an aromatic flavor to the tomatoes and the oil. Little hot peppers or pepper flakes spice up the tomatoes and oil nicely. My favorite combination follows.

Makes about 1½ pints

Put the sun-dried tomatoes in a bowl and cover with hot, but not boiling, water. Let rest for 30 minutes. Drain in a colander and gently press out any excess water with your hands.

Pour ¼ to ½ cup of olive oil into the bottom of a 1-quart glass jar with a wide opening. Add a layer of sun-dried tomatoes, a few pieces of slivered garlic, 2 basil leaves, a pinch each of oregano and salt, and ¼ teaspoon Parmesan cheese. Repeat the layers, adding the ingredients in the same order until all the sun-dried tomatoes are used. Cover with more olive oil—the ingredients must be completely covered by the oil or a mold will develop on top.

Seal the jar tightly and store in a cool, dark place for one week before using them. After opening the jar, it's best to keep the tomatoes in the refrigerator. The olive oil will solidify in the refrigerator. Just let the jar rest at room temperature for about 1 hour, and the olive oil will return to liquid. The sun-dried tomatoes keep for about two weeks.

Tonno Sott' Olio

(Preserved or Homemade Tuna Fish)

2 pounds 1½-inch-thick pieces
    fresh tuna steaks, skins
    removed
Salt
Best-quality olive oil

*W*e found this recipe for Tonno Sott' Olio in my grandmother Giovanna's old recipe book. Mamma said she remembered that it was excellent and considered a great delicacy at home, since Gangivecchio is so far from the sea. To have fresh fish of any kind in the interior is to possess a genuine treasure. Years ago, when someone went to Palermo, he or she would bring back a tremendous amount of tuna or other fish. We still bring fish and seafood home from Palermo, but not in such quantity.

The preserved tuna is delicious eaten plain, seasoned only with salt and pepper, perhaps a sprinkling of freshly chopped herbs, like parsley or dried oregano, and a spray of lemon juice. And we always eat it with bread to soak up the rich olive oil. If preserved tuna is served as part of an antipasti, it will disappear first.

The tuna can also be used in salads with cold vegetables, like green beans, tomatoes, and potatoes, or in pasta dishes. The flavor of fresh preserved tuna is more subtle than that of the canned variety, so we normally use canned tuna in pasta dishes for a bigger flavor.

Tonno Sott' Olio makes a truly delicious filling for *panini* (sandwiches). Mix the chopped tuna with a small amount of mayonnaise, and season it to taste with salt and pepper. For a more sumptuous version, replace the mayonnaise with softened butter.

The prepared tuna, completely covered with olive oil, must rest at least one week, to bring out the flavor, before it can be eaten. In Granny Giovanna's recipe she said to weight the tuna down with a big silver spoon. No weight is needed in our recipe.

When kept in the refrigerator, the olive oil covering the tuna will solidify. Don't concern yourself about this. Just let it rest at room temperature for about 1 hour before using. The oil will return to liquid.

Serves 6 to 8

Put the tuna pieces in a shallow bowl and cover with cold water. Sprinkle with a generous amount of salt and turn each piece. Let rest for 10 minutes.

Meanwhile, bring about 3 quarts of water to a rolling boil in a large, nonreactive saucepan. Season the water with 3 tablespoons of salt and stir. Add the tuna and bring the water back to the boil. Immediately reduce the heat to a simmer and cook for about 25 minutes, until the fish is well done, with no pinkness in the middle. Carefully transfer the fish to a baking rack to drain and cool thoroughly.

Arrange the pieces of tuna, fit snugly together but not pressed, in a glass container or ceramic pot in one or two layers. Completely cover the tuna with olive oil. Cover the dish and refrigerate for one week before serving. Allow the tuna to return to room temperature in the oil before serving or using it. The preserved tuna keeps for one more week in the refrigerator.

Funghi Sott' Olio

(Preserved Mushrooms)

1½ cups dry red wine
½ cup white wine vinegar
2 pounds medium-sized Portobello mushrooms, cut into ¼-inch-thick slices
1 garlic clove
10 black peppercorns
5 bay leaves
Best-quality olive oil

*P*reserved mushrooms, and the following recipe for preserved mushrooms, must be prepared one month in advance. Both are wonderful dishes to include with other dishes in an antipasti, and when served on top of grilled bread, they also make terrific *bruschetta.*

Makes about 1 quart

Bring the wine and vinegar to a boil in a large frying pan. Add the mushrooms and cook over high heat for 2 minutes. Drain the mushrooms well in a colander. Transfer to a baking rack set over a baking sheet with sides, in one layer, and let dry at room temperature for 12 hours.

The next day, put the garlic, peppercorns, bay leaves, and the mushrooms into a quart-size glass jar with a wide-mouthed opening. Completely cover the ingredients with olive oil. Seal jar tightly.

Store the jar in a cool, dark place and let rest for one month. After opening the container, keep the preserved mushrooms refrigerated. Before using them, let rest at room temperature for 1 hour. They will keep for about two weeks.

Melanzane Sott' Aceto di Peppe

Makes about 1 quart

(Peppe's Preserved Pickled Eggplant)

Cut the eggplants lengthwise into ½-inch-thick slices. Then cut the slices into pieces that are 1 inch wide by 2 inches long.

Bring the wine and vinegar to a boil in a large pot. Add the eggplant and cook over high heat for 2 minutes, stirring often. Drain the eggplant well in a colander, then transfer to a baking rack set over a baking sheet with sides, in one layer, and let dry at room temperature for 12 hours.

In a quart-size glass jar with a wide-mouthed opening, put the garlic clove, peppercorns, basil leaves, and the eggplant. Completely cover the ingredients with olive oil and seal the jar tightly.

Store the jar in a cool, dark place and let rest for one month. Refrigerate after opening. Before using the pickled eggplant again, let rest at room temperature for about 1 hour before serving. It will keep for about two weeks.

3 medium eggplants, with stem
   ends removed
1 cup dry red wine
1 cup red wine vinegar
1 garlic clove
10 black peppercorns
6 fresh basil leaves
Best-quality olive oil

Minestre

(Soups)

U'Maccu *(Fava Bean Soup with Fennel and Pasta)* • Olio Santo *(Hot Oil)* • Minestra di Lenticchie e Ditalini *(Lentil and Ditalini Soup)* • Minestra di Zucchine con Spaghetti *(Fresh Zucchini Soup with Spaghetti)* • Pasta con Finocchietti in Brodo *(Pasta with Fennel in Broth)* • Pancetta • Minestra di Fagioli con Pasta *(Borlotti Bean Soup with Pasta)* • Minestrone di Verdure Fresche *(Fresh Garden Vegetable Soup)* • Le Preziose Scorze di Parmigiano *(Valuable Parmesan Cheese Rinds)* • Minestra di Patate con Pasta *(Potato Soup with Pasta)* • Minestra di Ceci con Pasta *(Chick-pea Soup with Pasta)* • Palline di Riso in Brodo *(Rice Balls in Chicken Broth)* • Pesce in Brodo con Pasta *(Fish Soup with Pasta)* • Tuoni e Fulmini *(Thunder and Lightning—Chick-pea and Cabbage Soup)*

My father disliked soups for a reason we thought strange. "Why must they always be so hot?" I remember him grumbling. So, when Mamma prepared soup, we all sat at the table eating contentedly except Papà, who took his bowl outside on the balcony, watching impatiently until it stopped steaming.

Soup to me means warm comfort on cold winter evenings when there is snow outside on the ground, and inside, on the table, there is a bowl of one of my favorites—*u'maccu* (fava bean soup with fennel and pasta), very ancient and hearty, or *minestra di fagioli* (a tasty soup of borlotti beans and pasta). Either soup can be served with or without the pasta, but I like my *minestra di fagioli* with ditalini and infused with many drops of Olio Santo (Hot Oil, recipe on page 76), and topped with a mountain of grated pecorino. Normally, people are disgusted by the idea of so much cheese and hot oil with beans, but try it.

In the summertime we enjoy the produce from our home gardens by making fresh, light soups. Early on sunny mornings Peppe leaves the abbey with his big basket to collect what has ripened overnight as if he were going off to market.

Just when we have started asking each other if he has perished among the vegetables, he finally returns with a heaping basket, which might contain zucchini and zucchini blossoms, tomatoes, eggplants, sweet and hot peppers, green beans, and arugula. (I am sure that part of Peppe's garden marketing ritual includes a nap under the shade of a tree.) It is always the same anticipation: When will Peppe return so that we can begin to cook the harvest of the day?

Summer days call for *minestrone di verdure fresche* (fresh vegetable soup) that we, like Papa, favor cooled and without pasta, but, for me, always with some cheese sprinkled on top.

You will notice that we do not always use chicken or beef broth in our soup recipes. Instead, pure cool water, slowly heated, draws the flavors from the ingredients into a subtle or intense natural broth bouquet, depending on the particular soup. This classic process works wonderfully well.

To make a good chicken or beef broth requires chickens and cows. In the leaner times of the past, chickens at Gangivecchio were needed exclusively for their eggs or to raise chicks for more chickens and more eggs. Cows were kept for their precious milk, which was used to produce cheese and butter.

To complicate matters, this family cannot kill any animal that has been given a name. The moment a dog, cat, chicken, or cow appears here, either by just wandering onto the property or as a gift from neighbors or friends, Mamma always immediately asks, "What shall we name it?" We know that this creature, once named, will be with us until death. So, when we do make chicken or beef broth, we must buy the meat from the butcher in Gangi.

In Sicily, canned broths are not available as they are in America. We rely on bouillon cubes. For the American kitchen we suggest homemade or canned chicken or beef broth or stock, or a bouillon cube or two, usually vegetable, stirred into the water when a richer broth is wanted. Of course, there is nothing as good as a homemade, natural-flavored meat stock or broth as a soup base. Our recipe for *palline di riso in brodo* (rice balls in chicken broth) has a soothing homemade broth enhanced with little balls of rice.

U'Maccu

(Fava Bean Soup with Fennel and Pasta)

3 cups (about 1½ pounds) dried fava beans
½ cup best-quality olive oil, plus extra for topping
Salt
½ cup chopped dark green fennel tops
6 ounces ditali or tagliatelle or spaghetti; if using one of the two latter pastas, break them into small pieces, about 1 inch in length
Freshly ground pepper

U', Maccu is a humble, thick, and delicious soup that has been the mainstay of the Sicilian country peasant's diet for centuries. In winter, when farmers' gardens and plots of land were barren, the dried fava beans provided healthy, hearty sustenance. The only ingredients required for *u'maccu* were dried fava beans, water, salt, pepper, and olive oil, if this "liquid gold" was available. More recently, pasta and fennel were added to fortify and add flavor to *u'maccu.* The supply of dried fava beans was also shared with farm animals, especially the sheep. Nourishing the sheep was crucial, since the rich milk was essential for making cheese to eat and sell.

Everyone loves *u'maccu,* so we serve it regularly at home and in both restaurants at Gangivecchio in the wintertime.

In Sicily, we use skinned and dried fava beans (*fave sgusciate*) to make *u'maccu,* but since they aren't sold skinned in the United States in many markets (sometimes they are available in Middle Eastern or specialty food shops), our recipe gives instructions for using dried fava beans with the skins still intact. After soaking the fava beans in water overnight, these skins must be removed. But don't worry, it's easy work and takes only a few minutes to slip off the tough little jackets. (Read more about fava beans on page 240.)

Serves 6

Soak the fava beans overnight in a large bowl covered with 3 inches of cool water.

Drain the beans and remove the tough outer skins. They will slip off very easily. Also pinch off the dark germ, or sprout, at one end of each bean.

Put the beans into a pot with the olive oil and enough water to cover by about 2 inches. Add 2 teaspoons of salt and bring to a boil. Immediately reduce the heat and simmer for 1 hour, stirring occasionally.

Add the chopped fennel tops and continue cooking for about 30 minutes, or until the beans are very tender and literally fall apart. Soup must be stirred often as it thickens.

In another pot, bring 2 quarts of water to a rolling boil, add 2 teaspoons of salt, stir, and add the pasta. Cook the pasta until al dente, or just tender, stirring often.

Meanwhile, purée 3 cups of the soup in a blender or food processor and return to the pot. Stir the soup vigorously with a wooden spoon so that there are no whole beans or large pieces left.

Reserve 2 cups of the hot water that the pasta was cooked in. Drain the pasta and stir it into the soup. Season to taste with salt and pepper, and simmer for about 10 minutes. The soup should be thick, but if too thick, thin the mixture by stirring in the reserved hot pasta water, a little at a time, until the desired consistency is reached. Taste again for seasoning.

Serve *u'maccu* very hot and drizzle individual servings with olive oil. Accompany with bread or *grissini* (breadsticks). Normally, if pasta is included in the soup, we don't serve any bread.

Olio Santo
(Hot Oil)

Although *olio santo* is more commonly used in Calabria, many Sicilians are very partial to the zesty spirit it adds to many dishes like soups, stews, pasta, rice, and salad dressings.

You make *olio santo* by dropping 2 tablespoons *peperoncini* (tiny dried hot peppers) or 1 tablespoon dried hot pepper flakes into a small glass jar. Pour 2 cups best-quality olive oil over the peppers, seal the lid tightly, and store in a cool, dark place for one week, stirring occasionally.

For a garlic- and herb-scented *olio santo,* add 4 peeled garlic cloves and 1 teaspoon dried oregano and/or basil to the peppers before pouring in the olive oil.

After the oil steeps for one week, strain and throw away the hot peppers and the other ingredients, if you used them. Pour the oil back into the washed and thoroughly dried jar and reseal. *Olio santo* will keep for two months.

Dispense this liquid fire with caution, adding only a few drops at a time.

Minestra di Lenticchie e Ditalini

(Lentil and Ditalini Soup)

*S*ince this robust soup improves in flavor on the second day, and is even more delicious by the third, we always cook a large quantity, but you can prepare only half the recipe to serve 6 if you prefer.

For an interesting change of texture and flavor, we sometimes substitute rice for the ditalini in the soup, and also add garlic and lots of parsley. The instructions for this variation follows the recipe.

Giovanna has added Parmesan cheese to the list of ingredients because, to her, soup is always married to cheese, but this is not typical. She also adds a little cheese to fish or seafood soups, which is a mortal sin throughout all of Italy. —w.t.

Serves 12

2 pounds lentils
1 medium potato, peeled and diced
2 medium onions, chopped
2 carrots, scraped and diced
½ teaspoon baking soda
1 cup best-quality olive oil, plus extra for topping
Salt and freshly ground pepper
Few drops of Olio Santo (page 76) or pinch of cayenne pepper
¼ cup tomato paste
1 cup chopped dark green fennel tops
1½ cups ditalini
Freshly grated Parmesan cheese (optional)

Put the lentils, potato, onions, and carrots into a large pot and cover with enough cool water to rise 1 inch above the ingredients. Bring the water to a boil and stir in the baking soda, olive oil, a light amount of salt and pepper, and Olio Santo or cayenne pepper. Simmer for about 30 minutes, or until the lentils are almost tender. Add the tomato paste and fennel, and simmer 20 minutes more. Add water to desired thickness and bring to a boil. Add ditalini and cook over medium-high heat until the pasta is done, about 10 minutes. Remove from the heat and cover. Let the soup rest at least 10 minutes before serving. Pass the olive oil for individual diners to pour a little over the top. Also pass freshly grated Parmesan cheese and Olio Santo, if desired.

VARIATION FOR
Minestra di Lenticchie e Riso *(Lentil Soup with Rice)*

Heat 1 cup of olive oil in large pot and cook 2 chopped garlic cloves and ½ cup finely chopped Italian parsley for 5 minutes, stirring over medium heat. Add the lentils and proceed with the directions as given above, but don't add any more olive oil. When the ditalini is called for in the recipe, substitute 1 cup of Arborio rice. The rice will take 20 minutes to cook. This recipe also serves 12.

Minestra di Zucchine con Spaghetti

(Fresh Zucchini Soup with Spaghetti)

2½ pounds zucchini, washed, scrubbed, and cut into ½-inch cubes
1 large onion, chopped
¼ cup olive oil
Salt and freshly ground pepper
2 cups fresh tomatoes, peeled and diced, or canned tomatoes, drained and chopped
½ cup freshly chopped basil
Pinch of sugar
2 vegetable bouillon cubes, or 6 cups chicken broth, homemade or canned
¼ pound spaghetti, broken into 1–1½-inch lengths
Freshly grated Parmesan cheese

*M*ost home gardeners plant lots of zucchini seeds in the spring and then spend the late summer and fall in torture, searching for new ways to use up this lovely, prolific vegetable.

I made up this fragrant soup for dinner one evening a long time ago, when I discovered a pile of zucchini in the vegetable basket but only a few other ingredients in the kitchen. In my household I try to use up everything, wasting nothing.

Our supper that night was a big bowl of zucchini soup with pasta, followed by some of our caciocavallo cheese, served with bread and fruit. For a sweet I brought out a tin box of *biscotti* I always keep in an old vitrine we have in the dining room. We dipped the *biscotti* in little glasses of beautiful Moscato wine. Although not a banquet, our meal was very very *gustoso* (tasty).

Improvising from just what there is in the garden and pantry has always been my favorite way of inventing recipes. One day, when you think you have nothing for a meal, stop and look in the refrigerator and pantry. Unless you don't cook at all, you will be surprised to see how many meals are hiding right in your own kitchen. Spontaneity in the kitchen is as rewarding as it is in life.

I should tell you that this soup, although thick with zucchini and spaghetti pieces, has a relatively small amount of liquid. It's almost a light vegetable and pasta stew. If you want more liquid, just add more water or broth. Instructions are in the recipe.

Serves 6

Put the zucchini, onion, olive oil, and light amount of salt and pepper into a large saucepan. Add 1 cup of water and slowly bring to a boil. Reduce heat to a simmer and cook for 5 minutes.

Add the tomatoes, basil, sugar, 6 cups of cold water, and vegetable bouillon cubes, or canned chicken broth. Gently combine the ingredients and slowly bring to a boil. Add the spaghetti pieces, stir, and cook over medium to medium-high heat, with the water just popping bubbles, until the spaghetti is cooked, about 15 minutes. (Add extra boiling water or broth before adding the pasta if more liquid in the soup is desired.) Stir once in a while. Taste for salt and pepper seasoning. Serve the soup very hot and pass the Parmesan cheese.

Pasta con Finocchietti in Brodo

Serves 6 (*Pasta with Fennel in Broth*)

Put the fennel bulbs and tops and onion into a large saucepan with 7 cups of water and bring to a boil. Simmer for 10 minutes.

Add the tomatoes and olive oil, stir, and return to a boil. Season with salt and pepper to taste and add the spaghetti. Cook over medium-high heat until the pasta is done, about 15 minutes. Discard the onion. Stir in a pinch of cayenne pepper, if you like, and serve very hot. Garnish the top of each serving with a drizzle of olive oil.

3 cups chopped white fennel bulbs
½ cup chopped dark green fennel tops
1 medium onion, peeled and left whole
1 cup fresh tomatoes, peeled and chopped, or canned tomatoes, drained and chopped
¼ cup olive oil, plus extra for topping individual servings
Salt and freshly ground pepper
½ pound spaghetti, broken into 1-inch lengths
Cayenne pepper (optional)

Pancetta

Pancetta (meaning "little belly" in Italian) is cured and is the same cut of pork as bacon. In Sicily, it is either unsmoked or smoked, lightly seasoned with salt and pepper, and comes rolled up. Most of our recipes call for smoked pancetta, a taste we admire very much. Since it tastes nothing like American bacon, there is no point in making a substitution. Instead, use unsmoked pancetta or prosciutto. Prosciutto is not smoked, but it is closer to the texture and taste of pancetta than bacon. Many Italian butcher shops and specialty food stores carry pancetta, and you will also find it nowadays in some large supermarkets.

Minestra di Fagioli con Pasta

(Borlotti Bean Soup with Pasta)

Serves 6 to 8

2 cups dried borlotti or pinto
    beans, covered with cool
    water and soaked overnight
½ cup chopped pancetta
1 medium onion, chopped
½ cup olive oil
3 stalks celery, chopped
½ teaspoon baking soda
Salt and freshly ground pepper
¼ cup tomato paste
½ teaspoon sugar
8 ounces ditalini
Freshly grated Parmesan cheese

Put the pancetta, onion, and olive oil into a large pot and cook over medium-high heat for 5 minutes. Add the soaked and drained beans, celery, and 2½ quarts of cool water. Bring to a boil and remove from the heat. Stir in the baking soda and season lightly with salt and pepper.

Return the soup to medium-low heat and cook until the beans are done, about 2 hours, stirring often.

Stir in the tomato paste and sugar, and simmer for 10 minutes. Depending on how much water is left and how thick you like your soup, you may want to add a few cups of boiling water. The starch from the pasta thickens the soup somewhat, which is how we like it. Stir in the ditalini and cook until done, about 15 minutes. Taste again for seasoning. Serve hot and pass the Parmesan cheese.

Minestrone di Verdure Fresche

(Fresh Garden Vegetable Soup)

$\mathcal{T}$his beautiful soup is a true minestrone—a bouquet of fresh garden vegetable flavors. Other vegetables can be added or substituted in the recipe, depending on what your garden is producing or what your local farmers' market has to sell, so consider asparagus, zucchini, broccoli, cabbage, scallions, leeks, and corn.

Serves 6 to 8

Put all the ingredients through the olive oil into a large pot, cover the vegetables with cool water or homemade or canned chicken stock or broth, and season lightly with salt and pepper. Simmer over medium heat for 30 minutes, or until the vegetables are tender. Add a little more water, if necessary. Discard any remaining pieces of cheese rind. Taste for seasoning again and sprinkle with the parsley.

The soup can be served hot, at room temperature, or cool. Accompany the soup with croutons (grilled or toasted bread slices) and pass the hot oil and Parmesan cheese.

1¼ pounds boiling potatoes, peeled and cubed
2 large carrots, scraped and cubed
1 cup chopped fresh spinach
3 stalks celery, thinly sliced
1 medium onion, chopped
1¼ pounds fresh tomatoes, peeled and chopped
1 pound green beans, cut into 1-inch lengths
1 cup green peas
1 garlic clove, minced
¼ cup freshly chopped basil
One 3-ounce piece Parmesan cheese rind (page 82)
¼ cup olive oil
Salt and freshly ground pepper
1 tablespoon freshly chopped Italian parsley
Croutons
Olio Santo (page 76)
Freshly grated Parmesan cheese

Le Preziose Scorze di Parmigiano

(Valuable Parmesan Cheese Rinds)

Although Parmigiano Reggiano is not a native cheese, today Sicilians use Parmigiano (which we refer to in this book as Parmesan) and our local excellent pecorino equally in our home kitchens. At Gangivecchio, we have used Parmesan for as long as I can remember because my great-grandmother Giulia was born in Bologna in Emilia, the home of this admirable cheese. Made from cow's milk, world-famous Parmesan is a grana cheese, indispensable in Italian cooking. Occasionally we like to combine pecorino and Parmesan in individual recipes. Pecorino, a stronger-flavored cheese, can overpower a dish if not used with discrimination. (Read more about pecorino on page 179.)

We religiously save all the rinds from the Parmesan cheese that we use. The rinds are covered and kept stored in the refrigerator. So often discarded, Parmesan rinds have as intense a flavor as the edible part of the cheese.

We add small chunks of hard Parmesan rind to many dishes such as soups—*minestrone di verdure fresche* and *minestra di patate con pasta*—stews, and even risotto. In our Bolognese sauce, *ragù di tritato,* we include a piece of cheese rind instead of milk to help produce the delicate flavor and creamy texture of the dish.

There are two procedures to remember when using the rinds. On the exterior, exposed side of the rind, where the words "Parmigiano Reggiano" are impressed, a thin layer of the rind must be scraped off with a sharp knife or vegetable peeler to clean away impurities. The small, cleaned piece of cheese rind, usually from 2 to 4 ounces, can simply be tossed into stews, sauces, soups, or braised dishes, adding an interesting flavor dimension.

Most of the cheese will melt during the cooking process, but the hardest part of the rind often remains in the form of one or more softened lumps. So the second procedure to remember is to discard these little bits at the end of cooking. We save any remaining rinds for Giorgina, our wild boar. One of Giorgina's pails, in which we collect food for her next breakfast or dinner, is kept in the kitchen at all times. Giorgina's meals include food scraps and leftovers from the restaurant and our own dining rooms. Many repeat guests never leave Gangivecchio without visiting Giorgina in her pen. Some have claimed to have seen her smile.

Minestra di Patate con Pasta

Serves 6

(Potato Soup with Pasta)

Put the potatoes, olive oil, onion, and cheese rind in a large saucepan. Cook over medium heat for 2 minutes, mixing the ingredients well. Add the vegetable bouillon cube, stir. Cover the ingredients with cold water and season lightly with salt and pepper. Bring to a boil. Immediately reduce the heat to medium and cook for 10 minutes, stirring occasionally.

Stir in the tomato paste and cook for 15 minutes.

Add 2 cups of boiling water and the ditalini. Cook at a low boil until the pasta is done, about 15 minutes, stirring often. Discard any remaining pieces of cheese rind.

Remove from the heat and taste for seasoning. Sprinkle with parsley and pecorino or Parmesan cheese and serve hot.

2 pounds boiling potatoes, peeled and cubed
¼ cup olive oil
1 medium onion, chopped
One 3-ounce Parmesan cheese rind (page 82)
1 vegetable bouillon cube
Salt and freshly ground pepper
¼ cup tomato paste
1½ cups ditalini
Freshly chopped Italian parsley
Freshly grated pecorino or Parmesan cheese

Minestra di Ceci con Pasta

Serves 6 to 8

(Chick-pea Soup with Pasta)

Put the drained chick-peas, olive oil, and onion in a large saucepan. Cover with cool water, season lightly with salt and pepper, and add the vegetable bouillon cube. Bring to a boil. Off the heat, stir in the baking soda.

Return to the heat and simmer until the chick-peas are tender, about 2½ hours. Add more boiling water, if necessary.

Stir in the ditalini and chopped fennel bulb and greens, and cook at a low boil until the pasta is cooked, about 15 minutes. Check the taste of the soup for seasoning. Pass the olive oil, cheese, and Olio Santo if you like it spicy.

2 cups dried chick-peas (about 1 pound), covered with cool water and soaked overnight
¼ cup olive oil, plus extra for topping
1 medium-large onion, finely chopped
Salt and freshly ground pepper
1 vegetable bouillon cube
½ teaspoon baking soda
1 cup ditalini
1 cup chopped white fennel bulb
¼ cup chopped dark green fennel tops
Freshly grated pecorino or Parmesan cheese
Olio Santo (page 76)

Palline di Riso in Brodo

(Rice Balls in Chicken Broth)

One 3½-pound chicken, cut
    into serving pieces
1 large boiling potato, peeled
    and cubed
2 carrots, scraped and thinly
    sliced
2 celery stalks with leaves,
    coarsely chopped
Salt and freshly ground pepper
3 cups Il Mio Risotto (page
    143), cooked and cooled
2 large eggs, lightly beaten
Dried bread crumbs
Olive, sunflower, or vegetable
    oil, for deep-frying
Freshly grated Parmesan cheese

*D*elicious Palline di Riso in Brodo is, of course, served as a first course for a light lunch or dinner. But whenever Mamma cooks this soup, she can't help recalling an incident that happened three decades ago, when the soup unexpectedly became the main course. At the time, transportation here at Gangivecchio from Gangi was easier and more comfortable by horseback or on foot than in a car. We were grateful to have a telephone.

Back then, a day before we were expecting four friends for a winter weekend, they called to say that they would be arriving that very day. Their other surprising news was that they had grown in number from four to twelve. It was a freezing cold day, so they announced that they were hurrying along and should arrive before sunset.

Unprepared for company that day, and certainly not twelve, Mamma immediately fled to the kitchen. The two chickens she had planned to roast for dinner the following evening went into the pot to make a broth. She prepared an enormous amount of risotto, which she shaped into more *palline* than she could count. The dinner menu that evening began with a big cheese board laden with pecorino, ricotta salata (aged salted ricotta), and an immense wedge of Parmesan, preserved olives, olive oil, bread, and plenty of wine. Mamma was certain that this substantial appetizer would be more than enough. However, when she returned to the dining room not a morsel of food was left on the table. Now she worried that the delicate soup she was about to serve would not satisfy these starving people. Everyone ate heartily, appreciating the soup and rice balls. They were so happy to rest and warm up by the fire and have something hot to eat that they thought the humble dinner a grand feast.

Serves 6

To prepare the broth, put the chicken, potato, carrots, and celery in a large pot, season lightly with salt and pepper, and cover with cool water. Slowly bring to a boil. Reduce the heat to medium-low and cook for 1 hour and 15 minutes.

Meanwhile, shape the risotto into 1-inch balls. Coat with egg and then bread crumbs and let rest for 15 minutes.

Heat 2 inches of olive, sunflower, or vegetable oil in a large, deep-sided frying pan and fry the rice balls, in batches, until golden brown all over. Drain on paper towels as they are cooked.

Transfer the chicken to a side dish (reserve the chicken for another use*) and strain the broth.

Pour the broth into a clean pot and return to a boil. Taste the broth for seasoning. Add the golden rice balls and simmer for 2 minutes. Serve the soup very hot and pass the Parmesan cheese.

*Serve the boiled, skinned, and boned chicken meat with Salsa Verde (page 188) or mustard, or use to prepare a chicken salad.

Pesce in Brodo con Pasta

(Fish Soup with Pasta)

¾ cup chopped Italian parsley
1 pound grouper fillets, boned
1 pound monkfish steaks,
    boned
½ teaspoon salt
¼ cup olive oil
1 medium onion, chopped
2 garlic cloves, chopped
1 cup fresh or canned tomatoes,
    drained, peeled, and
    chopped
Freshly ground pepper
6 ounces spaghetti, broken into
    1–1½-inch lengths

Betty's Calabrian-born mother, Bruna Loiacono, who has lived in Palermo for many years, is still strongly influenced by the gastronomic specialties of her family's southern Italian region when it comes to cooking. Bruna is very *brava* in *cucina*. We are always happy when Betty tells us that her mother is coming because she loves to cook Calabrian dishes for us in Tenuta Gangivecchio's restaurant kitchen. We are always delighted to see Bruna, of course, but we can't help being excited to learn what she will prepare.

Bruna's Pesce in Brodo con Pasta calls for *cernia* and *scorfano* (grouper and scorpion fish). While you can find grouper in the States, it is unlikely you will find Mediterranean scorpion fish. So we have substituted monkfish for the *scorfano*.

Serves 4

Put 1½ quarts of cool water, ½ cup of the parsley, the fish, and salt into a large saucepan and bring to a boil. Reduce the heat to medium-low and simmer for 20 minutes. Turn off the heat and let the fish rest in the water until it has reached room temperature.

Transfer the fish to a plate and strain the cooking water. Pour it into a bowl. Cut the fish into bite-size pieces and transfer the fish to the same bowl.

Combine the olive oil, onion, garlic, tomatoes, the remaining ¼ cup of parsley, and pepper to taste in a large, clean saucepan, and simmer for 15 minutes. Add the fish and broth to the pan. Bring to a boil. Add the spaghetti, stir, and cook at a low boil until the pasta is done, about 15 minutes. (Add a little extra hot water, if necessary.)

Tuoni e Fulmini

*(Thunder and Lightning—
Chick-pea and Cabbage
Soup)*

This robust, flavorful soup was apparently given this amusing name because its combined two main ingredients—chick-peas and cabbage—can produce digestive "thunder and lightning." Our secret for helping cancel possible turbulent aftereffects is the addition of a small amount of baking soda during cooking.

Serves 8

1 pound dried chick-peas, covered with cool water and ½ teaspoon baking soda and soaked overnight
1 large onion, chopped
Salt and freshly ground pepper
½ teaspoon baking soda
1 quart shredded Savoy cabbage
Fried croutons
Olive oil
Freshly grated Parmesan cheese

Drain the chick-peas and transfer to a large pot. Add the onion, lightly season with salt and freshly ground pepper, and then add the baking soda and bring to a boil. Reduce the heat and cook at a low boil for about 2½ hours, until the chick-peas are tender, stirring occasionally.

Meanwhile, in another pot, bring 2 quarts of water to a boil. Add the cabbage and 1 teaspoon salt, stir, and simmer until tender, about 20 minutes.

Drain the cabbage and add to the cooked soup. Combine well. Taste for salt and pepper.

Serve with fried croutons and pass the olive oil and Parmesan cheese.

Pasta e Salse

(Pasta and Sauces)

Salse *(Sauces)*

Salsa di Pomodoro *(Fresh Tomato Sauce)* • Salsa di Concentrato di Pomodoro *(Concentrated Tomato Sauce)* • Estratto *(Concentrated Tomato Paste Extract)* • Salsa Besciamella Morbida *(Soft Béchamel Sauce)* • Salsa Besciamella Sostenuta *(Hard Béchamel Sauce)*

Pasta Fresca *(Fresh Pasta)*

Pasta Fatta in Casa *(Homemade Pasta)* • Ravioli di Ricotta di Papà *(Papa's Fresh Ravioli Stuffed with Ricotta)*

Pasta Secca *(Dried Pasta)*

Cucinare la Pasta *(To Cook the Pasta)* • Casareccia con la Frutta Secca *(Casareccia with Nut Pesto Sauce)* • Pinoli *(Pine Nuts)* • Spaghetti con il Nuovo Pesto di Rucola di Paolo *(Spaghetti with Paolo's New Arugula Pesto Sauce)* • Bucatini alla Palina *(Bucatini with Cauliflower, Currants, and Pine Nuts)* • Penne alla Renata *(Renata's Penne with Yellow and Red Pepper Cream Sauce)* • Spaghetti con Ricotta, Menta e Timo di Giovanna *(Giovanna's Spaghetti with Ricotta, Mint, and Thyme)* • Pennette alla Crema di Fave Fresche *(Pennette with Pancetta and Fresh Fava Bean Cream Sauce)* • Penne con Fave e Finocchielli *(Penne with Fava Bean and Fennel Sauce)* • Linguine con lo Scalogno *(Linguine with Scallions)* • Fusilli con Verdure Maritate *(Fusilli with Married Greens of Spinach and Escarole)* • Penne con Carciofi e Piselli *(Penne with Artichokes and Peas)* • Tagliatelle con Zucchine e Melanzane *(Tagliatelle with Zucchini and Eggplant with Spicy Herb Sauce)* • Gemelli con Erbe Aromatiche *(Gemelli with Aromatic Herbs)* • Spaghetti con Melanzane e Ricotta Salata *(Spaghetti with Eggplant and Ricotta Salata)* • La Pasta di Luciano *(Luciano's Spaghetti* with Zucchini, Tomatoes, and Pine Nuts) • I Rigatoni di Daniela (Daniela's Rigatoni with Pancetta, Tomato, and Hot Pepper Sauce) • La Pasta di Betty (Betty's Spaghetti with Baked Fresh Tomato Sauce) • Tagliatelle Mediterranee (Tagliatelle with Tomatoes, Black Olives, and Capers) • Spaghetti Estivi di Mariuccia (Mariuccia's Summer Spaghetti with Mozzarella and Tomato Cream Sauce with Basil) • Orecchiette alla Rucola e Salsa di Pomodoro di Betty (Betty's Orecchiette with Arugula and Tomato Sauce) • Rupa Santini (Conchiglioni with Eggplant, Three Cheeses, and Toasted Bread Crumbs) • MOLLICA (Bread Crumbs) • Tagliatelle con Salsa Picchio Pacchio (Tagliatelle with Picchio Pacchio Sauce) • La Pasta di Loretta (Loretta's Ditali with Spinach and Pancetta) • Bucatini con le Sarde Come la Faccio Io (My Bucatini with Sardines) • Pasta Trinacria (Spaghetti with Swordfish, Eggplant, and Mint) • Linguine con Gamberetti (Linguine with Small Shrimp and Puréed Onions) • Spaghetti di Mare di Maria-Angela al Cartoccio (Maria-Angela's Spaghetti with Seafood Baked in Foil) • Linguine del Mare (Linguine with Seafood) • Rigatoni alla Besciamella con Funghi e Gamberetti al Gratin (Rigatoni with Béchamel Sauce and Mushrooms and Shrimp au Gratin) • Spaghetti con Acciughe e Mollica Rossa (Spaghetti with Anchovy and Fresh Tomato Sauce and Toasted Bread Crumbs) • IL NOSTRO PASTIFICIO LOCALE (Our Local Pasta Mill) • Spaghetti con Bottarga (Spaghetti with Tuna Roe) • Anelletti al Forno (Baked Timbale of Anelletti with Veal and Vegetables) • Timballo di Rigatoni alla Gangivecchio (Gangivecchio's Rigatoni Timbale with Veal, Pork, and Fennel) • Spaghetti con Ragù di Tritato (Spaghetti with Bolognese-Style Veal Sauce) • Casareccia con Ragù di Carne (Casareccia with Pork or Veal Sauce) • Penne con Agnello e Finocchielli in Salsa (Penne with Lamb and Fennel in Tomato Sauce) • Lasagne Ricce con Ragù di Salsiccia (Lasagne Ricce with Fresh Sausage Sauce) • La Pasta di Paolo (Rigatoni with Pork, Green Peas, and Tomato Sauce au Gratin) • Farfalle alla Wanda con Prosciutto,

Spinaci e Pisellini *(Wanda's Farfalle with Prosciutto, Spinach, and Peas)* •
Gnocchetti alla Madonita *(Madonie-Style Gnocchetti with
Meat and Vegetables)*

∞

In Sicily, there are more pasta dishes than there are names for babies. We have read that an Arabian in the twelfth century wrote that *itriya* (later called *tria*), a pasta with a shape similar to vermicelli, was produced in Trabia, a little town near Palermo. We are not historians, but we like to think that after ancient Rome, Sicily was the first to produce Italy's national dish.

After *la pasta* it seems to us that the next great invention was the commercial pasta machine, widely used in Sicily and southern Italy by the nineteenth century.

The Sicilian people regard pasta as the most important dish on the table, to be eaten at any hour of the day. We say that two pastas will save any situation, even a troubled marriage. We have always served two pastas at Gangivecchio as part of our set menu: one with a green sauce and one with a red sauce. No one ever complains, and there are always several requests for seconds.

In Sicily, pastas are traditionally served as *primo piatto* (first courses), to be followed by *secondo* meat or seafood dishes. Today, however, pastas, especially hearty ones containing vegetables, meat, or seafood sauces, are wonderful, substantial main courses.

In our home we rarely have leftover pasta, but when we do, we save it for lunch the next day and cook it in a frying pan with a little oil. The pasta is heated through, then left in the pan to form a delicious crunchy crust on the bottom side. (Some people add beaten eggs to the mixture to make it more firm.) The fried pasta is inverted onto a dish and cut into wedges. It disappears quickly.

SALSE *(Sauces)*

When we think of sauces, tomatoes come to mind first. In Sicily, tomato sauce is the heart of pasta and brings to mind summertime and the intermingled cooking aromas of fresh tomatoes, onions, and basil.

When my brother and I were children, we thought the preserving process was a nightmare. Three days before the sauce-making day, ordinary green bottles (*bordolesi*), collected throughout the year, were scrubbed and washed. Early on the morning of the chosen day, a huge amount of tomatoes were gathered and thoroughly washed. Over wood fires on the stove, enormous pots sat filled to the top with simmering chopped tomatoes, big pieces of onions, and trees of basil. Then the painstaking work of passing this boiling hot mixture by hand through the strainer began. The sauce was immediately poured into bottles, tightly sealed, and sterilized in boiling water. Once filled, the bottles had to be placed into large, blanket-lined baskets, covered with more blankets, and left to slowly cool.

The heat outside in August was already like an oven, so you can imagine what the temperature was like inside. During the sterilization a bottle or two would often explode, blasting tomato sauce all over the kitchen, delighting Paolo and me—we were disappointed if at least one didn't detonate. The great reward for all this hard work was reaching to a shelf in the pantry during the dreary winter days for a taste of the fresh sweet Sicilian summer.

Today we make fresh tomato sauce for the restaurant all summer long. For the preserved Salsa di Pomodoro we send a big crop of tomatoes and our saved bottles to a neighbor, who has the time and the patience for this chore. She keeps half the sauce as payment for her labor.

Salsa di Pomodoro

(Fresh Tomato Sauce)

*F*resh tomato sauce is as indispensable to Sicilian cooking as flour is to making pasta. Salsa di Pomodoro, our most valuable basic and versatile sauce, is extended into hundreds of different sauces for pasta. It's also used extensively in meat and vegetable dishes.

Makes about 1 quart

Stir the tomatoes, onion, and chopped basil together in a large pot. Season to taste with salt. Cook over medium heat for about 15 minutes, stirring often.

A few cups at a time, pass the mixture through a food mill. Return the sauce to a clean pot with the olive oil, basil leaves, sugar, and salt and pepper to taste. Simmer for 30 minutes, stirring occasionally.

5 pounds ripe tomatoes, with stem ends removed, coarsely chopped
1 large onion, chopped
½ cup freshly chopped basil leaves, plus 6 whole fresh basil leaves
Salt
½ cup olive oil
1 teaspoon sugar
Freshly ground pepper

Salsa di Concentrato di Pomodoro

(Concentrated Tomato Sauce)

*I*n this book Concentrato di Pomodoro is given in recipes in place of *estratto,* a thick tomato extract paste, which we would normally use. (The recipe is on page 94.) *Estratto* is not easily found in America.

Makes about 1 quart

Heat the olive oil in a heavy-bottomed saucepan and cook the onion for 5 minutes over medium heat, stirring often. Stir in the remaining ingredients and season to taste with salt and pepper. Simmer over low heat for 1 hour. The sauce must be stirred frequently.

1 cup olive oil
1 medium onion, finely chopped
3 cups tomato paste
1 teaspoon sugar
Salt and freshly ground pepper

Estratto

(Concentrated Tomato Paste Extract)

Estratto is a rich, full-flavored concentrate of cooked fresh tomatoes seasoned only with salt and the sun. (Check the summer weather report in advance. You will need about five hot days of full sun and little humidity.) The cooked tomatoes are forced through a food mill and strainer. The tomato purée is spread onto a large wooden board out in the sun and is stirred throughout the day. Eventually the stirring process turns into spreading, as the moisture evaporates. The tomatoes are covered at night, and the process repeated for three to five days, depending on the strength of the sun. The weather must cooperate. You begin with 10 pounds of tomatoes and end up with about 1 pound of *estratto* for all your labor, but only a small amount is required in dishes to produce a rich tomato taste.

We haven't made *estratto* in several years, because we haven't the staff or time, but excellent-quality commercial *estratto* is available to us in Sicily. We use a large quantity in the restaurant at Gangivecchio. Since it isn't readily available in America, we have included a recipe for Salsa di Concentrato di Pomodoro, which has more of a likeness in taste to true *estratto* than tomato paste. In our book Salsa Concentrato di Pomodoro (page 93) is used in our recipes that would normally contain *estratto*.

Makes 1 pound

20 pounds ripe, full-flavored, Italian plum tomatoes
Salt
Olive oil

Remove the stem ends of the tomatoes. Chop the tomatoes and put them into a large pot. Bring to a boil, then immediately reduce the heat to low and season with salt. Cook for about 1 hour, stirring often to prevent burning.

Pass the tomatoes through a food mill. If any seeds remain, pour the mixture through a fine strainer. Season well with salt.

Since the mixture is quite liquid at the beginning, you can divide it among several large platters for the first drying stages. Place the platters in the sun and stir the tomatoes frequently, about every hour, until enough moisture evaporates to prevent the mixture from running off the sides of a wooden board. The board you need for the drying should be very large, about 2 × 4 feet. Spread the tomatoes across the surface and let them continue drying in the sun. Spread the tomatoes about every 30 minutes with a spatula, turning the mixture over and over.

At the end of the day, after 8 hours (for example, from 10 a.m. to 6 p.m.), bring the board inside the house and cover the tomatoes with filmy, sheer cloth, like cheesecloth or curtain material, that will allow the tomatoes to breathe—the cloth must not touch the tomatoes. The easiest way to achieve this is to put 4 large cans on each corner of the board, stretch the cloth taut, and tuck it underneath the board.

The next day, remove the cloth and return the board to the sun. Spread the mixture throughout the day, at half-hour or hourly intervals. Repeat the covering procedure at the end of the day, and repeat the process for about three more days—the time depends on the strength of the sun and lack of humidity. *Estratto* is done when it is dark red and has a thick, barely spreadable pastelike consistency.

Pack the *estratto* into a crock or glass jar and cover the top with olive oil. Cover and refrigerate. It will keep for two months.

Salse Besciamella

(Béchamel Sauces)

In Sicily, white sauces with pasta are not a tradition like they are in northern Italy. We mainly use white sauces as fillings, such as the stuffing for *arancine* or the creamy centers of *crocchè di latte* (milk croquettes). We also use Salsa Besciamella (béchamel sauce) for au gratin dishes.

The two kinds we prepare are hard (*sostenuta*) or soft (*morbida*), depending on which consistency is required. Of course, only *besciamella morbida* is used for pasta. Whenever we serve a white sauce with pasta at Gangivecchio, which Mamma and I enjoy once in a while for a change, Paolo wants to know, "Who is coming to dinner—a child or an invalid?"

For a delicious, creamy pasta sauce, prepare Salsa Besciamella Morbida. Stir ¾ cup of freshly grated Parmesan cheese into the hot sauce and toss with 1 pound cooked spaghetti or other long-shaped pasta. If you like, you can also add a cup of thinly sliced boiled ham and ½ cup cooked green peas to the sauce. Don't forget to season to taste with salt and pepper.

Makes about 2¼ cups

Salsa Besciamella Morbida *(Soft Béchamel Sauce)*

¼ cup sweet butter
¼ cup all-purpose flour
2 cups hot milk
Salt

Melt the butter in a saucepan. Stir in the flour and cook over low heat, constantly stirring until the flour has "cooked" for about 2 minutes. Slowly pour in the milk, whisking constantly, and turn the heat to high. Whisk until the sauce has thickened and season to taste with salt.

NOTE: This recipe is easily doubled.

Salsa Besciamella Sostenuta *(Hard Béchamel Sauce)*

The recipe for making hard béchamel is the same as for making soft, except that you use ½ cup all-purpose flour instead of ¼ cup.

NOTE: This recipe is easily doubled.

PASTA FRESCA *(Fresh Pasta)*

To make a large quantity of pasta by hand is a tremendous task requiring many more hands than just two. Nowadays at Gangivecchio we make fresh pasta only on holy days, other special occasions, or by advance request at the restaurant. The one consolation for this work is that it tones up the arm muscles.

Our dried *(secca)* pastas made with hard durum wheat flour are superb. Most Sicilians prefer dried rather than fresh pasta, for its al dente texture. As delicious as fresh pasta is, the result for us is always soft, because we only use "00" flour (similar to all-purpose flour) in the dough. Here we give two basic *pasta fresca* recipes—for tagliatelle and ravioli.

Pasta Fatta in Casa

(Homemade Pasta)

*F*or this recipe you can make any shape pasta you like. Mamma's instructions below are for tagliatelle. Sometimes Betty makes giant bucatini by pressing strips of rolled-out strips of dough around *busi* (knitting needles).

Hand-turned pasta machines are excellent work and time-savers, but Mamma refuses to use the "gadget," as she calls it. Everyone at Gangivecchio uses one but Mamma.

4 cups all-purpose flour
4 large eggs
Pinch of salt

Serves 4 for a main course and 6 for a first course

Put the flour into a large bowl. Make a hole in the center. Break the eggs into the hole and sprinkle with a pinch of salt. Mix the eggs together with a fork and, little by little, work the flour in from the side walls. Continue working until all the flour is incorporated into the dough, adding a little warm water when necessary. Shape the dough into a ball and knead it until smooth and silky. Let the dough rest at room temperature for 1 hour in a bowl covered with a damp cloth.

Roll the dough out on a lightly floured board to a little less than an ⅛-inch thickness. Sprinkle the dough lightly with flour. Starting at one end, fold the dough over itself 2 inches at a time. Cut through the dough crosswise with a sharp knife at ¼-inch intervals. Separate the noodles and either cook them immediately in boiling, salted water, or put them on a tray dusted lightly with flour. The pasta can be left, covered with a damp towel, for a day, but fresh pasta is always better cooked right away.

Fresh pasta has a very short cooking time—anywhere from 2 to 5 minutes, depending on the size and shape of the pasta. Cooked fresh pasta is never as firm to the bite as dried pasta. To tell when fresh pasta is done, you must watch the color of the dough—as it cooks, it brightens in color and becomes slightly opaque. The only real test is to taste it. When the raw-dough taste is gone, the pasta is done.

Ravioli Freschi di Papà

(Papa's Fresh Ravioli Stuffed with Ricotta)

2 cups drained ricotta (see
    instructions on page 39—
    must be prepared one to two
    days in advance)
Salt and freshly ground pepper
8 tablespoons sweet butter,
    melted and clarified
Freshly grated Parmesan cheese

PASTA DOUGH

6 cups all-purpose flour
4 large eggs, at room tempera-
    ture
Salt

*S*oon after my parents were married, they went to visit friends who lived in a villa in Taormina and had an accomplished Austrian cook. For dinner one evening the cook prepared fresh ravioli stuffed with ricotta and topped only with melted butter and Parmesan cheese, which my father thought wonderful—so pure, so simple. Mamma learned how to make the dish, and back at Gangivecchio, she carefully prepared the ravioli for the family. The ravioli dish both surprised and delighted my father's mother, Giovanna. I suspect that this is when the affectionate culinary competition between my mother and Granny was born.

Serves 4 to 6

Put the ricotta into a bowl and season it well with salt and pepper. Mix it vigorously with a fork for a minute and let rest.

To make the pasta dough, turn the flour into a large bowl and make a well in the center. Put the eggs into the well and add a pinch of salt. Mix the eggs together with a fork in a circle and, little by little, work the flour in from the side walls. Continue working until all the flour is incorporated into the dough, adding a little warm water when necessary. Shape the dough into a ball and knead it until smooth and silky on a lightly floured work surface, about 10 minutes.

Divide the dough in half and work into smooth, flattened rectangles about 1 inch thick. Cover the dough with a damp cloth and let rest for 1 hour.

Roll each half of the dough out into a long, ⅛-inch-thick rectangle, about 18 inches × 5 inches, on a work surface. Place rounded teaspoonfuls of the ricotta 1 inch from the lengthwise edge of the sheet of dough in two parallel rows the length of the dough. Place the other sheet of dough on top of the first. Make the ravioli by cutting the dough into 2-inch squares with the wheel of a serrated pastry cutter or square ravioli cutter. Lightly press the edges to seal. Place the ravioli on a baking sheet lightly dusted with flour.

Bring 4 quarts of water to a rolling boil. Stir in 1½ tablespoons of salt, stir, and, one by one, smoothly release the ravioli into the water and gently stir. Cook the pasta until done, stirring lightly but often. The ravioli cooks in 4 to 5 minutes.

Heat the clarified butter.

Transfer half the ravioli to a warmed serving platter with a slotted spoon. Pour half the heated butter over the top and sprinkle with Parmesan cheese. Put the remaining ravioli on top, pour the rest of the butter over them, and sprinkle again with Parmesan.

PASTA SECCA *(Dried Pasta)*

At Gangivecchio, we primarily use dried pasta. To best duplicate the finest Sicilian pasta, we recommend using imported Italian brands made from hard durum wheat (also called semolina). Most of the recipes were tested with DeCecco and Barilla brands, which are well distributed in the United States, but you can use any quality pasta you prefer.

Pastas are classified in two basic shapes—long and short. In Sicily, there is an enormous selection of pasta shapes. Among the most popular shapes are gemelli (open-sided twisted short shapes), casareccia (twin-twisted short shapes), bucatini (long hollow strands, also called perciatelli), anelletti (little rings), conchiglioni (snail shapes), ditalini (short hollow pieces with straight sides), sedani (wide hollow shapes with ridged, straight sides), tripolini, and margherita, or lasagne ricce (long, flat strips with curly sides or with a straight side and a curly or ribbon-shaped side). There are many others we use that will be more familiar to Americans, like linguine, penne, rigatoni, farfalle, fusilli, tagliatelle, ravioli, fettuccine, and, of course, spaghetti—the most popular shape in Sicily and the world. All regions of Italy have certain shapes they favor, such as pappardelle in Tuscany and orecchiette in Apulia. Generally the same basic types of pastas are interchangeable. For example, you can substitute penne for gemelli and linguine for spaghetti.

In our restaurant we normally use short-shaped pastas because they are easier to cook in large amounts—sometimes up to 40 pounds at a time for 150 people. Long shapes, like spaghetti, lasagne ricce, and linguine, we save for our home dining rooms. My brother, Paolo, would eat spaghetti every day of the year if Mamma, Betty, and I did not insist on variety at the table. But he can be very stubborn. None of us is surprised when he rises up from the table to cook his own spaghetti.

Cucinare la Pasta
(To Cook the Pasta)

Although it might seem that all Italians are born with an instinct for cooking pasta, it's really because from when we are tall enough to look into the pot, we are at our mother's side hungrily waiting for the pasta to be done. When we were children, near the end of cooking time, Mamma always let Paolo and me each taste a string of spaghetti—*uno spaghetto.* She would ask us, "*Che pensi, è cotta?* [What do you think? Is it done?]" She questioned us to teach us, but also because it was a game. She knew if I said yes, Paolo would say no, or vice versa.

There are only a few simple rules to follow when cooking dried pasta. First, it must be cooked in a generous amount of salty water. We recommend 4 quarts of water with 1½ tablespoons of salt for 1 pound of pasta. Salting the water is an important factor in flavoring the pasta, but you can reduce the amount of salt if you prefer.

Bring the water to a rolling boil in a large covered pot. When the water boils, stir in the salt, then add the pasta all at once and stir it again immediately. Keep the heat on high throughout the entire cooking process. Bring the water back to the boil and continue cooking and stirring the pasta often to prevent it from sticking together or to the bottom of the pot.

In Sicily, sometimes part or all of the water we use to cook the pasta in is the water that a vegetable has been cooked in, such as cauliflower or fennel, especially if the vegetable is featured in the sauce for the pasta.

Occasionally we add a small amount of olive oil to the water when we're cooking several pounds of large types of pasta like fettuccine or rigatoni, which helps prevent it from sticking together.

Long, thin strands of dried pasta, like capellini and spaghetti, and little shapes like tubettini cook the fastest. Conchiglie, rigatoni, and bucatini, to mention only a few of the thicker-shaped pastas, require more cooking time. However, the size of the pasta isn't always a determining factor. Our anelletti, tiny ring-shaped pasta, takes 12 minutes or more to cook. It is impossible to know exactly how long it will take to cook pasta, since you can't know how old the pasta is or how much moisture it contains.

After most pasta has boiled for 5 minutes, you must taste it frequently. Spaghetti takes anywhere from 6 to 8 minutes. Thicker, larger shapes usually take from 10 to 12 minutes or more.

Pasta should be cooked al dente, or to the tooth, and be slightly resistant to the bite. Even when my mother cooks spaghetti for the cats, she cooks it al dente.

When the pasta is done, quickly remove 1 to 2 cups of the hot water it cooked in and set aside. This simple, hot pasta cooking water is very useful when the sauce you are using doesn't blend in with the pasta smoothly or thoroughly enough, or if the sauced pasta, which has been sprinkled with bread crumbs or cheese, has dried out somewhat. Just add some of the hot pasta water, a little bit at a time, and toss. Try it. You'll see how well it works. Exceptions to this rule are when preparing a pasta that is to be served at room temperature or cold, such as for a salad, or for certain dishes using cream or those that are baked. For reasons of temperature, texture, and taste, it is better to add a small amount of extra olive oil to a pasta salad rather than water.

To drain cooked pasta, we use different methods for different shapes. For long pasta, such as spaghetti and linguine, we transfer it to a bowl with a big pasta fork, leaving a little water clinging to the strands. For draining short shapes, like gemelli, penne, or rigatoni, we use a colander placed in the sink, and then we shake it two or three times over the sink to eliminate most of the excess water hiding inside the hollow spaces.

Pasta must be sauced immediately after it is drained. For a pound of pasta we normally add a cup or so of sauce first, toss it, and then judge how much more is needed, adding ½ cup or so at a time and tossing the pasta after each addition. The reserved hot pasta water can then be added if necessary, a few tablespoons at a time. It's important, too, never to oversauce pasta. A big puddle of sauce on the bottom of the pasta serving bowl means that too much sauce has been added. At Gangivecchio, after the proper amount of sauce has been added, we like to present the dish with a little sauce spooned over the top as a garnish.

Casareccia con la Frutta Secca

(Casareccia with Nut Pesto Sauce)

½ cup almonds
½ cup hazelnuts
½ cup walnuts
½ cup pistachio nuts
½ cup pine nuts
6 garlic cloves, peeled
2 cups fresh basil leaves
⅓ cup freshly chopped Italian
    parsley
½ cup freshly grated Parmesan
    cheese, plus more for topping
½ cup freshly grated pecorino
Salt and freshly ground pepper
¾ cup olive oil, or as needed
2 pounds casareccia, gemelli, or
    penne
2 tablespoons sweet butter

This exquisite version of an Arab-inspired Sicilian pasta dish with a nut pesto sauce was given to us many years ago by an old family friend who insisted that its success lies in crushing each ingredient separately with a mortar and pestle. For a while we faithfully followed her instructions—a time-consuming, tedious job. Now we have become modern, or too lazy, so we accomplish the task quickly and efficiently in the food processor. The sauce tastes better than ever, and it is one of the most popular dishes at our restaurant.

When our friend tasted her sauce prepared by machine, she shrugged. Preserving the beloved past, she continues laboriously grinding the ingredients one by one. Although Mamma doesn't understand why her friend is so stubborn, Mamma herself still refuses to use the food processor, so I must always make the sauce.

Casareccia are twin-twisted short-shaped pasta pieces, very popular in Sicily, but gemelli, penne, or any other similar-size pasta can be used. The recipe below is the right amount for 2 pounds of pasta that will serve 8 to 12 people. The recipe can be cut in half to serve 4 to 6. The sauce freezes well, so you might want to make the larger amount and save half the sauce for another day. To use the frozen sauce, thaw it at room temperature. Reheat the sauce in the top pan of a double boiler, stirring it often, just until thoroughly heated.

Serves 8 to 12

Put all the ingredients, except the olive oil, pasta, and butter, into the bowl of a food processor. Turn on the machine and immediately begin pouring the olive oil through the feed tube in a slow, steady stream. The mixture should be a thick, creamy, spreadable consistency. Add a little extra olive oil, if necessary. Do not over-purée the sauce; the nuts should remain grainy in texture and crunchy. Transfer the sauce to a large saucepan or heatproof bowl and set it aside.

Bring 6 quarts of water to a rolling boil in a large pot. Stir in 3 tablespoons of salt, stir again, and add the pasta. Cook until al dente, or just tender, stirring often.

Meanwhile, add the butter and 2 cups of boiling water from the pasta pot to the sauce, and thoroughly combine.

Remove 1 cup of the hot pasta water and reserve it. Drain the pasta and transfer it to a large serving bowl. Adding 1 cup of the sauce at a time, toss the pasta until all the sauce is used. Add a little hot pasta water, if necessary. Taste for seasoning.

No extra cheese is required, but if you like, pass the Parmesan cheese.

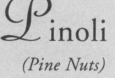

Pinoli
(Pine Nuts)

At Gangivecchio, we have very tall, ancient pine trees that yield a good crop of pine nuts each year. Pine nuts, the seeds of the tree, are found hidden inside its large pine cones. The shells are extremely hard and quite a task to crack open, especially since they are so tiny—that is the reason they cost as much as they do.

To collect the pine cones from the trees, Peppe, our houseman, leans a tall ladder against each tree and shakes the branches vigorously until the cones fall to the ground. He has spent hundreds of hours cracking pine nuts during his lifetime. These days, when he can't sleep at night, Peppe sits in front of his big color television set in his room cracking the nuts while watching old movies.

Spaghetti con il Nuovo Pesto di Rucola di Paolo

(Spaghetti with Paolo's New Arugula Pesto Sauce)

4 cups loosely packed fresh
    arugula, washed and dried
    and coarsely chopped
2 garlic cloves, chopped
½ cup chopped walnuts
½ cup olive oil
4 medium-sized firm, fresh ripe
    tomatoes
Salt and freshly ground pepper
1 pound spaghetti
1 tablespoon sweet butter
Freshly grated pecorino or
    Parmesan cheese

With kilos and kilos of arugula in our gardens this year, we searched for new ways to use this piquant peppery green. My brother, who regularly invents new pasta sauces, had an idea for an arugula pesto made with walnuts that would also include tomatoes, both puréed and cubed. The tasty outcome is below.

Also consider using the pesto sauce as a wonderful topping pâté for grilled or toasted bread slices for *bruschetta*. For the pâté, reduce the amount of olive oil in the recipe to 3 tablespoons.

Serves 6 as a first course and 4 as a main course

Put the arugula, garlic, walnuts, and olive oil into the bowl of a food processor and purée until smooth and creamy. Add 1 peeled, seeded, and chopped tomato and purée.

Turn the mixture into a bowl, season to taste with salt and pepper, and set aside. (The sauce can be made up to 1 hour in advance.)

Bring 4 quarts of water to a rolling boil in a large pot.

Meanwhile, cut each of the remaining 3 peeled and seeded tomatoes into small cubes and drain well.

When the water comes to the boil, stir in 1½ tablespoons of salt, stir, and add the spaghetti. Stir it again and cook the spaghetti until al dente, or just tender, stirring frequently.

Put the butter in the bottom of a large bowl with 1 tablespoon of the sauce.

When the pasta is done, reserve 1 cup of the hot cooking water. Drain the spaghetti lightly and turn it into the bowl. Add half the sauce and the tomatoes and toss. Add the remaining sauce and tomatoes and gently toss. If necessary, add a little of the hot water and toss again if the sauce is not blended thoroughly or the pasta has dried out. Serve immediately and pass the pecorino or Parmesan cheese.

Bucatini alla Palina

Serves 6 as a first course or 4 as a main course

(Bucatini with Cauliflower, Currants, and Pine Nuts)

Bring 1½ quarts of water to a rolling boil. Stir in 1 teaspoon salt and add the cauliflower. Cook at a slow boil for about 5 minutes. Transfer the cauliflower to a bowl with a slotted spoon. Reserve 1 quart of cooking water.

In a large saucepan, heat the olive oil and cook the shallots or onion and anchovies over medium heat for 5 minutes. Add the cauliflower water, saffron, currants, and pine nuts. Combine well and season to taste with salt and pepper. Simmer for 15 minutes.

Meanwhile, combine 3 quarts of water and the reserved quart of cauliflower cooking water and bring to a rolling boil in a large pot. Stir in 1½ tablespoons of salt and add the bucatini. Cook until al dente, or just tender, stirring often.

Reserve 1 cup of the pasta water, drain the pasta, and return it to the pot. Immediately add the sauce and gently toss. Add more pasta water, as needed, if a thinner sauce is preferred. Cover and let the pasta rest, off the heat, for 5 minutes. Toss again and serve with the toasted bread crumbs.

Salt
1 small cauliflower, with florets cut into small pieces
¾ cup olive oil
½ cup finely chopped shallots or onion
2 tablespoons minced anchovy fillets
¼ teaspoon powdered saffron
½ cup currants, soaked in hot water for 10 minutes and drained
¼ cup pine nuts
Freshly ground pepper
1 pound bucatini, broken in half
¾ cup toasted bread crumbs (page 121)

Penne alla Renata

(Renata's Penne with Yellow and Red Pepper Cream Sauce)

2 large red bell peppers
2 large yellow bell peppers
2 tablespoons sweet butter
½ cup olive oil
1 medium onion, grated
3 tablespoons heavy cream
Salt and freshly ground pepper
1 pound penne
Freshly ground Parmesan cheese

I have a friend in Palermo who invented this wonderful creamy yellow-and-red pepper sauce for pasta. I asked her for the recipe several times, but she would never give it to me. When I was alone one day with her ten-year-old daughter, Renata, I asked if she knew how her mother prepared the sauce. Renata gave me the recipe. When I told her mother that I had the recipe, she just laughed and said, "Renata gave you her recipe, she would never give you mine." —G.T.

Serves 6 as a first course or 4 as a main course

Blacken the whole peppers a few inches from the heat source under the broiler. Cool slightly and peel off the skins.

Cut out the stem ends of the peppers and quarter each. Remove the seeds and white membranes.

Purée the pepper quarters in a food processor.

In a large saucepan, heat the butter and olive oil with 1 teaspoon of water. Add the onion and cook to a thick paste, about 15 minutes. Stir in the pepper purée and simmer, without boiling. Add the cream and season with salt and pepper to taste. Simmer over very low heat for 5 minutes, stirring occasionally.

Meanwhile, bring 4 quarts of water to a rolling boil. Stir in 1½ tablespoons of salt and add the penne. Cook until al dente, or just tender, stirring often.

Reserve 1 cup of the pasta water. Drain the penne and add it to the pepper sauce. Cook over low heat for 2 minutes, stirring frequently. Add a little more pasta water, if necessary. Taste again for seasoning. Pass the Parmesan cheese.

Spaghetti con Ricotta, Menta e Timo di Giovanna

(Giovanna's Spaghetti with Ricotta, Mint, and Thyme)

*T*his is an excellent recipe Giovanna created for an American couple who arrived at Gangivecchio for lunch unexpectedly on a day that we are always closed—Monday. After often preparing meals for as many as one hundred for Sunday's lunch, we need to rest and recover for a day. I am very strict about this. But on this particular day, a very pleasant American couple arrived, exhausted from their long drive all the way from Siracusa. So Giovanna, who is always kind, thought that we should feed them. I told her they were welcome to stay for lunch if she cooked the entire meal. To my surprise, she did.

Serves 6 as a first course or 4 as a main course

Bring 4 quarts of water to a rolling boil.

While waiting for the water to boil, heat the olive oil and butter with the garlic cloves in a large frying pan over low heat, stirring often. When the garlic cloves begin to turn golden, discard them, stir in the ricotta with a wooden spoon.

Add the tomato sauce, chopped mint, and chopped thyme, and season to taste with salt and pepper. Simmer for 10 minutes, stirring occasionally.

Stir 1½ tablespoons of salt into the boiling water and add the spaghetti. Cook until al dente, or just tender, stirring often.

Reserve 1 cup of the pasta water. Transfer the spaghetti to a serving bowl. Add 1 cup of the sauce and toss. Turn the remaining sauce over the top and toss well. Garnish the bowl with a little bouquet of fresh mint and thyme sprigs, and serve with Parmesan cheese.

½ cup olive oil
2 tablespoons butter
4 whole garlic cloves, peeled
2 cups drained ricotta (see instructions on page 39—must be prepared one to two days in advance)
¾ cup fresh tomato sauce (Salsa di Pomodoro, page 93)
¼ cup fresh mint, finely chopped, plus 2 sprigs for garnish
1 tablespoon fresh thyme leaves, finely chopped, plus 2 sprigs for garnish
Salt and freshly ground pepper
1 pound spaghetti
Freshly grated Parmesan cheese

Pennette alla Crema di Fave Fresche

(Pennette with Pancetta and Fresh Fava Bean Cream Sauce)

½ cup olive oil
1¼ cups cubed smoked
    pancetta
3 cups fresh fava beans, shelled
¾ cup diced white bulb of
    fennel
½ cup heavy cream
1 tablespoon sweet butter
½ cup dry white wine
Salt and freshly ground pepper
1 pound pennette or penne
Freshly grated pecorino

*H*ere is an exquisite pasta invented by my brother, Paolo. When fava beans are in season, he often cooks the dish for the guests in the restaurant of the *albergo*. The aroma of the combined simmering fava beans, fennel, and smoked pancetta wafting through the corridors always brings guests to dinner early.

Serves 6 as a first course or 4 as a main course

Heat the olive oil in a large frying pan and cook the pancetta for 5 minutes over medium heat. Transfer to a dish.

Bring 2 quarts of lightly salted water to a boil and cook the fava beans and fennel until tender, about 5 minutes. Drain the beans and fennel through a strainer over a pot that will be used for cooking the pasta. Purée the vegetables in the food processor.

Heat the purée in a frying pan with the cream and butter, stirring constantly for a few minutes. Pour in the wine and cook over high heat for 1 minute, stirring constantly. Season to taste with salt and pepper. Add the pancetta and simmer over very low heat while cooking the pasta.

Add 2 quarts of water to the vegetable water in the pot and bring it to a rolling boil. Stir in 1½ tablespoons of salt, stir, and add the pasta. Cook until al dente, or just tender, stirring often.

Reserve 2 cups of the pasta water. Drain the pasta and transfer to a large serving bowl. Turn the sauce onto the pasta, sprinkle lightly with pecorino, and toss well. Add a little pasta water, if necessary, if a thinner sauce is preferred. Taste for seasoning.

Serve immediately and pass the pecorino.

"In artichoke season we prepare many
of Mamma's artichoke recipes, especially her wonderful tarts."

Sformato di Carciofi, page 59

"The preserved tuna is excellent eaten plain or as a truly delicious filling for *panini*."

Tonno Sott' Olio (before and after), page 69

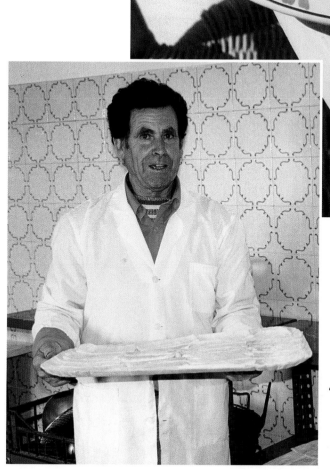

Above: "*Ricotta* (which means 'recooked') is made from the whey that is left over from the *tuma* production."

"Peppe Bevacqua, our houseman, farmer, cook, and do-everything man, whom we consider a family member, has been at Gangivecchio for thirty years."

"With absolute confidence I can boast that my Frittelle di Fiori di
Zucca are the best in the world."

Frittelle di Fiori di Zucca, page 54

"Soup to me means warm comfort on cold winter evenings when there is snow on the ground, and inside, on the table, there is a bowl of one of my favorites."

Minestra di Patate con Pasta, page 83

"Paolo, who regularly invents new pasta sauces, had an idea for an arugula pesto made with walnuts."

Spaghetti con il Nuovo Pesto di Rucola di Paolo, page 104

"Fresh tomato sauce is as indispensible to Sicilian cooking as flour is to making pasta."

Salsa di Pomodoro, page 93

"This exquisite version of an Arab-inspired Sicilian dish with a nut pesto sauce was given to us many years ago by an old family friend."

Casareccia con la Frutta Secca, page 102

"In Sicily there are more pasta dishes than there are names for babies."

Bucatini con le Sarde, Come la Faccio Io, page 124

"*Estratto* is a rich, full-flavored concentrate of cooked fresh tomatoes seasoned only with salt and the sun."

Estratto, page 94

"Risotto is not a Sicilian tradition, but when Sicilians come to the restaurant and learn that risotto is on the menu, they always respond with happy sighs."

Risotto con Funghi, page 149

"In Sicily, our favorite way of eating rice is when it is transformed into charming balls called *arancine*."

Arancine II, page 146

Penne con Fave e Finocchielli

(Penne with Fava Bean and Fennel Sauce)

Salt
2 cups fresh fava beans, shelled
2 cups chopped white fennel
    bulb
1 tablespoon sweet butter,
    softened
Olive oil
1 medium onion, chopped
6 ounces chopped boiled ham
Cayenne pepper (optional)
½ cup dry white wine
1 pound penne
Freshly grated pecorino

*T*his is our adaptation of a typical pasta dish prepared by shepherds in the Madonie region in the spring, when the fava beans are young and tender. Sometimes the shepherds like to add creamy fresh ricotta made from their sheep's milk. Wild fennel is normally used in the recipe, but we use white-bulb fennel. Of course, the shepherds here would never use butter, ham, or wine, but we like adding these ingredients. The ham can be omitted.

Serves 6 as a first course or 4 as a main course

Bring 1 quart of water to a boil. Add in 1 teaspoon of salt, stir, and add the fava beans and fennel. Simmer about 10 minutes, until the vegetables are very tender.

Using a strainer, drain the water from the beans and fennel into a large pot to be used for cooking the pasta.

Purée the beans, fennel, and butter with ½ cup olive oil in the food processor and set aside.

Add 3 quarts of water to the vegetable water in the pot and bring to a rolling boil.

Meanwhile, heat ¼ cup olive oil in a large frying pan and cook the onion until it begins to turn golden brown, stirring often. This will take only a few minutes. Add the ham, a pinch of cayenne pepper, if you like, and the wine. Stir well and cook for 2 minutes over high heat. Reduce the heat and fold in the purée. Simmer over very low heat for 5 minutes.

Stir 1½ tablespoons of salt into the boiling water, stir again, and add the penne. Cook until al dente, or just tender, stirring often.

Reserve 1 cup of the pasta water from the pot. Drain the penne and return it to the pot. Add the sauce, toss well, and simmer for 1 minute over low heat. Add a little extra pasta water, if a thinner sauce is preferred.

Serve hot and pass the pecorino.

Linguine con lo Scalogno

(Linguine with Scallions)

Serves 6 as a first course or 4 as a main course

3 cups scallions, using white
    parts and 2 inches of green
    tops, cut into 1-inch pieces
1 cup olive oil
Salt and freshly ground pepper
⅛ teaspoon powdered saffron
1 pound linguine
Freshly grated pecorino or
    Parmesan cheese

Bring 4 quarts of water to a rolling boil.

Meanwhile, put the scallions into a frying pan with the olive oil, plus 2 tablespoons of water, and cook over medium heat. Season to taste with salt and pepper. Cover the pan and cook about 5 minutes, until the scallions have softened.

Remove the cover and cook over high heat until the scallions begin to turn golden brown. Remove from the heat.

Stir 1½ tablespoons of salt and the saffron into the boiling water and add the pasta. Cook until al dente, or just tender, stirring often.

Reserve 1 cup of pasta water. Drain the spaghetti and transfer to the scallion sauce in the pan. Add ¼ cup of the hot pasta water. Toss the pasta well and season to taste with salt and pepper. Add a little more hot water, if a thinner sauce is desired. Serve with grated pecorino or Parmesan cheese.

Fusilli con Verdure Maritate

*(Fusilli with Married Greens
of Spinach and Escarole)*

1 pound fresh spinach, washed,
    with stems cut off
1 pound escarole, washed and
    coarsely chopped
1½ cups olive oil
6 garlic cloves
6 anchovy fillets, chopped
Salt and freshly ground pepper
Pinch of cayenne pepper
    (optional)
1¼ cups chopped peeled fresh
    or canned tomatoes
1 pound fusilli
Freshly grated Parmesan cheese

*W*e normally prepare this aromatic pasta dish with wild greens and borage, but both are difficult to find in America. Native to the Middle East, borage grows wild in Sicily and other countries of the Mediterranean and in Europe in the spring. Many visitors think that we are gathering flowers when they see us collecting bouquets of tiny blue borage flowers along the roads. We use both borage flowers and the delicate leaves in cooking.

We have substituted spinach and escarole, which are also delicious, for the wild greens and borage.

Serves 4 to 6

Bring 2 quarts of water to a rolling boil and add the spinach and escarole. Reduce the heat and simmer for 5 minutes. Drain well and squeeze dry, then chop fine.

Heat the olive oil and garlic in a large frying pan and cook for 5 minutes, stirring often. Don't let the garlic burn. Stir in the anchovies and the greens, and simmer for 15 minutes.

Meanwhile, bring 4 quarts of water to a rolling boil. Stir in 1 tablespoon of salt, stir again, and add the pasta. Cook until al dente, or just tender, stirring often.

Reserve 1 cup of the pasta water. Drain the pasta and transfer it to the greens. Toss, adding a little pasta water, if a thinner sauce is desired. Serve with Parmesan cheese.

VARIATION: Other greens like Swiss chard, beet tops, or kale can be substituted or added to the spinach and escarole.

Penne con Carciofi e Piselli

(Penne with Artichokes and Peas)

Serves 6 as a first course or 4 as a main course

Put the artichokes into a saucepan with the onion, 1 cup of olive oil, and the garlic. Lightly season with salt and pepper, and simmer over low heat until the artichokes are cooked, about 10 minutes. (If using thawed frozen artichoke hearts, they need to cook for only 5 minutes.) Discard the garlic cloves. Mix in the parsley and set aside.

Put the peas into a small saucepan with the onion and 1 tablespoon each of water, olive oil, and butter, and season lightly with salt and pepper. Cook over medium-low heat until done—about 10 minutes for fresh peas, 5 minutes for frozen peas. Discard the onion and add the peas to the artichokes. Gently combine the ingredients and simmer over very low heat.

Bring 4 quarts of water to a rolling boil. Stir in 1½ tablespoons of salt and add the penne. Cook until al dente, or just tender, stirring often.

Reserve 1 cup of the pasta water. Drain the pasta and return it to the pot. Add 1 cup of the sauce and toss. Add the remaining sauce and toss. Add a little pasta water, if a thinner sauce is desired. Season to taste with salt and pepper. Serve immediately with Parmesan cheese.

6 large fresh artichoke hearts, chopped, or two 10-ounce packages frozen artichoke hearts, thawed, well drained, and chopped
1 small onion, thinly sliced
Olive oil
2 garlic cloves, peeled
Salt and freshly ground pepper
⅓ cup freshly chopped Italian parsley
2 cups fresh or frozen (thawed) green peas
1 small whole onion
1 tablespoon sweet butter
1 pound penne
Freshly grated Parmesan cheese

Tagliatelle con Zucchine e Melanzane

(Tagliatelle with Zucchini and Eggplant with Spicy Herb Sauce)

Serves 6 as a first course or 4 as a main course

Olive oil
2 medium eggplants, peeled and
　　cut into 1-inch cubes
Salt
3 medium zucchini, sliced into
　　¼-inch rounds
4 garlic cloves, peeled
1 medium onion, chopped
⅓ cup freshly chopped mint
　　leaves
⅓ cup freshly chopped basil
¼ cup freshly chopped Italian
　　parsley
1¾ pounds fresh tomatoes,
　　peeled and seeded, or one
　　28-ounce can Italian plum
　　tomatoes, well drained, with
　　extra liquid gently squeezed
　　out, and chopped
Freshly ground black pepper
⅛ teaspoon cayenne pepper, or
　　to taste (optional)
1 pound tagliatelle
Freshly grated pecorino or
　　Parmesan cheese

Heat 3 inches of olive oil in a large, deep-sided frying pan until the oil is hot but not smoking. Fry the eggplant cubes, in batches, until lightly browned. Drain on paper towels and sprinkle sparingly with salt. Set aside.

In the same oil, add more olive oil as needed for a 2-inch depth in pan, then fry the zucchini, in batches, until golden. Drain and sprinkle with salt. Set aside.

Heat 1 cup of olive oil in a large frying pan and cook the garlic and onion over medium-high heat until golden. Stir in the mint, basil, and parsley, and simmer for 5 minutes. Add the fried eggplant, zucchini, and tomatoes. Gently stir and season to taste with salt, black pepper, and cayenne pepper, if you like. Simmer over low heat.

Bring 4 quarts of water to a rolling boil. Stir in 1½ tablespoons of salt and add the pasta. Cook until al dente, or just tender, stirring often.

Reserve 1 cup of the pasta water from the pot. Drain the pasta and transfer it to a serving bowl. Turn the sauce over the pasta and gently toss. Add a little pasta water, if a thinner sauce is desired. Season to taste with salt and pepper. Pass the pecorino or Parmesan cheese.

Gemelli con Erbe Aromatiche

(Gemelli with Aromatic Herbs)

*W*e found this old handwritten recipe on a piece of paper in the middle of a religious book that belonged to my grandmother Giovanna. Mamma and I didn't remember her ever having cooked the dish for us, but we immediately tried it. It was quite wonderful, so we added it to our family recipe book and are happy to include it here.

Serves 6 as a first course or 4 as a main course

Heat the olive oil and butter in a large frying pan and cook the onion over medium heat until it becomes transparent, stirring often.

Stir in the anchovies and herbs, and simmer for 5 minutes.

Stir in the wine and cook for 3 minutes. Add the tomato sauce and season to taste with salt and pepper. Simmer for 10 minutes.

Meanwhile, bring 4 quarts of water to a rolling boil in a large pot. Stir in 1½ tablespoons of salt, stir, and add the pasta. Cook until al dente, or just tender, stirring often.

Reserve 1 cup of the pasta water. Drain the gemelli or penne and turn it into a serving bowl and top with the sauce. Toss well. Season to taste with salt and pepper. Add a little hot pasta water, if a thinner sauce is desired, and toss again. Serve with freshly grated Parmesan cheese.

½ cup olive oil
2 tablespoons sweet butter
1 large onion, finely chopped
12 anchovy fillets, coarsely chopped
½ cup finely chopped celery leaves
¼ cup freshly chopped Italian parsley
5 whole sage leaves
1 tablespoon fresh rosemary, finely chopped
½ cup dry white wine
3 tablespoons fresh tomato sauce (Salsa di Pomodoro, page 93)
Salt and freshly ground pepper
1 pound gemelli or penne
Freshly grated Parmesan cheese

Spaghetti con Melanzane e Ricotta Salata

(Spaghetti with Eggplant and Ricotta Salata)

Olive oil, for deep-frying
2 medium eggplants, cut into strips ½ inch thick, 1 inch wide, and no more than 4 inches long
3 cups fresh tomato sauce (Salsa di Pomodoro, page 93)
1 pound spaghetti
Salt and freshly ground pepper
Sprig of fresh basil leaves
½ cup grated ricotta salata

*T*his wonderful, simple pasta is one of Sicily's most popular dishes. In Catania, the dish is known as Spaghetti alla Norma, named after the heroine of the great opera composed by Catania-born Vincenzo Bellini. My mother has always wondered if Bellini, the great composer, ever actually cooked it himself.

Serves 6 as a first course or 4 as a main course

Heat 3 inches of olive oil in a deep-sided frying pan until the oil is hot but not smoking, and fry the eggplant pieces, in batches, until golden brown. Drain on paper towels and let rest.

While slowly heating the sauce, bring 4 quarts of water to a rolling boil in a large pot. Stir in 1½ tablespoons of salt and add the spaghetti. Cook until al dente, or just tender, stirring often.

Stir the eggplant into the sauce.

Reserve 1 cup of the pasta water. Drain the spaghetti and return it to the pot. Add half the sauce and toss. Reserve 1 cup of the sauce and turn the rest over the pasta and toss.

Transfer the pasta to a serving bowl and spoon the remaining sauce over the top. Garnish with the basil sprig and pass the ricotta salata.

La Pasta di Luciano

(Luciano's Spaghetti with Zucchini, Tomatoes, and Pine Nuts)

⅓ cup olive oil
4 tablespoons sweet butter
3 medium zucchini, scrubbed clean and diced
Salt and freshly ground pepper

*L*uciano, a friend from Palermo, loves good food, but his wife has always refused to cook. This is very rare among Sicilian women, but it happens. Out of hunger, Luciano was forced to learn to cook. He is very *bravo* in the kitchen, so his wife eats very well.

Serves 6 as a first course or 4 as a main course

Bring 4 quarts of water to a rolling boil in a large pot.

Meanwhile, heat the olive oil and butter in a large frying pan.

Add the zucchini and salt to taste, stirring constantly over high heat, and cook for 5 minutes.

With a slotted spoon, transfer the zucchini to a bowl, leaving as much liquid in the pan as possible.

Put the onion, garlic, and tomatoes into the saucepan and season to taste with salt and pepper. Cook for 5 minutes over medium heat.

Mix in the cooked zucchini and the basil and set aside.

Stir 1½ tablespoons of salt into the boiling water and add the spaghetti. Cook until al dente, or just tender, stirring often.

Ladle 1 cup of the sauce onto the bottom of a large serving bowl.

Reserve 1 cup of the hot pasta water from the pot. Drain the spaghetti and turn it into the bowl. Add all but ½ cup of the sauce and toss. Add a little pasta water, if a thinner sauce is desired. Toss and season to taste with salt and pepper. Spoon the remaining sauce on top and sprinkle with the pine nuts. Serve immediately and pass the Parmesan.

1 medium onion, minced
4 garlic cloves, minced
2 cups fresh tomatoes, peeled and chopped, or canned Italian plum tomatoes, drained and chopped
½ cup freshly chopped basil
1 pound spaghetti
½ cup pine nuts
Freshly grated Parmesan cheese

I Rigatoni di Daniela

(Daniela's Rigatoni with Pancetta, Tomato, and Hot Pepper Sauce)

$\mathcal{P}$aolo once had a fascination for a model named Daniela who cooked this pasta for him whenever they were together. But she normally didn't eat it with him, because she had to starve herself to stay thin for fashion shows in Palermo in the spring and fall. When the shows were over, she would splurge on this dish. I was very jealous of Daniela after she and Paolo became engaged, so I learned to make her pasta and cooked it for him at Gangivecchio to please him in her absence. After they broke up, I was glad to have learned her dish and very happy that Paolo waited for Betty. —G.T.

Serves 6 as a first course or 4 as a main course

Heat the olive oil and butter in a large frying pan. Add the onion and pancetta. Cook over low heat until the pancetta is cooked and

½ cup olive oil
1 tablespoon sweet butter
1 medium onion, chopped
1½ cups smoked pancetta, cut into ½-inch cubes
One 28-ounce can Italian plum tomatoes, drained, with excess juice gently pressed out
¼ cup Scotch whisky
3 tablespoons heavy cream
Salt and freshly ground pepper

I Rigatoni di Daniela (cont.)

Pinch of cayenne pepper
   (optional)
1 pound rigatoni
Freshly grated Parmesan cheese

the onions have softened. Stir in the tomatoes and simmer for 10 minutes.

Pour in the Scotch whisky and cook over high heat for 2 or 3 minutes, or until the whisky evaporates. Add the cream, salt and pepper to taste, and cayenne pepper, if you like. Simmer over very low heat while cooking the rigatoni.

Bring 4 quarts of water to a rolling boil. Add 1½ tablespoons of salt, stir, and add the pasta. Cook the pasta until al dente, or just tender, stirring often. Right before draining the pasta, put 1 cup of the sauce into a large bowl.

Reserve 1 cup of the hot pasta water. Drain the pasta and transfer to bowl with the sauce and toss well. Add the remaining sauce and toss. Add a little pasta water, if a thinner sauce is desired. Season to taste with salt and pepper.

Serve immediately and pass freshly grated Parmesan cheese.

La Pasta di Betty

(Betty's Spaghetti with Baked Fresh Tomato Sauce)

Serves 6 as a first course or 4 as a main course

2¼ pounds fresh, ripe tomatoes,
   peeled and chopped
¾ cup freshly grated pecorino,
   plus extra for topping
½ cup freshly chopped basil or
   Italian parsley
3 garlic cloves, chopped
Salt and freshly ground pepper
⅛ teaspoon cayenne pepper, or
   to taste (optional)
Dried bread crumbs
Olive oil
1 pound spaghetti

Preheat the oven to 350°F.

Put the tomatoes into a shallow baking dish and sprinkle with the pecorino, basil or parsley, garlic, salt and pepper to taste, and the cayenne pepper, if you like. Mix well and smooth down. Sprinkle lightly with bread crumbs and drizzle with olive oil

Cook in the preheated oven for 45 minutes, or until fairly dry.

Bring 4 quarts of water to a rolling boil in a large pot. Stir in 1½ tablespoons of salt and add the spaghetti. Cook the pasta until al dente, or just tender, stirring often.

Reserve 1 cup of the hot pasta water. Transfer the spaghetti to a serving bowl. Top with the sauce and toss. Add a little pasta water, if a thinner sauce is desired. You can also add a little olive oil, if you like. Pass the pecorino.

Tagliatelle Mediterranee

Serves 6 as a first course or 4 as a main course

(Tagliatelle with Tomatoes, Black Olives, and Capers)

Heat the olive oil in a large saucepan and add the onion. Cook over medium heat for 5 minutes, stirring often.

Add the anchovies, tomatoes with the liquid, and sugar, season lightly with salt and pepper, and simmer for 20 minutes.

Add the black olives and simmer for another 10 minutes.

Stir in the capers and taste for seasoning. Simmer for 10 minutes more. Sprinkle with oregano, cover, and let rest for 30 minutes off the heat.

Bring 4 quarts of water to a rolling boil. Stir in 1½ tablespoons of salt and add the pasta. Cook until al dente, or just tender, stirring often.

Reheat the sauce. Remove 1 cup of the hot pasta water, drain the pasta, and turn it into a serving bowl. Top with all but 1 cup of the sauce. Toss. Spoon the remaining sauce on top and serve immediately.

Serve with freshly grated Parmesan cheese.

½ cup olive oil
1 medium onion, chopped
6 anchovy fillets, finely chopped
One 35-ounce can Italian plum tomatoes with liquid—tomatoes should be chopped, with stem ends removed
2 teaspoons sugar
Salt and freshly ground pepper
1 cup pitted black olives, cut into quarters
⅔ cup capers, washed and drained
½ teaspoon dried oregano
1 pound tagliatelle
Freshly grated Parmesan cheese

Spaghetti Estivi di Mariuccia

(Mariuccia's Summer Spaghetti with Mozzarella and Tomato Cream Sauce with Basil)

1 pound mozzarella, fresh if possible, cubed
1½ cups heavy cream
2 tablespoons sweet butter
1½ cups fresh tomatoes, peeled, seeded, and chopped (only use fresh, ripe tomatoes)
½ cup freshly chopped basil leaves, plus basil sprigs for garnish
Salt and freshly ground pepper
1½ pounds spaghetti
Freshly grated Parmesan cheese

*M*y aunt Mariuccia who lives in Palermo gave me the recipe for this fragrant pasta dish. It is not typically Sicilian, because of the cream it contains. Aunt Mary lives in a beautiful house that has a kitchen with doors opening out onto a terrace. The perfume of the sauce cooking passes through these doors and spreads throughout the neighborhood. As people pass by, they always look up and smile hungrily. —G.T.

Serves 8 as a first course or 6 as a main course

Bring 6 quarts of water to a rolling boil in a large pot.

Meanwhile, put the mozzarella, cream, and butter into a large, nonstick saucepan and heat it slowly.

When the cheese has melted, add the tomatoes, basil, and salt and pepper to taste. Simmer over very low heat while the pasta cooks.

Stir 2 tablespoons of salt into the boiling water and add the spaghetti. Cook until al dente, or just tender, stirring often.

Drain the pasta and turn into a serving bowl. Pour half the sauce over the top and toss well. Add the remaining sauce and toss again. Season to taste with salt and pepper. Serve hot and garnish with basil sprigs. Pass the Parmesan cheese.

Orecchiette alla Rucola e Salsa di Pomodoro di Betty

(Betty's Orecchiette with Arugula and Tomato Sauce)

*B*etty's simple, slightly spicy pasta dish made with an uncooked tomato sauce is excellent served on a hot summer day. She and Paolo serve dinners at Tenuta Gangivecchio's restaurant outside, at tables under the stars, in the summertime. What a magical setting it is.

Serves 6 as a first course or 4 as a main course

Thoroughly combine the ingredients from the garlic through the cayenne pepper in a large bowl and let rest.

Bring 4 quarts of water to a rolling boil. Stir in 1½ tablespoons of salt and add the pasta. Cook until al dente, or just tender, stirring often.

Reserve 1 cup of the hot pasta water. Drain the pasta and turn it into the bowl with the tomato sauce. Toss it well. Sprinkle the top with the ribbons of arugula and freshly grated pecorino. Toss again. Taste for seasoning. Add a little pasta water, if a thinner sauce is desired.

2 garlic cloves, minced
2 cups fresh tomatoes, peeled, seeded, and diced
1 tablespoon freshly chopped basil
Salt and freshly ground pepper
¾ cup olive oil
Pinch of cayenne pepper (optional)
1 pound orecchiette
12 arugula leaves, snipped crosswise with scissors into very thin ribbons
Freshly grated pecorino

Rupa Santini

(Conchiglioni with Eggplant, Three Cheeses, and Toasted Bread Crumbs)

*L*ate one morning at Gangivecchio, when Michele and I were going over the manuscript in the very last stages of finishing this book, wonderful smells permeated our office. We followed the aromas nearby to the kitchen where Mamma, in a very good mood because her work was done, was cooking two dishes for lunch—conchiglioni (snail-shaped pasta) with eggplant, pecorino, Parmesan, and mozzarella cheeses with toasted bread crumbs, and small fresh sardines roasted with garlic, parsley, and olive oil. These two recipes were not in the book.

Olive oil
1 medium eggplant, cut into 1-inch cubes
2 cups fresh tomato sauce (Salsa di Pomodoro, page 93)
Pinch of cayenne pepper (optional)

1 pound conchiglioni (snail-
shaped pasta) or conchiglie
(shell-shaped pasta)
Salt
¼ cup freshly grated Parmesan
cheese
¼ cup freshly grated pecorino
8 ounces mozzarella, diced
¼ cup toasted bread crumbs
(page 121)
1 tablespoon sweet butter
Freshly ground pepper

After our delicious lunch, almost simultaneously Michele and I agreed to add, "Just two more recipes?" Mamma replied in English, "Certainly." Here is the recipe for the pasta dish, which I named after the room Michele always stays in at Gangivecchio in the *albergo,* Rupa Santini. The recipe for Sarde per Augusto is on page 210.

Serves 6 as a first course and 4 as a main course

Bring 4 quarts of water to a rolling boil in a large pot.

Meanwhile, heat 2 inches of olive oil in a large, deep saucepan. Fry the eggplant cubes until golden brown, in batches, if necessary. Drain on paper towels and set aside.

When the water for the pasta is boiling, stir in 1½ tablespoons of salt, then add the pasta. Cook until al dente, or just tender, stirring often.

Heat the tomato sauce with the cayenne pepper, if you like, in a small saucepan.

Reserve 1 cup of hot cooking water from the pasta. Drain the pasta and return it to the pot. Immediately add the tomato sauce and eggplant and toss. Stir in the three cheeses. Add the bread crumbs and butter and toss again. Add a little of the hot cooking water, if a thinner sauce is desired. Season the pasta to taste with salt and pepper, and serve immediately.

Mollica
(Bread Crumbs)

Humble bread crumbs are an important element of Sicilian cuisine. They are vital for breading our famous *arancine* (rice croquettes), fritters, vegetables, meats, and seafood. We Sicilians are fond of all kinds of stuffings, in which bread crumbs are indispensable. But our most notable and charming use of bread crumbs in Sicily is toasting and sprinkling them on top of cooked pasta dishes. This custom was probably invented by clever poor people who couldn't afford cheese to grate over their pasta. The addition of toasted bread crumbs to pasta adds texture and a faint nutty flavor.

Traditionally, toasted bread crumbs are served on certain pastas such as Bucatini con le Sarde Come la Faccio Io (My Bucatini with Sardines) on page 124 and Bucatini alla Palina (Bucatini with Cauliflower, Currants, and Pine Nuts) on page 105. Once in a while we also sprinkle toasted bread crumbs on cooked vegetables at Gangivecchio—even over eggs. Mamma calls toasted bread crumbs *mollica rossa* because after they are toasted, they blush.

To make toasted bread crumbs, grate thoroughly dry two- or three-day-old firm Italian country bread—with or without the crust. (We always include the crust for the slight variety of colors it produces and, perhaps, a hint of extra flavor.) Bread crumbs can also be efficiently made in the food processor, or you can buy a small bag in an Italian grocery store. Commercial plain bread crumbs found in packages and containers aren't as good, because they aren't as fresh and sometimes are too finely processed, but you can use them as a last resort.

One cup of bread crumbs is a sufficient amount for 4 servings of pasta. Heat 1½ tablespoons of olive oil in a frying pan and swirl it all over the bottom of the pan. Stir in the crumbs with a wooden spoon. Turn them repeatedly over medium-high heat, spreading them across the pan, until they blush a rosy golden-brown color. This takes only 2 or 3 minutes. (Double the amount of olive oil for 2 cups of crumbs.) Spread the toasted bread crumbs onto a plate, allowing them to cool, stirring once or twice before using them.

Serve toasted bread crumbs in a little bowl sitting on a saucer with a small spoon, or in a grated cheese dish with a spoon. Place the bowl on the table and pass it around so the crumbs can be sprinkled on top of the pasta as you would Parmesan cheese.

We have found that toasted bread crumbs keep well for only a day, so they must be made the same day they are used.

Tagliatelle con Salsa Picchio Pacchio

(Tagliatelle with Picchio Pacchio Sauce)

2¼ pounds fresh tomatoes,
    peeled
¼ cup olive oil
2 garlic cloves
Salt and freshly ground pepper
1 teaspoon sugar
1 pound tagliatelle
¼ cup freshly chopped Italian
    parsley
Freshly grated Parmesan cheese

We don't know why the musical name *picchio pacchio* was given to this delicious fresh tomato sauce. But we do know that it is an excellent way to use up a big harvest of ripe tomatoes.

Although the simple recipe below is the one we prefer, other herbs such as fresh basil or dried oregano can be added. Add ¼ cup freshly chopped basil or 1 teaspoon dried oregano. Taste, adding a little more of one or the other, if you like.

Serves 6 as a first course or 4 as a main course

Bring 4 quarts of water to a rolling boil in a large pot.

While waiting for the water to boil, cut the tomatoes into wedges and squeeze out the seeds and as much juice and liquid as possible. Cut the tomatoes into small cubes.

Heat the olive oil with the garlic in a large frying pan and cook for 5 minutes. Stir in the tomatoes, salt and pepper to taste, and sugar. Cook over medium heat for 10 minutes, stirring often.

Stir 1½ tablespoons of salt into the boiling water. Add the tagliatelle and stir. Cook until al dente, or just tender, stirring often.

When the sauce is done, remove from heat and blend in the parsley and taste for seasoning. Set aside.

Reserve 1 cup of the hot pasta water and drain the pasta. Turn into a bowl, add half the sauce and toss. Add the remaining sauce and toss again. Add a little hot pasta water if a thinner sauce is desired. Pass the cheese.

La Pasta di Loretta

(Loretta's Ditali with Spinach and Pancetta)

Serves 6 as a first course or 4 as a main course

Cook the spinach with ½ cup of lightly salted, boiling water in a large saucepan, stirring often. Drain the spinach and, when cool enough to handle, press out the excess water in a strainer. Chop the spinach very well.

Heat the butter and olive oil in a frying pan. Add the spinach and garlic, and season to taste with salt and pepper. Cook over very low heat for 10 minutes, stirring occasionally.

Meanwhile, cook the pancetta in a frying pan until lightly browned.

Add the pancetta and the Parmesan cheese to the spinach mixture and toss. Remove from the heat.

Bring 4 quarts of water to a rolling boil in a large pot. Stir in 1½ tablespoons of salt and add the pasta. Cook until al dente, or just tender, stirring often.

Remove 1 cup of the pasta water. Drain the pasta and turn into a serving bowl. Top with the sauce and toss well. Add a little hot pasta water, if necessary. Season to taste with salt and pepper. Serve immediately. Pass the Parmesan cheese.

1 pound fresh young spinach, washed and dried, with stems removed
Salt
⅓ cup butter
1 tablespoon olive oil
2 garlic cloves
Salt and freshly ground pepper
¾ cup diced smoked pancetta
½ cup freshly grated Parmesan cheese, plus extra for topping
1 pound ditali

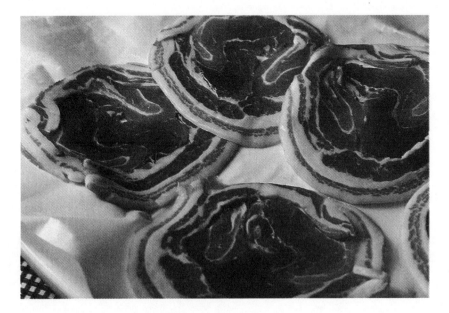

Bucatini con le Sarde Come la Faccio Io

(My Bucatini with Sardines)

2 medium fennel bulbs, white
    parts only plus ¾ cup dark
    green fennel tops, finely
    chopped (discard tough
    stalks)
1 large onion, finely chopped
1 cup olive oil
6 anchovy fillets
Salt and freshly ground pepper
2½ pounds whole fresh sar-
    dines, or frozen (thawed)
    sardines, scaled, cleaned,
    boned, finned, and deheaded
    (After cleaning, only 1
    pound of fillets will remain.
    If your fishmonger will pre-
    pare them for you, all the
    better. Ask for 1 pound fil-
    leted sardines.) Cut the fil-
    lets into bite-size pieces.
½ cup currants, soaked in ½
    cup lukewarm water for 10
    minutes
½ cup pine nuts
1 pound bucatini or perciatelli
½ teaspoon ground saffron
1 cup toasted bread crumbs
    (page 121)

The woman in every Sicilian house has her own way of preparing Bucatini con le Sarde, one of the island's most famous and appreciated pasta dishes. If two Sicilian women discuss their special version, each will insist, "Mine is better." My grandmother used to serve it the old-fashioned Sicilian way, which meant covering the top of the sauced pasta with the sardines. We don't do it this way anymore—we mix the sardines with the sauce, but it can be done either way.

Serves 6 as a first course or 4 as a main course

Place the whole fennel bulbs and green tops in a saucepan with 1½ quarts of water and bring to a boil. Reduce to a low boil and cook the fennel until tender, about 10 minutes. With a slotted spoon, transfer the fennel to a cutting board and reserve 1 quart of the cooking water. When cool enough to handle, chop the fennel and set aside.

Put the onion and ½ cup of water in a large saucepan and cook over medium heat, stirring often, for 5 minutes, until the water has almost evaporated. Add the olive oil and anchovies. Cook over medium heat for 5 minutes, until thickened. Stir in the sardines. Season to taste with salt and pepper. Simmer for 10 minutes.

Stir in the currants, pine nuts, fennel bulbs and dark green tops. Simmer for 5 minutes and let rest.

Bring 3 quarts of water and the reserved quart of fennel water to a rolling boil. Break the bucatini or perciatelli in half (making them much more manageable to eat). Stir in 1½ tablespoons of salt and the saffron and add the pasta. Cook until al dente, or just tender, stirring often.

Drain the pasta. Return it to the pot and add two thirds of the sauce with about ¼ cup olive oil. Gently toss, cover, and let rest off the heat for 5 minutes. Gently toss again and serve with the extra sauce and toasted bread crumbs. If you want to be *raffinato* and add a touch of class, sprinkle the pasta with finely chopped, toasted almonds instead of the bread crumbs.

Pasta Trinacria

(Spaghetti with Swordfish, Eggplant, and Mint)

½ cup olive oil
3 garlic cloves, cut into slivers
One 28-ounce can whole imported Italian plum tomatoes, including juice from the can
Salt and freshly ground pepper
2 medium eggplants, cut into 1-inch cubes
Sunflower or vegetable oil, for deep-frying
1 pound swordfish steaks, skinned and cut into ½-inch cubes
¼ cup freshly chopped mint, plus 2 sprigs for garnish
1 pound spaghetti

*W*e named Betty's delicious spaghetti dish after the three-legged symbol of Sicily, the *trinacria* (each leg represents one of the three corners of our triangular-shaped island), because the three foods featured in the recipe—swordfish, eggplant, and mint—are characteristic ingredients in Sicilian cooking. Many versions of this dish exist, but we think Betty's is fantastic.

Fresh tuna can be substituted for the swordfish.

Serves 6 as a first course or 4 as a main course

Heat the olive oil with the garlic in a saucepan and cook for 3 minutes, stirring often. With your fingers, squeeze the tomatoes into little pieces in a large bowl and be sure to include the juice from the can. Season to taste with salt and pepper, and simmer for 10 minutes.

Meanwhile, fry the eggplant, in batches, in 2 inches of hot, but not smoking, sunflower or vegetable oil until golden, stirring often. Drain on paper towels and season lightly with salt. Set aside.

Bring 4 quarts of water to a rolling boil in a large pot.

While waiting for the water to boil, stir the swordfish and chopped mint into the tomato sauce and simmer over very low heat for about 10 minutes. When the swordfish is cooked, remove from heat.

Stir 1½ tablespoons of salt into the boiling water and add the spaghetti. Cook until al dente, or just tender, stirring frequently.

A minute or two before the pasta is done, stir the fried eggplant into the sauce and taste for seasoning.

Reserve 1 cup of the pasta water. Drain the pasta and turn it into a serving bowl. Add three quarters of the sauce and gently toss, adding a little pasta water, if a thinner sauce is desired. Spoon the remaining sauce over the top and garnish with the mint sprigs. Serve immediately.

Linguine con Gamberetti

(Linguine with Small Shrimp and Puréed Onions)

1 large onion, coarsely chopped
¾ cup olive oil
2 garlic cloves, minced
½ cup freshly chopped Italian parsley
Salt and freshly ground pepper
1¼ pounds small shrimp, shelled and deveined
1 pound linguine

Serves 6 as a first course or 4 as a main course

Purée the onion in a food processor until creamy. Put the onion, olive oil, garlic, and ¾ cup of water into a large, deep-sided frying pan. Cook over medium-low heat for 30 minutes, until the water has almost evaporated, stirring often.

Add the parsley and salt and pepper to taste. Stir in the shrimp and simmer for 10 minutes.

Meanwhile, bring 4 quarts of water to a rolling boil in a large pot. Stir in 1½ tablespoons of salt and add the linguine. Cook until al dente, or just tender, stirring often.

Reserve 1 cup of the pasta water. Drain the pasta and put it into the frying pan and toss well. Let it cook over low heat for 1 minute. Add a little hot pasta water, if a thinner sauce is desired. Season to taste with salt and pepper. Serve immediately.

Spaghetti di Mare di Maria-Angela al Cartoccio

(Maria-Angela's Spaghetti with Seafood Baked in Foil)

1 pound mussels, cleaned, debearded, and washed
1 pound cherrystone clams, cleaned very well
Olive oil
3 garlic cloves, crushed
1 pound squid rings
½ cup dry white wine
3 cups fresh or canned Italian plum tomatoes, peeled and chopped

Serves 6 as a first course or 4 as a main course

Put the mussels and clams into a large pot with 2 tablespoons of olive oil and ½ cup of water, cover with a lid, and cook over medium-high heat, stirring occasionally, until the shells open. Remove the mussels and clams from their shells. Pass the liquid from the pan through a strainer lined with two thicknesses of cheesecloth and set aside.

Pour ½ cup of olive oil into a large saucepan and cook the garlic for 5 minutes, over medium heat, stirring often. Add the squid rings and cook over low heat for 5 minutes. Add the white wine and cook 5 minutes more. Add the tomatoes, season to taste with salt and pepper, and simmer for 20 minutes. Add the parsley, mussels, clams, and reserved broth. Simmer, covered, for a minute or two, then remove from the heat.

Preheat the oven to 350°F.

Bring 4 quarts of water to a rolling boil. Stir in 1½ tablespoons of salt and add the spaghetti. Cook for only 6 minutes, stirring often. Drain and turn the spaghetti into a bowl. Drizzle a small amount of olive oil over the pasta and toss. Spoon half the seafood sauce over the pasta and mix well.

Rub the inside (the unshiny side) of a large sheet of heavy-duty aluminum foil (or 4 individual smaller sheets) with olive oil. Turn the sides up along the edges, forming a 3- or 4-inch collar, so that the sauce won't run out. Spoon all the pasta and liquid into the large sheet, or divide equally among the small sheets. Seal the edges of the foil carefully over the center of the filled foil pieces to form 1 large or 4 individual small packages.

Place the large package or the individual ones on a baking sheet and bake in the preheated oven for 10 minutes.

If you cooked a large package, put it onto a large serving dish. If you cooked the individual packages, place one on each of 4 dinner plates. Let each diner open his or her own seafood pasta packages. If serving the large size, slit the top open with a knife and serve.

⅓ cup freshly chopped Italian parsley
Salt and freshly ground pepper
1 pound spaghetti

Linguine del Mare

(Linguine with Seafood)

Serves 6 as a first course or 4 as a main course

Heat the olive oil with the garlic in a large, deep-sided frying pan, and cook for about 5 minutes, stirring often. Don't allow the garlic to brown. Add the mussels and cook over medium-high heat for 10 minutes, until the mussel shells open, stirring often. Add the shrimp and tomatoes, stir, and season to taste with salt and pepper. Simmer for about 5 minutes, until the shrimp are cooked. Let rest off the heat while cooking the pasta.

Bring 4 quarts of water to a rolling boil. Stir in 1½ tablespoons of salt and add the linguine. Cook until al dente, or just tender, stirring often.

Meanwhile, warm the sauce over low heat.

When the pasta is done, reserve 1 cup of the pasta water. Drain

½ cup olive oil
3 garlic cloves, minced
2 pounds mussels, scrubbed, debearded, and washed well
1 pound medium shrimp, shelled and deveined
1 cup fresh tomatoes, peeled and diced
Salt and freshly ground pepper
¼ cup freshly chopped Italian parsley
1 pound linguine

the pasta and turn it into the pan with the sauce and toss well. Add the parsley and toss again. Cook over high heat for 1 minute. Add a little hot pasta water, if necessary. Season to taste with salt and pepper.

Rigatoni alla Besciamella con Funghi e Gamberetti al Gratin

(Rigatoni with Béchamel Sauce and Mushroom and Shrimp au Gratin)

Serves 6 as a first course or 4 as a main course

3 tablespoons olive oil
1 small onion, minced
1 garlic clove, minced
¼ pound cremini mushrooms, thinly sliced
2 tablespoons finely chopped Italian parsley
¾ pound boiled shrimp, coarsely chopped
Salt and freshly ground pepper
1 pound rigatoni
2½ cups Salsa Besciamella Morbida (page 96)
4 tablespoons butter
Few grates of nutmeg
Freshly grated Parmesan cheese

Heat the olive oil and sauté the onion and garlic for 1 minute. Add in the mushrooms and parsley, and cook over medium heat for 5 minutes, stirring often. Stir in the shrimp and set aside.

Bring 4 quarts of water to a rolling boil. Stir in 1½ tablespoons of salt and the rigatoni. Cook until al dente, just tender, stirring often.

Meanwhile, heat the Salsa Besciamella Morbida in the top pan of a double boiler. Stir in 2 tablespoons of the butter, the mushroom-and-shrimp mixture, and the nutmeg. Simmer over very low heat, stirring constantly.

Drain the rigatoni and return to the pot. Add the sauce, except for ¾ cup, and toss it well. (The dish can be seasoned with salt and pepper to taste and eaten at this point. Pass the Parmesan.) Turn the pasta into a greased au gratin pan and spoon the remaining sauce over the top. Sprinkle lightly with Parmesan cheese, dot with the remaining 2 tablespoons of butter, and pass under the broiler until the top is golden brown.

VARIATIONS: Any number of foods can be added or substituted for the mushrooms and shrimp in the recipe, such as peeled and diced fresh tomatoes, cooked green peas, or any diced cooked meat or fish.

Spaghetti con Acciughe e Mollica Rossa

Serves 6 as a first course or 4 as a main course

(Spaghetti with Anchovy and Fresh Tomato Sauce and Toasted Bread Crumbs)

Heat 1 tablespoon of the olive oil in a large frying pan. Add the bread crumbs and cook over medium heat, constantly stirring, until the bread crumbs are toasted to a golden reddish brown. Spread over a large plate to cool.

Bring 4 quarts of water to a rolling boil in a large pot.

Meanwhile, heat the remaining ½ cup of olive oil in a large saucepan with the anchovies, concentrated tomato sauce, and pepper to taste. Simmer for 10 minutes.

Stir 1½ tablespoons of salt into the boiling water and add the spaghetti. Cook until al dente, or just tender, stirring often.

Reserve 1 cup of the hot pasta water. Drain the pasta and transfer it to a bowl. Top it with the sauce and toss. Add a little hot pasta water, if a thinner sauce is desired. Serve the bread crumbs in a bowl and sprinkle them on top of individual pasta servings like freshly grated cheese.

½ cup plus 1 tablespoon olive oil
1 cup dried bread crumbs
1 dozen anchovy fillets, finely chopped
2 cups concentrated tomato sauce (Salsa di Concentrato di Pomodoro, page 93)
Salt and freshly ground pepper
1 pound spaghetti

Il Nostro Pastificio Locale

(Our Local Pasta Mill)

We buy all our dried pasta from a *pastificio* (pasta maker) near us in the town of Petralia Sottana, owned and operated by the Castagna brothers. The oldest, Santo, always smiles shyly when asked to tell the mill factory's history, but he is happy to repeat it.

In the valley at Petralia there was once a rushing river where twenty water mills were built in the sixteenth century. The energy the water mills created enabled the *pastifici* to mill flour. They had all closed by the beginning of the last century because the river had become a trickling stream.

In 1808, near the ruins of one of these water mills, Baron Pucci and Signor Calascibetta built a new mill. At that time, farm animals provided the energy for grinding the wheat into flour. The mill continued operating through various Pucci and Calascibetta generations and different owners until electricity came to the area in the thirties. (At Gangivecchio, we first had electricity in 1970.) Santo Castagna and his brothers bought the mill in 1965 and spent several years remodeling, including the installation of modern equipment and machinery to produce pasta.

Today the Castagna mill produces 60,000 pounds of pasta a day, made from esteemed hard durum wheat harvested in the Madonie and other regions of Sicily. The Castagnas proudly distribute their pasta thoughout Sicily; in Italy, from the southern tip to Naples; and to several northern European countries.

Spaghetti con Bottarga

(Spaghetti with Tuna Roe)

*B*ottarga is dried, salted, and pressed tuna eggs. It comes in the form of a little hard brick encased in thick, airtight plastic wrapping. It is dark brownish-red in color and quite unattractive. Mamma always says it's incredible that something so ugly is so good and costs so much. The compressed eggs are shaved or grated over hot cooked pasta—a dish highly esteemed in Sicily.

Bottarga isn't readily available in America, but when you visit Sicily, you can buy a little block to take home. Elegant restaurants in Sicily serve spaghetti with *bottarga,* especially in Trapani, where the great tuna hauls are made.

1 cup olive oil, or as needed
3 garlic cloves, chopped
½ cup grated *bottarga,* plus
    extra for topping
½ cup freshly chopped Italian
    parsley
Freshly ground pepper
Salt
1 pound spaghetti

Serves 6 as a first course or 4 as a main course

Put the olive oil and garlic in a frying pan and cook over medium heat for 5 minutes, stirring often. Add the *bottarga.* Toss and cook for 1 minute. Add the parsley and season to taste with pepper. No salt is necessary, because *bottarga* is very salty. Set aside.

Bring 4 quarts of water to a rolling boil. Stir in 1½ tablespoons of salt and add the spaghetti. Cook until al dente, or just tender, stirring often.

Reserve 1 cup of the pasta water. Drain the pasta and turn it into the pan with the sauce. Toss and cook over high heat for 1 minute, adding a little pasta water, if necessary. Transfer the spaghetti to a serving dish and sprinkle with a little grated or shaved *bottarga.* Serve immediately.

Anelletti al Forno

(Baked Timbale of Anelletti with Veal and Vegetables)

3 cooked Polpette alla Wanda (meatballs, page 172)
2¼ pounds anelletti (Anelletti are small ring-shaped pasta. They can be found in Italian markets, but if not available, substitute rigatoni—an entirely different shape, but it is what we use.)
Salt
3 cups Ragù di Tritato (page 134)
2 cups cooked small green peas
1 cup boiled or cooked ham, coarsely chopped
1 cup diced sweet provolone
1 quart fresh tomato sauce (Salsa di Pomodoro, page 93)
½ cup freshly grated pecorino
4 tablespoons sweet butter, softened, plus extra for greasing the pan
½ cup grated Parmesan cheese
Freshly grated pepper
1 cup Salsa di Besciamella Morbida (page 96)
¾ cup fresh bread crumbs

*H*istorically, Anelletti al Forno was the richest dish poor people could offer family and friends on holidays or festival days in Sicily. Long ago, because few had ovens in the countryside, the timbale was cooked in a hole in the ground that was completely encased in coal—a most effective makeshift oven.

Since this hearty molded casserole contains pasta, meat, and vegetables, all that is required to complete the meal is a crisp green salad and a fruit tart for dessert.

Serves 12

Preheat the oven to 450°F. Break up the Polpette alla Wanda, or meatballs, very well with a fork.

Bring 8 quarts of water to a rolling boil. Stir in 3 tablespoons of salt, stir, and add the pasta. Stir and cook until al dente, or just tender. Drain and return to the pot.

Off the heat, add the Ragù di Tritato and the remaining ingredients, except for the bread crumbs. Combine thoroughly but gently.

Butter the bottom and sides of a 12–14-inch round baking dish with 4-inch sides. Add the bread crumbs and coat the bottom and sides, tapping out any extra crumbs.

Gently spoon the pasta into the pan, evenly smoothing the top and patting it down lightly.

Bake in the preheated oven for 30 minutes, or until golden brown on top.

Remove the timbale from the oven and let it rest for 10 minutes. Run a thin knife around the edge of the pan to release any sticking part. Place a round serving platter, 4 to 6 inches larger than the diameter of the pan, on top of the timbale. Invert the dish and gently lift off the pan. Serve immediately.

Timballo di Rigatoni alla Gangivecchio

Serves 8

Put ½ cup of the olive oil in a large saucepan with 1 chopped onion, the sausage, and 1 cup of the *estratto* or 2 cups of the Salsa di Concentrato di Pomodoro or the tomato paste. Cook over medium heat for 5 minutes, stirring often. Add 2 cups of water and simmer for 1 hour. Season to taste with salt and pepper.

In another saucepan, add the other chopped onion, the remaining ½ cup of olive oil, and the ground veal. Mix well and cook over high heat until the veal is golden. Add the remaining *estratto*, Salsa di Concentrato di Pomodoro, or tomato paste, a pinch of sugar, and 4 cups of water, and cook over low heat for 1 hour.

Bring 2 quarts of water to a rolling boil. Stir in 1 teaspoon of salt and cook the fennel bulb and tops for 5 minutes, or until tender. Drain.

Preheat the oven to 375°F.

Bring 4½ quarts of water to a rolling boil. Stir in 1 tablespoon of salt and add the rigatoni. Cook until al dente, or just tender. Drain and return the pasta to the pot it cooked in. Add the two sauces and the fennel. Stir in the cheeses and mix throughly.

Butter the sides and bottom of a round 12–14-inch baking dish with 4-inch sides. Add ½ cup of bread crumbs to the pan, and coat the bottom and sides of the pan evenly by tipping and rotating the pan. Tap out the extra crumbs.

Turn the pasta into the pan and spread evenly. Sprinkle lightly with bread crumbs and bake for 30 minutes, or until the top is golden brown.

Remove the timbale from the oven and let rest for 5 minutes.

Run the thin blade of a knife along the edges inside the pan to release any sticking bits. Place a serving platter 4 to 6 inches wider in diameter than the baking pan and carefully invert the pan and platter. Remove the pan. Let the timbale rest a few minutes before serving.

(Gangivecchio's Rigatoni Timbale with Veal, Pork, and Fennel)

1 cup olive oil
2 medium onions, finely chopped
1¼ pounds ground pork sausage
1½ cups *estratto* (page 94), or 2¾ cups Salsa di Concentrato di Pomodoro (page 93) or tomato paste
Salt and freshly ground pepper
1¼ pounds ground veal
Pinch of sugar
2½ cups fresh white fennel bulb, finely chopped
½ cup dark green fennel tops, finely chopped
1½ pounds rigatoni
⅓ cup each freshly grated pecorino and Parmesan cheese
Sweet butter
Bread crumbs

Spaghetti con Ragù di Tritato

(Spaghetti with Bolognese-Style Veal Sauce)

½ cup olive oil
2½ pounds ground veal
1 medium onion, finely
   chopped
2 vegetable bouillon cubes
1 cup tomato paste
One 6-ounce piece Parmesan
   cheese rind (page 82)
2 carrots, peeled and quartered
1 teaspoon sugar
3 cups cool water
Salt and freshly ground pepper
2 pounds spaghetti
Freshly grated Parmesan cheese

*M*y mother-in-law's mother-in-law, Giulia, was born in Bologna, where this great sauce was also born. My husband's Sicilian mother, Giovanna, loved Ragù di Tritato and taught me her version. For all its simplicity, a glorious, bold flavor is produced. Aside from pasta, Giovanna put the *ragù* to good use in many many ways—as a filling for Sformato di Riso (a wonderful baked rice mold, page 147) and to stuff sweet peppers or her Arancine (Rice Ball Croquettes Stuffed with Meat, page 145).

We have always prepared the *ragù* with veal instead of the traditional beef, because the tender veal married with the Parmesan cheese rind gives the sauce a more delicate flavor and creamier texture. Of course, beef can be substituted. —w.т.

Serves 10 to 12 as a first course or 8 to 10 as a main course

Cook the olive oil, veal, and onion in a large, heavy-bottomed saucepan over high heat, stirring often, until the veal loses its pink color.

Add the remaining ingredients through the 3 cups of cool water and mix well. Simmer for about 1½ hours, stirring every 15 minutes.

When the sauce is done, discard the carrots and any remaining pieces of cheese rind. Taste for seasoning.

Stir 2 tablespoons of salt into 8 quarts of boiling water. Add the spaghetti, stir, and cook until al dente, or just tender. Reserve 1 cup of the hot pasta water and drain the spaghetti.

Put a big ladleful of sauce into a large bowl, add the pasta, and top with several more ladlesful. Toss well. Add the rest of the sauce and reserved pasta water, if a thinner sauce is desired. Serve immediately and pass the cheese.

NOTE: The recipe is easily cut in half to serve 6 to 8 as a first course or 4 to 5 as a main course.

Casareccia con Ragù di Carne

Serves 6 as first course or 4 as a main course

(Casareccia with Pork or Veal Sauce)

Heat the olive oil and the onion in a medium-sized, heavy-bottomed saucepan over medium heat until the onion begins to brown. Add the wine and cook for 5 minutes, stirring occasionally.

Add the sugar, *estratto,* Salsa di Concentrato di Pomodoro, or tomato paste, ¾ cup of water, and season to taste with salt and pepper.

Put the pork or veal and the vegetables into the sauce. Add enough water to cover all but the top of the meat, and stir, turning the meat over once or twice. Sprinkle flour lightly over the top of the meat and don't stir.

Cook over low heat for about 30 minutes, partially covered. Remove the cover, stir the sauce, and turn the meat. Simmer, uncovered, for about 1 hour, stirring the sauce and turning the meat occasionally, until the meat is very tender.

Pick up the meat with a fork and hold it over the pan, scraping off as much of the sauce as possible into the pan. Chop the meat into small pieces or shred it, and return the meat to the sauce and heat it thoroughly. Taste for seasoning.

Bring 4 quarts of water to a rolling boil in a large pot. Stir in 1½ tablespoons of salt and cook the pasta until al dente, stirring often. Reserve 1 cup of the hot pasta water, drain, and turn the pasta into a serving bowl with 1 cup of the sauce. Add another 1½ cups of sauce and toss. Add a little pasta water, if a thinner sauce is desired. Pass extra sauce and Parmesan cheese.

½ cup olive oil
1 medium onion, finely chopped
½ cup dry red wine
1 teaspoon sugar
½ cup *estratto* (page 94), or 1 cup Salsa di Concentrato di Pomodoro (page 93) or tomato paste
Salt and freshly ground pepper
1¼ pounds boneless pork shoulder or veal
1 carrot, scraped and diced
2 small potatoes, peeled and diced
1 stalk celery, thinly sliced
Flour
1 pound casareccia, gemelli, or penne
Freshly grated Parmesan cheese

Penne con Agnello e Finocchielli in Salsa

(Penne with Lamb and Fennel in Tomato Sauce)

1 medium onion, chopped
1½ pounds leg of lamb or lean lamb shoulder, coarsely chopped into small pieces
2 lamb bones from leg, shoulder, or rib
½ cup olive oil
½ cup dry red wine
½ cup Salsa di Concentrato di Pomodoro (page 93) or tomato paste
1 quart fresh tomato sauce (Salsa di Pomodoro, page 93)
Salt and freshly ground pepper
Pinch of cayenne pepper (optional)
2 cups dark green fennel tops, finely chopped
1¼ pounds penne
¼ cup diced provolone
¼ cup freshly grated caciocavallo or pecorino cheese, plus extra to pass

The beautiful aromatic sauce for this recipe is actually a simplified version of an old typical Madonie mountain lamb *ragù*. The bold-flavored, fennel-infused sauce served as a pasta dish has become a favorite at Gangivecchio because, while Sicilians still appreciate the flavor, they rarely take the time to cook lamb *ragù* at home any longer.

Serves 6 to 8 as a first course or 4 to 6 as a main course

Cook the onion and lamb in the olive oil in a large, heavy-bottomed pot for 5 minutes, stirring often. Add the wine and cook 5 minutes more over medium-high heat, stirring occasionally.

Stir in the Salsa di Concentrato di Pomodoro or tomato paste and the Salsa di Pomodoro, 2 cups of cool water, salt and pepper to taste, and a pinch of cayenne pepper, if you like. Bring to a boil, then reduce the heat and simmer over very low heat for 1½ hours, stirring once in a while.

Bring 1 quart of water to a boil and cook the fennel tops for 10 minutes over medium heat. Drain well and stir into the sauce.

When the sauce is done, discard the lamb bones (if any meat is left on the bone, dice and add to the sauce) and taste for seasoning.

Bring 4½ quarts of water to a rolling boil in a large pot. Stir in 1½ tablespoons of salt and add the penne. Stir again and cook the pasta until al dente, or just tender. Stir often during cooking time.

Reserve 1 cup of the hot pasta water from the pot. Drain the pasta and turn it into a large serving bowl. Pour half the sauce over the pasta and toss it well. Add as much of the remaining sauce as needed, and toss with the provolone and the caciocavallo or pecorino cheese. Add some hot pasta water, if a thinner sauce is desired. Serve the extra sauce in a little bowl and pass the caciocavallo or pecorino.

Lasagne Ricce con Ragù di Salsiccia

(Lasagne Ricce with Fresh Sausage Sauce)

$\mathcal{M}$y uncle Eugenio always looks at the steaming bowl of this pasta as if it were a naked woman. In fact, everyone—men, women, and children—loves this pasta. —G.T.

Serves 6 as a first course or 4 as a main course

Heat the olive oil and *estratto* or Salsa di Concentrato di Pomodoro or tomato paste in a large saucepan, slowly adding about 1 cup of hot water. Stir constantly, until the *estratto* has melted and the mixture is smooth. (If substituting Salsa di Concentrato di Pomodoro or tomato paste for the *estratto,* only ½ cup of water is necessary.)

Add the sausage, celery, onion, and sugar. Add enough water to just cover the ingredients and combine well. Season to taste with salt and pepper, and simmer for 1 hour.

Bring 4 quarts of water to a rolling boil. Stir in 1½ tablespoons of salt and add the pasta. Cook until al dente, or just tender, stirring often.

Reserve 1 cup of the hot pasta water. Drain the pasta and transfer to a serving bowl. Add the sauce and toss well, adding a little pasta water, if a thinner sauce is desired. Pass the caciocavallo or pecorino.

⅓ cup olive oil
1 cup *estratto* (page 94), or 1½ cups Salsa di Concentrato di Pomodoro (page 93) or tomato paste
1½ pounds fresh Italian sweet sausage, cut into 1-inch lengths
2 stalks celery, diced
1 small onion, chopped
¼ teaspoon sugar
Salt and freshly ground pepper
1 pound lasagne ricce (½-inch-wide, long ribbon-edged pasta) or fettuccine
Freshly grated caciocavallo or pecorino cheese

La Pasta di Paolo

(Rigatoni with Pork, Green Peas, and Tomato Sauce au Gratin)

Serves 4 to 6

Heat the olive oil in a large frying pan and cook the onion until golden. Stir in the pork and season lightly with salt and pepper. Cook the mixture for 10 minutes, stirring occasionally.

Add the *estratto,* Salsa di Concentrato di Pomodoro, or tomato paste and mix well. Stir in the wine and simmer for 5 minutes.

Add the peas, stir, and simmer for 10 minutes.

Off the heat, stir in the Salsa Besciamella Morbida.

½ cup olive oil
1 small onion, finely chopped
2 cups minced pork
Salt and freshly ground pepper

La Pasta di Paolo *(cont.)*

2 tablespoons *estratto* (page 94)
  or ¼ cup Salsa di
  Concentrato di Pomodoro
  (page 93) or tomato paste
½ cup dry red wine
1 cup fresh or frozen (thawed)
  green peas
1 cup Salsa Besciamella Morbida (page 96)
1 pound rigatoni
Freshly grated pecorino or
  Parmesan cheese

Preheat the oven to 350°F.

Bring 4 quarts of water to a rolling boil in a large pot. Stir in 1½ tablespoons of salt, stir, and add the rigatoni. Cook until al dente, or just tender, stirring often.

Drain the pasta and add it to the sauce in the pan. Toss it well.

Transfer the mixture to a shallow baking dish or pan. Bake in the preheated oven for 30 minutes.

Sprinkle the top of the dish with the pecorino or Parmesan cheese and pass under the broiler for a few minutes, or until the top is golden.

Farfalle alla Wanda con Prosciutto, Spinaci e Pisellini

(Wanda's Farfalle with Prosciutto, Spinach, and Peas)

1½ cups fresh or frozen (thawed
  and drained) green peas
1 small onion, minced
½ cup sweet butter
Salt and freshly ground pepper
½ cup olive oil
½ pound fresh spinach leaves,
  chopped
2 tablespoons freshly grated
  Parmesan cheese
1 pound farfalle
½ cup thinly sliced prosciutto
  or boiled ham, cut into thin
  strips about 1 inch long
Freshly grated Parmesan cheese

Serves 6 as a first course or 4 as a main course

Put the peas, onion, and butter in a saucepan and season lightly with salt and pepper. Cook over medium heat, stirring often, for about 5 minutes, or until done.

Meanwhile, bring 4 quarts of water to a rolling boil.

Heat the olive oil with the spinach and Parmesan cheese in a large frying pan, stirring often, for 5 minutes. Set aside.

When the water is boiling, stir in 1½ tablespoons of salt, stir, and add the farfalle. Cook until al dente, or just tender, stirring often.

Reserve 1 cup of the hot pasta water. Drain the pasta and return to the same pan. Add the peas and spinach and the prosciutto or ham and toss well. Add a little hot pasta water, if necessary. Season to taste with salt and pepper. Cover and let rest 5 minutes.

Toss again and serve sprinkled with freshly grated Parmesan cheese.

Gnocchetti alla Madonita

Serves 8 as a first course or 6 as a main course

(Madonie-Style Gnocchetti with Meat and Vegetables)

Combine the onion through the tomato paste in a large saucepan and cook over low heat for 10 minutes. Add 1 quart of water, salt and pepper to taste, and simmer for 50 minutes, stirring occasionally until the sauce is creamy. Stir in the peas and cook 10 minutes more. Off the heat, stir in the butter, parsley, and pecorino or Parmesan cheese. Let rest.

Bring 6 quarts of water to a rolling boil in a large pot. Stir in 2 tablespoons of salt and add the gnocchetti. Cook the pasta until al dente, or just tender, stirring often.

Reserve 1 cup of the hot pasta water. Drain the pasta and turn over the sauce. Toss together and heat for a few minutes. Add a little hot pasta water, if a thinner sauce is desired. Serve immediately with the extra cheese for sprinkling on top.

1 medium onion, finely
  chopped
¾ cup cooked chicken breast,
  finely chopped
¾ cup cooked sweet Italian
  sausage, finely chopped
1 medium carrot, scraped and
  thinly sliced
2 cups chopped fresh spinach
½ cup finely chopped ham
½ cup diced Napoli salami
1 cup olive oil
1 cup ground veal
1 tablespoon tomato paste
Salt and freshly ground pepper
¾ cup fresh or frozen (thawed)
  green peas
1 tablespoon sweet butter
⅓ cup freshly chopped Italian
  parsley
½ cup freshly grated pecorino
  or Parmesan cheese, plus
  extra for topping
1½ pounds gnocchetti

Riso

(Rice)

Il Mio Risotto *(My Saffron Risotto)* • TRE FORME D'ARANCINE *(The Three Arancine Shapes)* • Arancine I *(Rice Ball Croquettes Stuffed with Meat)* • Arancine II *(Oval Rice Croquettes Stuffed with Béchamel, Ham, and Mozzarella)* • Sformato di Riso *(Baked Risotto Timbale with Veal Ragù Filling)* • Risotto Lardellato *(Molded Rice Ring of Risotto Covered with Ham and Green Peas)* • Risotto con Funghi *(Risotto with Mushrooms)* • Risotto con Zucca e Noci di Betty *(Betty's Risotto with Pumpkin and Walnuts)* • APRIAMO UN ALBERGO ED UN NUOVO RISTORANTE *(We Open a Hotel and a New Restaurant)* • Risotto con Carciofi *(Risotto with Artichokes)* • Risotto con Spinaci e Pecorino *(Risotto with Spinach and Pecorino)* • Risotto alla Marinara *(Seafood Risotto)* • Risotto con la Verza di Betty *(Betty's Risotto with Savoy Cabbage)*

In Sicily, our favorite way of eating rice is when it is transformed into charming balls called *arancine* (meaning "little oranges" in Italian), with a meat or thick béchamel sauce laced with a ham-and-mozzarella filling inside. *Arancine* are simply stuffed risotto shapes coated with bread crumbs and fried until golden. If you stick a tiny twig of an orange tree with a shiny green leaf attached into the top of one of these rust-colored rice croquettes, it does resemble an orange. We sometimes serve *arancine* on a tray this way, also garnished with orange blossoms. Read about the different shapes of *arancine* on page 145.

Arancine are the triumph of Palermo, where they are sold everywhere—at food stalls, market stands, *tavola calda,* the train station, and even at the airport. You cannot escape them. Oh, you will find all qualities of *arancine*—some wonderful, fragrant-flavored delicacies, and others like cannonballs, practically inedible. Good *arancine* can't be eaten too long after they are cooked. Like people, when they sit too long, they grow in weight.

Legend has it that on December 13, 1582, Saint Lucia created a miracle in

Palermo's harbor, where a fleet of ships carrying a priceless cargo of grain appeared. The grain saved the starving population from a terrible famine. On December 13, Saint Lucia's Day, it is very bad luck to eat anything made of flour—so, no pasta or bread. Palermo celebrates Saint Lucia's Day with a diet of grains. Wheat berries and rice are featured in three special dishes always associated with this day—*arancine, panelle* (chick-pea fritters), and *cuccia* (a soft custardy dessert made with wheat berries and ricotta).

At Gangivecchio, occasionally we organize *arancine* parties and serve only *arancine* of different shapes and sizes, with various stuffings, followed by seasonal fruit. Our friends have to be gravely ill or out of the country to give up the fun of one of our *arancine* parties because Mamma's are the best. There is always a contest to see who can eat the most large ones. Six is the record.

The second way we prepare rice is risotto, which everyone in our family loves. Risotto is not a Sicilian tradition, but when Sicilians come to the restaurant and learn that risotto is on the menu, they always respond with happy sighs. We serve a risotto at the restaurant as a first course only when there are twelve people or less.

Recently a risotto battle has begun between my mother and Paolo and Betty. Mamma always insists on using the classic, short-grain Arborio rice for risotto, but Paolo and Betty use another short-grain rice called Blond, or long-grain rices like Uncle Ben's, which are readily available in Sicily. Betty and Paolo insist the cooking time for these rices is more predictable, exactly 18 minutes, which, no matter what anyone says, is not always true for the different varieties of Arborio rice—which usually take up to 30 minutes. They argue further that not only are these other rices easier on the budget but, when properly cooked, they produce excellent creamy risottos. Mamma counters that this idea is absurd, that other rices stay separated and won't blend together as they should. Substituting other short- or long-grain rices for Arborio in risotto, of course, doesn't produce the same result, but you should try it; you might be very surprised and like it, too.

When Paolo or Betty prepare one of their risottos for dinner at Tenuta Gangivecchio, throughout the meal Mamma and the two of them continue discussing until death the subject of rice for risotto, because not one of the three will change his or her mind. I always remain uncommitted during the war of the rices, preferring to concentrate on my Risotto con Funghi (page 149) and reflect upon the poetic meeting between the creamy rice and mushrooms in my mouth.

G.T.

Il Mio Risotto

(My Saffron Risotto)

*T*his basic risotto is fantastic on its own, but it's a wonderfully adaptable recipe. You can convert this basic recipe into dozens of risottos by simply adding a small amount of vegetables, meat, seafood, herbs, or spices at the point in the recipe after you have melted the butter and cooked the rice for 2 minutes. You can, for example, add 1 cup of chopped leeks or scallions for a leek or scallion risotto; 1 small minced onion and 2 cups of grated cooked beets for a rosy-red risotto; and 1 small minced onion and 2 cups of chopped cooked broccoli or asparagus for a broccoli or asparagus risotto. Adding 1½ cups of cooked sweet sausage to the basic recipe produces an incredibly delicious risotto. Sometimes, when I don't have sausage, I toss in a few fennel seeds. The list of possibilities goes on and on—mixed spring vegetables, tomato and fresh basil. So be inventive with this recipe and experiment with your favorite foods. We have a friend who makes a strawberry risotto—not something I believe I would care for, but why not.

Il Mio Risotto is also used to make *arancine* and two molded dishes—Sformato di Riso (page 147) and Risotto Lardellato (page 148). As you see, it is a most useful recipe.

Serves 10 to 12 as a first course or 8 to 10 as a main course

10–12 cups homemade beef or chicken stock or canned broth (Vegetable stock or broth can be used, too.)
¼ teaspoon ground saffron
8 tablespoons sweet butter
3 cups (about 1½ pounds) Arborio rice
One 6-ounce piece Parmesan cheese rind, quartered (see information on page 82)
Salt and freshly ground pepper
1 large egg yolk, at room temperature
Freshly grated Parmesan cheese

Heat the beef or chicken stock or broth almost to a boil in a saucepan, then turn the heat to very low and stir in the saffron. Put a ladle into the pan and place it next to the burner on which you are going to cook the risotto.

In a large saucepan, melt 6 tablespoons of the butter. Immediately stir in the rice and cook over medium-high heat, stirring until the rice just begins to turn translucent, about 2 minutes. Take care not to let it burn. Adjust the heat as needed, but for the most part, the rice is cooked over medium-high heat. Add 2 ladlesful (each ladleful is about ½ cup) of the simmering broth and the Parmesan cheese rind. Constantly stir the rice with a wooden spoon until the liquid has almost been absorbed. Add another ladleful or two of the hot broth, and continue stirring and adding broth until it has been absorbed. Keep repeating this procedure until the rice is al dente, or just tender, using only as much of the broth as you need. If you happen to need more, you can add some boiling hot water to the broth pan and keep it simmering. Cooking time is about 20 minutes. Risotto can be cooked and served *all'onda* (like waves) and slightly runny, or it may have a firmer consistency. For *arancine,* a firmer-cooked rice mixture is required. This is achieved by simply cooking the risotto a little longer after the last of the broth is added.

Five minutes before the risotto is done, call everyone to the dining table.

When the rice is cooked and the desired consistency is reached, remove from the heat and season to taste with salt and pepper. Discard any leftover pieces of cheese rind. Add the remaining 2 tablespoons of butter and the egg yolk, and immediately mix very well. Normally, extra cheese isn't needed in the risotto, but taste it, and if you'd like more of a cheese flavor, add a small amount of Parmesan cheese and stir in well. (When preparing *arancine,* stir in ¼ cup grated Parmesan cheese at the end.) Serve the risotto immediately, while steaming hot, and pass the cheese.

NOTE: I have given this recipe in such a large quantity because it is the exact amount needed in the *arancine* recipes that follow. Simply cut the recipe in half to serve 6 as a first-course or 4 as a main-course risotto. —W.T.

Tre Forme D'Arancine

(The Three Arancine Shapes)

In recent years the shape of *arancine* has become a food language that reveals what stuffing is inside. These forms are either round, oval, or conical. The classic round-shaped *arancine* signifies a meat filling—either beef or veal *ragù*. An oval *arancine* has a creamy béchamel stuffing (with or without the ham and cheese). A conical-shaped *arancine*, with one flat side to rest on, indicates a chicken or other meat *ragù* center.

When you are in Sicily, you must sample *arancine* at a *friggitoria* (street food stall), but be sure to remember these shapes so you won't be disappointed to find an unexpected filling inside. And if you don't actually see the *arancine* removed from the frying pot, inquire from the seller when they were cooked. If you simply ask, "Are they fresh?" the answer you will always receive is "Si."

In the summer, when Paolo and I were children, Mamma would pack a basket with *arancine* and fruit for a picnic. We'd all ride with Papa on his tractor to la Balza di Gangivecchio—the high ridge above us on our property. On a clear day from there you can see Mount Etna far off to the east, nearly eighty miles away. After we ate our fill of *arancine* and fruit, everyone slept like angels in the shade of a tree.

It takes some advance preparation to make *arancine*. Two separate dishes must be made—the risotto and the meat *ragù*— but the *ragù* can be made a day in advance. Mamma uses Ragù di Tritato as a filling, but Ragù di Carne (page 135) is more traditional.

Arancine I

(Rice Ball Croquettes Stuffed with Meat)

1 recipe Il Mio Risotto (page 143)
½ recipe Ragù di Tritato (page 134), at room temperature
4 large egg whites
Dried bread crumbs
Sunflower or vegetable oil, for deep-frying

Our *arancine* are quite large in size, so one or two are plenty for a meal. We also make small, walnut-size *arancinette* (page 49) to serve as an appetizer or in a mixed antipasto.

Serves 4 to 6

Prepare the risotto to a slightly firm or dry consistency (not *all'onda,* or wavy and slightly runny) and cool completely. Take a scant cup of rice and flatten it into a cup or tulip shape in the palm of one hand. Spoon 1 generous tablespoonful of the *ragù* sauce into the center, then fold the outer edge of the rice over the filling, completely enclosing it. Otherwise the filling will leak out. You may need to add a little more rice. Shape into a perfect ball about 3 inches in diameter. Make 7 more *arancine* in the same manner.

Thoroughly coat each ball with egg white and then with bread crumbs. Put the *arancine* on a tray and refrigerate for 30 minutes.

Heat 4 inches of sunflower or vegetable oil in a large, deep-sided frying pan until the oil is hot but not smoking. Gently lower 4 *arancine* into the hot oil with a slotted spoon and cook until golden brown all over, rolling over often. Drain on paper towels. Cook the remaining *arancine* the same way. Serve immediately. We always eat *arancine* with a paper napkin in our hands. Somehow they are tastier that way.

Arancine II

(Oval Rice Croquettes Stuffed with Béchamel, Ham, and Mozzarella)

*T*hese *arancine* are prepared exactly in the same manner as Arancine I, except that the filling is a firm béchamel sauce (Salsa Besciamella Sostenuta) with ham and mozzarella, and the croquettes are oval rather than round.

Serves 4 to 6

Prepare the Salsa Besciamella Sostenuta (page 96) and, while still hot, stir in ¾ cup minced boiled ham and ¾ cup diced mozzarella.

Cool thoroughly. (This filling can be made a day ahead and kept in the refrigerator.)

Flatten a scant cup of rice into a cup or tulip shape in the palm of one hand, spoon a generous tablespoonful of the béchamel mixture into the center, and thoroughly enclose the filling. Proceed as directed in the previous recipe, but shape each *arancine* into an oval, about 3 inches in diameter at the center and 5 inches in length. Make 8 *arancine*. Follow the instructions for coating, refrigerating, and cooking the *arancine*. Serve hot.

Sformato di Riso

(Baked Risotto Timbale with Veal Ragù Filling)

Serves 8 to 10

½ cup olive oil
1 pound ground veal
1 medium onion, chopped
Salt and freshly ground pepper
2 cups tomato paste
1 teaspoon sugar
1 tablespoon sweet butter, plus extra for greasing the pan
½ cup freshly grated Parmesan cheese
Dried bread crumbs
1 recipe Il Mio Risotto, without egg (page 143), cooked and cooled

In a large, heavy saucepan, combine the olive oil, veal, and onion, and season lightly with salt and pepper. Cook over high heat, stirring often, until the veal is no longer pink. Add the tomato paste, sugar, and 1 quart of water. Simmer for 1 hour, stirring often, or until the sauce is reduced to about 2½ cups.

Stir in the butter and cheese and mix well. Transfer the mixture to a bowl and let it cool.

Preheat the oven to 375°F.

Liberally grease a round baking dish or pan about 12 inches in diameter and 3 to 4 inches deep. Add 3 tablespoons of bread crumbs and evenly coat the bottom and sides of the pan. Knock out the extra crumbs.

Turn half the risotto into the pan and evenly smooth it across the bottom and 2 inches up the side of the pan. Spoon the veal *ragù* onto the rice and smooth it down evenly. Gently spoon the remaining risotto over the top and gently pat it down.

Sprinkle the top with bread crumbs, pressing down slightly. Let rest for 10 minutes. (The recipe can be prepared to this stage up to 1½ hours in advance.)

Cook the timbale on a baking sheet in the preheated oven for about 45 minutes, or until golden brown on top.

Remove the *sformato* and let it rest 15 minutes. (If you want to serve the dish later, do not unmold it until just before you're ready.

It can be served at room temperature. We tested the *sformato* recipe in St. Thomas with Michele and took it to the beach as the main course of a picnic lunch.)

Run a knife along the sides of the pan. Cover the *sformato* with a dish (preferably round) several inches wider than the pan and invert the baked risotto onto it. Hold the sides of the dish and the pan securely and give it one good shake. This should release the timbale. Remove the pan. Cut servings into squares or wedges like a cake. Serve hot or at room temperature.

Risotto Lardellato

*(Molded Rice Ring of Risotto
Covered with Ham and
Green Peas)*

Serves 6 to 8

Softened sweet butter
¾–1 pound boiled ham, thinly
 sliced
1 recipe Il Mio Risotto, cooked
 with chicken broth (page
 143), at room temperature
3 cups cooked green peas

Generously butter a 12-inch ring mold. Line the mold with an overlapping layer of the ham slices, with the ends of each slice hanging over the center and outer edges of the mold.

Spoon the risotto into the mold and gently press down. Fold the ends of the ham over the risotto. Let rest 10 minutes.

Place a platter (preferably round) several inches wider than the mold over it, and while securely holding both, invert the mold onto the platter. Fill the center of the mold with green peas and spoon the extra peas around the mold. Serve at room temperature.

VARIATIONS: The mold can be covered with thin slices of smoked salmon instead of ham, although the salmon makes the dish rather expensive. It makes a beautiful and delicious presentation.

The risotto can be prepared as in Il Mio Risotto except near the end of the cooking time, stir in 2 tablespoons finely chopped basil and 2 small tomatoes, peeled and diced.

Risotto con Funghi

(Risotto with Mushrooms)

*I*f we are lucky, for a short period in the spring and in the fall, the earth at Gangivecchio gives us magnificent ferla mushrooms (page 234). First we want to grill some ferlas plain, just to savor the unique flavor of these incredible mushrooms, then Mamma always prepares a ferla risotto for dinner. In Sicily, we are fond of saying that when the pasta is served, there is finally silence at the table. The same can be said for risottos, but especially one prepared with ferla mushrooms.

Ferla mushrooms can't be found in America, so we have substituted dried porcini mushrooms in the following recipe. However, ferlas don't taste like porcini at all. There is really no equivalent. Any mushroom can be used in this recipe—chopped Portobello, cremini, or cultivated white mushrooms. Wild field mushrooms, if you can find them, would be an excellent choice.

Serves 6 as a first course or 4 as a main course

½ ounce dried porcini mushrooms, soaked in 3 cups lukewarm water for 30 minutes, rinsed, well drained, and finely chopped, or 3 cups fresh mushrooms, chopped

4–6 cups homemade beef or chicken stock or broth (depending on whether you use dried or fresh mushrooms)

4 tablespoons olive oil

4 tablespoons sweet butter

2 garlic cloves, minced

1 small onion, finely chopped

1½ cups Arborio rice

⅓ cup freshly chopped Italian parsley

½ cup freshly grated Parmesan cheese

Salt and freshly ground pepper

If you are using dried porcini mushrooms, reserve 2 cups of the soaking water and strain it through a fine strainer lined with a double layer of cheesecloth. You will need only 4 cups of stock or broth because the strained mushroom soaking water will be added to the stock. If you are using fresh mushrooms, you will need 6 cups stock or broth.

Heat the broth and 2 cups of the strained mushroom water in a saucepan and let simmer. Put a ½-cup ladle into the pan and leave it next to the burner on which you'll be cooking the risotto.

Heat the olive oil and 2 tablespoons of the butter with the garlic and onion in a heavy saucepan. Cook about 3 minutes, stirring often. Stir in the rice and cook over medium-high heat for 2 minutes, stirring constantly.

Add 2 ladlesful of broth and the chopped mushrooms, and stir vigorously until the water has almost been absorbed. Add another ladleful of broth, stir, and continue letting the rice absorb the broth and adding 1 ladleful of broth at a time. Cook until the rice is cooked al dente, or just tender, and the mixture is thick and creamy, about 20 to 25 minutes. Never stop stirring the rice. If you happen to run out of broth, add boiling water to the broth pan and keep it simmering.

Five minutes before the end of cooking time, call everyone to the table.

Remove the risotto from the heat and stir in the remaining 2 tablespoons of butter, the parsley, and the freshly grated Parmesan cheese. Season to taste with salt and pepper, and serve immediately.

Risotto con Zucca e Noci di Betty

(Betty's Risotto with Pumpkin and Walnuts)

Serves 6 as a first course or 4 as a main course

3 cups fresh calabaza (West Indian pumpkin), or butternut or acorn squash, peeled and diced
6 cups homemade beef or chicken stock, or canned chicken broth
⅛ teaspoon ground saffron
4 tablespoons olive oil
1 small onion, finely chopped
1½ cups Arborio rice
2 tablespoons sweet butter
½ cup freshly grated Parmesan cheese
Salt and freshly ground pepper
⅓ cup freshly chopped walnuts

Bring 6 cups of water to a boil. Add the calabaza or squash and simmer until just tender, about 10 minutes. Drain well.

Heat the stock or broth in a saucepan, add the saffron, and let simmer on a burner next to where you are cooking. Put a ladle in the pan and keep it near the burner where you'll be cooking the risotto.

Heat the olive oil with the onion in a heavy saucepan and cook for about 3 minutes, stirring often. Add the rice and stir constantly for about 2 minutes over medium-high heat. Add 2 ladlesful of simmering broth to the rice and stir vigorously. Stir in the calabaza and continue stirring until the liquid has been absorbed. Add another ladleful of broth and stir. Continue letting the rice absorb the broth before adding another ladleful of broth.

Cook the rice this way until it is al dente, or just tender, and the mixture is thick and creamy, about 20 to 25 minutes. If necessary, add boiling water to the broth pan and keep it simmering.

Five minutes before the end of cooking time, call everyone to the table.

Remove the risotto from the heat and stir in the butter and Parmesan cheese. Season to taste with salt and pepper. Transfer the risotto to a warmed serving dish or bowl, sprinkle with walnuts, and serve immediately.

Apriamo un Albergo ed un Nuovo Ristorante

(We Open a Hotel and a New Restaurant)

About four years ago my brother, Paolo, made the decision that the time was perfect for us to open a small hotel, with the hope of generating more income. Paolo thought an ancient stable about one hundred meters east of the abbey would be the ideal location for it. We invested all our savings in this project, and the result is a charming nine-room hotel called Tenuta Gangivecchio (Estate Gangivecchio), which opened in the fall of 1992.

The building itself has ocher-colored masonry walls with a curved tile roof, accented with natural stonework with some outside connecting stone walls. Eight rooms are situated in the main building. The ninth, and largest, room is in a separate, small stone building adjacent to the reception and lobby entrance. This lodging was constructed as the manager's private accommodation, but before one was hired, Paolo and Betty discovered that not only were they capable of operating the hotel on their own, they enjoyed it. Betty does the accounting and oversees the housekeeping and kitchen staff. Paolo organizes the rest, like greeting guests, showing them to their rooms, answering any questions, solving any problems, or seeing to repairs. The long list of their hotel responsibilities never seems to end, including buying supplies and food and doing all the cooking.

Tenuta's lobby room, with high wood-beamed ceilings, has homelike sitting areas, a large table and chairs, potted plants, and lots of wood-framed windows so the sun can shine inside. In one corner is a fireplace, where we and our guests like to gather before or after dinner on cold winter evenings to have a glass of wine or grappa and talk or sing.

The atmosphere at Tenuta Gangivecchio is very friendly, as it is in all places in the countryside. Sicilians who repeatedly come here feel more like our friends than paying guests. And people arrive from all over the island, from as far away as Trapani, Agrigento, Siracusa, Taormina, and Palermo. Many foreigners have begun to come, too.

Paolo and my sister-in-law are very *bravi* in the kitchen. Their restaurant at Tenuta Gangivecchio accommodates their guests, serving three meals a day, and as in Gangivecchio's main restaurant, lunch is at 1:30 p.m. and dinner at 8:30 p.m.

Their dining room can serve up to forty people. We celebrate Christmas and New Year's Eve there.

In Tenuta Gangivecchio's wonderful new professional kitchen Betty excels at salads, vegetable dishes, risottos, main courses, and desserts. Paolo is the pasta sauce and grilled meat specialist. Their menu, like ours, varies with the seasons. At times, there is a sort of affectionate cooking contest between the two restaurants, Gangivecchio versus Tenuta Gangivecchio, especially during the holidays. And of course, we often help each other out, one team cooking for the other, but it is more likely that it is Mamma and I who will bring cakes, a sauce, or antipasti over to the hotel when some unexpected crisis occurs.

Mamma and I always dine with Paolo and Betty in the evenings in our private quarters, unless there are guests at the *albergo,* which there usually are on weekends, or unless Mamma and I have guests at our restaurant. We walk over with Puffo, Mamma's Yorkshire terrier, at about 8:00 p.m. Candles are already flickering on the tables. Paolo has a small bar, where he plays taped music softly. After dinner he prepares excellent espresso. Tenuta's dining room is bright and sunny during the day. In the summertime, when it gets warm, all meals are served at tables outside.

Tenuta Gangivecchio is part of a European government-sponsored program called *Agriturismo,* which offers travelers the opportunity to experience an intimate taste of authentic local living. *Agriturismo* accommodations are usually at farms in the countryside, operated by the owners who serve meals made mostly from what they produce. Rates are always reasonable, and lower than at bigger, more elaborate hotels. *Agriturismo* is prospering in Italy and spreading across Sicily now, too. Our hotel is doing so nicely that Paolo and Betty are contemplating adding another six rooms. And there is now a small swimming pool.

Horseback riding is a favorite activity here, but lots of guests, like two visiting schoolteachers from California, come to Tenuta Gangivecchio to rest, breathe in the mountain air, take long walks through the vine-covered arbor pathways, read in the shade by the fountain and pool, visit with our animals, take afternoon naps, and enjoy fresh Sicilian food. Anyway, we are very proud of our little *albergo* and Paolo and Betty's new restaurant. If you come to Sicily and like the idea of a quiet country setting and respite, we are always here.

Risotto con Carciofi

Serves 6 as a first course or 4 as a main course

(Risotto with Artichokes)

Heat the chicken stock in a saucepan and let simmer. Put a ladle into the pot and keep it close to the burner where you'll be cooking the risotto.

Heat 4 tablespoons of the butter with the onion in a heavy saucepan and cook for 2 minutes, stirring constantly. Add the rice and stir vigorously for 2 minutes. Add the artichokes and 2 ladlesful of broth. Stir constantly until the liquid is absorbed. Add another ladleful of stock and stir. Continue letting the rice absorb the stock one ladleful at a time, always stirring. Cook until the rice is al dente, or just tender, and the mixture is thick and creamy, about 20 to 25 minutes. If you happen to run out of stock, add boiling water to the stock pan and keep it simmering.

Five minutes before the end of cooking time, call everyone to the table.

Remove the risotto from the heat and stir in the remaining 2 tablespoons of butter, the parsley, and the Parmesan cheese. Season to taste with salt and pepper, and serve immediately.

6 cups homemade chicken stock or canned broth
6 tablespoons sweet butter
1 small onion
1½ cups Arborio rice
8 fresh artichoke hearts, cleaned and chopped (instructions on page 58) or two 10-ounce packages frozen artichoke hearts, thawed, well drained, and chopped
½ cup freshly chopped Italian parsley
½ cup freshly grated Parmesan cheese
Salt and freshly ground pepper

Risotto con Spinaci e Pecorino

(Risotto with Spinach and Pecorino)

Serves 6 as a first course or 4 as a main course

1 tablespoon sweet butter

1 tablespoon olive oil

1 pound fresh spinach, washed, stemmed, steamed, well drained, and finely chopped (One 10-ounce package frozen chopped spinach, cooked and well drained, can also be used.)

½ cup freshly grated Parmesan cheese, plus extra to pass at the table

Salt and freshly ground pepper

½ recipe Il Mio Risotto (page 143)

6 ounces sweet pecorino or provolone, cut into ¼-inch-thick slices, then cut into thin strips

Heat the butter and olive oil in a saucepan with the well-drained, cooked spinach over medium-low heat for 5 minutes, stirring often. Off the heat, stir in the ½ cup of Parmesan cheese and season to taste with salt and pepper. Let rest.

Begin cooking Il Mio Risotto. When it is half cooked, stir in the spinach and continue cooking the risotto as directed.

Five minutes before the risotto is cooked, call everyone to the table.

Spoon individual servings of the risotto onto warmed dinner or first-course plates in equal amounts. Very quickly press the pecorino or provolone into the top of each serving of risotto in a circle, in equal portions. Serve immediately and pass the Parmesan cheese.

Risotto alla Marinara

(Seafood Risotto)

Serves 6 as a first course or 4 as a main course

Heat ½ cup of the olive oil, the onion, and garlic in a large frying pan, and cook over medium heat, stirring often, for 3 minutes. Add the fish fillets and cook over low heat for 4 minutes, stirring occasionally. Set aside.

Put the clams and mussels into a large pot with ½ cup of water and the white wine and cook, covered, over medium-high heat until the shells have opened, stirring occasionally.

Remove the mussels and clams from their shells and add to the pan with the fish. Strain the juices from the pan the clams and mussels cooked in through a fine strainer lined with a double layer of cheesecloth into a saucepan. Add 5 cups of water and bring the seafood broth to a boil. Reduce heat to a simmer. Put a ladle into the pan and keep it close to the burner on which you'll be cooking the risotto.

Heat 4 tablespoons of the olive oil in a heavy-bottomed saucepan and add the rice. Stir constantly for 2 minutes. Ladle in 1 cup of seafood broth and, stirring vigorously and constantly, cook until the liquid has been absorbed. Add another ladleful of broth and stir the rice until the liquid has been absorbed. Add the cooked seafood, shrimp, tomatoes, parsley, cayenne pepper, if you like, and 2 ladlesful of broth to the risotto. Stir and continue adding the broth, ½ cup at a time, stirring until the liquid has been absorbed and the risotto is done. If necessary, add boiling water to the seafood broth and keep it simmering.

Five minutes before the risotto is ready, call everyone to the table.

Season the cooked risotto to taste with salt and pepper and stir in the butter. Turn the risotto into a warmed serving dish or bowl and garnish with the parsley sprigs. Serve at once.

NOTE: It is always considered uncivilized to serve Parmesan cheese with any seafood pasta or risotto, but I always sprinkle both with cheese because I like it. It's up to you. —G.T.

Olive oil
1 small onion, minced
1 garlic clove, minced
¼ pound fresh fish fillets, such as mullet or snapper, cut into small pieces
1 pound cherrystone clams, scrubbed and washed
1 pound mussels, scrubbed, debearded, and washed
½ cup dry white wine
1½ cups Arborio rice
½ pound small shrimp, shelled and deveined
1 cup fresh peeled or canned tomatoes, chopped
¼ cup freshly chopped Italian parsley, plus 2 sprigs for garnish
Pinch of cayenne pepper (optional)
Salt and freshly ground pepper
2 tablespoons sweet butter

Risotto con la Verza di Betty

(Betty's Risotto with Savoy Cabbage)

Serves 6 as a first course and 4 as a main course

3 cups Savoy cabbage, finely
   shredded and chopped
1 small onion, minced
Olive oil
Salt and freshly ground pepper
3 cups milk
2 vegetable bouillon cubes
4 tablespoons sweet butter
1½ cups Arborio rice
¼ cup freshly grated Parmesan
   cheese, plus extra to pass at
   the table

Put the Savoy cabbage, onion, and 4 tablespoons of olive oil into a large, heavy-bottomed saucepan with ½ cup of water and bring to a boil, stirring constantly. Season the cabbage to taste with salt and pepper. Lower the heat to medium, cover, and simmer until the cabbage is cooked, about 10 minutes.

Meanwhile, heat the milk in a saucepan with 3 cups of water and the vegetable bouillon cubes. Stir until the cubes have dissolved. Put a ½-cup ladle into the pan and keep the liquid simmering over very low heat close to where you'll be cooking the risotto.

In a clean, heavy-bottomed pan, heat 2 tablespoons of olive oil and 2 tablespoons of the butter. Add the rice and stir vigorously for 2 minutes. Add 2 ladlesful of the milk broth and the cabbage. Stir and cook over medium-high heat until the liquid has been absorbed. Continue adding a ladleful of broth and stirring until the liquid is absorbed and the risotto is cooked.

Five minutes before the risotto is ready, call everyone to the table.

Remove the risotto from the heat. Stir in the remaining 2 tablespoons of butter, the ¼ cup of Parmesan cheese, and season to taste with salt and pepper. Serve immediately and pass the Parmesan cheese.

Secondi di Carne

(Meat Main-Course Dishes)

Vitello *(Veal)*

Involtini alla Benedettina *(Veal Rolls Stuffed with Ham)* • Falsomagro di Donna Giulia *(Giulia's Braised Stuffed Veal)* • Medaglioni di Vitello di Gangivecchio *(Gangivecchio's Veal Medallions Stuffed with Mortadella and Mozzarella)* • Cotoletta Siciliana *(Sicilian-Style Veal Cutlets with Tomatoes and Parsley)* • Spezzatino di Vitello *(Veal Stew with Onions)* • Spiedini di Vitello *(Veal Kebabs)* • Lacerto *(Braised Veal with Puréed Vegetable Sauce)* • I Giorni del Mercato a Gangi: Passato e Presente *(Past and Present Market Days in Gangi)* • Filetto in Casseruola con Cognac *(Fillet of Veal Cooked in a Casserole with Cognac)* • Polpette alla Wanda *(Wanda's Veal and Pork Meatballs)* • Carne ad Antipasto *(Veal and Pumpkin Stew)* • Carne alle Cipolline alla Giovanna *(Giovanna's Veal Scallops Braised with Pearl Onions)* • Tritato alla Pizzaiola *(Baked Chopped Veal Steak with Pizza Sauce)*

Maiale *(Pork)*

Costolette di Maiale con Marsala, Aglio ed Erbe *(Pork Chops with Marsala, Garlic, and Herbs)* • Costate di Maiale con Rosmarino e Vino *(Sautéed Pork Chops with Rosemary and Wine)* • Salsiccia con Patate e Pomodori di Paolo *(Paolo's Baked Pork Sausages with Potatoes and Tomatoes)* • Iudisco al Latte *(Pork Loin Braised in Milk)* • Formaggi Locali e il Caciocavallo di Gangivecchio *(Gangivecchio's Caciocavallo and Local Cheese Production)*

Agnello *(Lamb)*

Agnello della Nonna Giovanna *(Grandmother Giovanna's Lamb Stew with Rosemary and Red Wine)* • Fricassea di Agnello di Bruna *(Bruna's Lamb Fricassee au Gratin)* • Interiora d'Agnello *(Lamb Kidneys Braised in Red Wine Sauce)* •

Un Principe Viene a Pranzo a Gangivecchio *(A Prince Comes to Lunch at Gangivecchio)*

Pollo   *(Chicken)*

Polletti Arrosto al Rosmarino *(Roast Cornish Hens with Rosemary)* • Pollo alla Tornabene *(Baked Chicken Legs and Thighs with Tomatoes and Onions)* • Scaloppine di Pollo con Spinaci *(Sautéed Chicken Breasts with Spinach)* • Pollo della Nonna Elena *(Grandmother Elena's Braised Chicken with Potatoes)* • Involtini del Monastero *(Chicken Breasts Stuffed with Smoked Pancetta and Caciocavallo)*

Tacchino   *(Turkey)*

Lesso Misto *(Turkey and Mixed Meat Casserole with Vegetables)*

Coniglio   *(Rabbit)*

Coniglio di Santina *(Santina's Stewed Rabbit)* • Coniglio con Olive e Capperi *(Sautéed Rabbit with Olives and Capers)*

Meat is the curse and delight of our table. We say this because it has not traditionally been a major part of the Sicilian diet. In the past, unless we had our own animals to butcher, little meat was available to us. What meat could be found came at a very dear price. Today we have plenty of exceptional meat, but it remains very expensive. Since we live in the interior, away from our island's great seafood, we have always been forced to rely on meat for the main course for holidays and special occasions and, of course, in our restaurant. Most of the protein in our diet has been provided by beans, legumes, and cheeses.

When we opened our restaurant, for the *secondi di carne* (meat main course) we served a large quantity of pork, excellent in quality in our region, so it seemed a good idea to breed our own pigs. The pig is a banquet. Every portion of the animal, from the foot to the head, is delicious and can be eaten. My grandmother Giovanna used to prepare a fantastic jellied pork head.

We bought a male and two female pigs, but as happens with all animals at Gangivecchio, they soon became members of the family with names—Little Esther, Emerald, and Merlin. Everyone coming here wanted to photograph them, scratch their backs, and feed them biscuits. When Esther and Emerald had babies—the Blue Bells and the Country Boys—it became impossible to kill and butcher any of them. While the pigs lived the

good country life, we spent a lot of money feeding them and buying pork from the butcher.

On a trip to Genoa, Paolo bought a female wild boar, which he planned to mate with a male pig, because he had heard that the meat produced from this union is highly prized. The boar, Giorgina, made a meal of her first litter. (Our veterinarian told us this was normal.) Giorgina had no milk for her second litter, and because she ferociously kept everyone away, protecting her babies, they soon died. The male pig, Gastone, developed arthritic hind legs, so no more babies came. We had to give up our grand plan. Gastone eventually died, but Giorgina lives on, still being photographed and consuming tremendous amounts of food. She eats all the leftovers from the restaurant.

In the summertime we serve mainly veal at Gangivecchio's restaurant. The quality of our veal in the Madonie region is extraordinarily tender and delicious because the animals have grazed on the rich greens of our mountain pastures. We serve simple dishes, as you will see, but they are all very much appreciated by our guests. Mamma insists on a special cut of veal for her famous *involtini* (Involtini alla Benedettina, page 163), which comes from the hind section of the animal, called *fare spese*. The meat is flattened into splendid, large, thin pieces. In New York, when buying veal for this dish, we stood silently by as Mamma and the butcher argued back and forth in Italian about the precise cut. "*Finalmente trovo il pezzo giusto* [Finally he got it right]," Mamma triumphed.

Unfortunately, most of what Sicilian beef we have is on the tough side. Therefore, we have no recipes for beef in this collection. If we happen to obtain an inferior piece of veal and my brother tastes it, he asks suspiciously, "Is this beef?"

Since we raise an enormous number of sheep in the Madonie, grazing on fertile mountain pastures, our lamb is choice. Several of our favorite lamb dishes are in this chapter, like Agnello della Nonna Giovanna (page 180), a fragrant lamb stew, as well as a typical and wonderful Madonie ragù sauce for a pasta dish (on page 136).

We eat a small amount of chicken at home but rarely serve it in the restaurant. When Sicilians dine out, they want to have something special that they don't generally have at home. For most, chicken is considered too ordinary. Every Wednesday afternoon, when grocery stores and butcher shops are closed throughout the island, many Sicilians in Palermo and other cities and villages buy chickens cooked on rotisseries—*polli allo spiedo*—to take home. We have tried serving chicken several times in the restaurant but without much success. However, one special guest relished the chicken we served. When Prince Charles dined at Gangivecchio, he requested in advance something light, so Mamma created a chicken dish for him—Polletti Arrosto al Rosmarino (page 184).

We have two kinds of rabbits available to us in Sicily: wild rabbits, small and delicious, and the domestic ones, which are larger and not as tender or as good. We consider wild rabbit a delicacy and serve it at home and when guests ask for it in advance at the restaurant.

Our butchers in Gangi are our main meat source, but on Tuesdays at our weekly street market, when the meat truck arrives, we have a bigger selection. Aside from superior veal, lamb, rabbit, turkey, and sausages, the meat vendor also carries an excellent selection of fresh cheeses and prosciutto and many other quality items.

To be honest, for us, meat is much more a delight than a curse. Contrary to what many people believe, Sicilians are meat lovers.

VITELLO *(Veal)*

Involtini alla Benedettina

(Veal Rolls Stuffed with Ham)

*I*nvoltini alla Benedettina is our customers' favorite meat dish at Gangivecchio. When people call to make a reservation, many ask if it will be on the menu. (Our menus are set.) Of all the recipes in this book, aside from my beloved desserts, I hold Involtini alla Benedettina closest to my heart. I have never given anyone outside the family my recipe, and I resisted including it here, but Giovanna convinced me that our collection of Gangivecchio's family recipes would be incomplete without it. I suppose she is right, so I finally agreed. Then I want to change my mind again, like I did yesterday. After Sunday lunch in the restaurant that included my *involtini,* a Sicilian man who comes here often asked me again for the recipe. I told him that he must wait for the book. Then I warned him that it would be of no help to him, because the book is going to be published only in English. He said he would be happy to pay for a translator.

When you smell Involtini alla Benedettina cooking and then taste it, know that you are also in the kitchen and dining room here at Gangivecchio. Pay close attention to the cut of the veal and the directions for preparing the veal. —w.t.

Serves 6

Mix the stuffing ingredients together in a bowl.

Spread out the pieces of veal on a marble or other work area. At the widest end of the veal scallop, put a piece of ham. Place a rounded spoonful of the stuffing a little over an inch from the edge of the veal on top of the ham. Fold over the end piece of the veal with the stuffing and roll up snugly to the opposite end. Secure by sticking a toothpick through the loose end of the veal and through the center. Make the remaining *involtini* in the same manner.

Heat ⅓ cup of olive oil in a large frying pan and brown the veal

STUFFING

2 cups fresh bread crumbs (soaked in a little water for a few seconds and squeezed dry)

⅓ cup freshly chopped Italian parsley

1 small onion, finely chopped

4–6 thin slices boiled ham, cut lengthwise into 1½-inch-wide pieces

2 tablespoons canned Italian plum tomatoes, finely chopped and squeezed dry

18 thin veal scallops (about 2½ ounces each) (The veal must be cut from the thigh section of the leg and flattened very thin. There must be no breaks or holes in the meat, or the cheese in the stuffing will leak out. If the veal isn't flattened thin enough and if the muscle isn't broken down, the *involtini* won't be tender enough. Insist that the butcher cut and prepare the veal in this manner. Once you have taught him

the correct method, it will be more convenient for you to use the same butcher, so you won't have to explain repeatedly how you like the veal.)

Olive oil

Salt and freshly ground pepper

2 teaspoons dried rosemary

1 cup finely chopped onions

½ cup tomato paste

Flour

6 small fresh rosemary sprigs

rolls on all sides over medium-high heat. Cook them in batches, if necessary.

Transfer the veal to a large, heavy pot, season to taste with salt and pepper, add the dried rosemary, and toss gently.

In the same pan, combine the onions, tomato paste, and 1 cup of water, and simmer over low heat for 5 minutes. Pour the sauce over the *involtini* and then add enough water to almost cover the veal rolls. Sprinkle the tops of the rolls, which are sticking out of the water, lightly with flour and bring to a boil. Partially cover and cook over medium heat for about one hour, until the veal is very tender. After the first 15 minutes of cooking time, stir the *involtini* often to prevent any from sticking to the bottom of the pan—the flour will have dissolved and begun to thicken the sauce.

With tongs, transfer the cooked *involtini* to a dish, shaking any extra sauce back into the pot. Remove the toothpicks from the rolls. Arrange the *involtini* in rows or in a circle in a serving dish and spoon about 1 cup of sauce over the top. Garnish with rosemary sprigs. Pass the extra sauce in a bowl. Any remaining sauce is excellent on spaghetti for another meal, and it freezes well.

Falsomagro di Donna Giulia

(Giulia's Braised Stuffed Veal)

One 3-pound veal breast, cut open to within 1 inch of one side, butterfly style

1 tablespoon sweet butter, melted

1 large onion, thinly sliced

½ cup grated pecorino

¾ cup diced caciocavallo or provolone cheese

1 cup diced Napoli salami

3 hard-boiled eggs, cut crosswise into thin slices

*F*alsomagro means "false lean." No one can figure out exactly why this dish was given the strange name. Perhaps because there is a big stuffing and only a little meat in the portions served.

Serves 8

Open up the butterflied piece of veal on a countertop, skin side down. Brush the inside with the melted butter. Arrange the sliced onion over the surface, about 1 inch from the sides of the meat. Equally distribute the pecorino, caciocavallo or provolone cheese, salami, eggs, bread crumbs, and parsley over the top, and sprinkle with salt and pepper.

Carefully begin turning the veal over the stuffing into a roll we call *braciolone.* You can stick toothpicks into the seam to hold it together while you tie it up with string. Discard the toothpicks.

Heat the olive oil in an oval casserole pan just large enough to hold the veal. Brown the veal on all sides. Add the tomato sauce and ½ cup of hot water and bring to a boil. Reduce the heat, cover, and simmer for about 1½ hours until tender, turning the veal once in a while.

Transfer the veal to a platter and let cool for 15 minutes.

Remove the string and slice the meat into ½-inch slices. Serve with the heated sauce from the pan.

1½ cups toasted bread crumbs (page 121)
⅓ cup freshly chopped Italian parsley
Salt and freshly ground pepper
¼ cup olive oil
2 cups fresh tomato sauce (Salsa di Pomodoro, page 93)

Medaglioni di Vitello di Gangivecchio

(Gangivecchio's Veal Medallions Stuffed with Mortadella and Mozzarella)

Serves 6

Spread veal medallions onto a work surface. Place a slice of mortadella and a slice of mozzarella in the center of each. If the mortadella slice is larger than the piece of veal, trim off the extra mortadella.

Fold the stuffed veal medallion in half crosswise, carefully dip into the eggs, then coat with the bread crumbs.

Heat the butter and olive oil in a large frying pan and sauté the veal until golden brown on each side, adding a little extra butter and oil, in equal amounts, if necessary.

In summer, serve the veal with a tomato salad with oregano. In winter, serve with green beans and boiled potatoes.

12 veal medallions (about 2½ ounces each), flattened as directed on page 163
6 thin slices mortadella, cut into strips about 3 inches wide
6 thin slices mozzarella, cut in half lengthwise
2 large eggs, beaten and seasoned lightly with salt
Dried bread crumbs
2 tablespoons sweet butter, plus more as needed
2 tablespoons olive oil, plus more as needed

Cotoletta Siciliana

*(Sicilian-Style Veal Cutlets
with Tomatoes and Parsley)*

Serves 6

2 cups dried bread crumbs
⅓ cup freshly grated pecorino
    or Parmesan cheese
1 medium-sized ripe but firm
    fresh tomato, peeled and cut
    into small dice, with seeds
    and liquid squeezed out
½ cup freshly chopped Italian
    parsley
Salt and freshly ground pepper
2½ pounds veal cutlets, flat-
    tened (directions are on page
    163)
2 large eggs, lightly beaten with
    a pinch of salt
3 tablespoons sweet butter
3 tablespoons vegetable oil
1 large lemon, cut into 6 wedges
    and seeded

Mix together the bread crumbs with the pecorino or Parmesan cheese, tomato, and parsley. Season well with salt and pepper.

Dip the cutlets into the eggs and coat with the bread-crumb mixture, pressing it lightly onto both sides. Let rest for 10 minutes.

Heat the butter and vegetable oil in a large frying pan. Fry the cutlets over medium-low heat, a few at a time, until tender and golden brown on each side.

Garnish each cooked cutlet with a lemon wedge.

VARIATION: You can substitute boned, skinned, and flattened, chicken breasts for the veal cutlets in this recipe.

Spezzatino di Vitello

(Stewed Veal with Onions)

¾ cup olive oil
3½ pounds lean stewing veal,
    cut into 1-inch pieces
    (remove any gristle or excess
    fat)
1 large onion, chopped
Salt and freshly ground pepper
½ cup tomato paste
2 vegetable bouillon cubes
½ teaspoon sugar
2½ tablespoons flour

*I*n the early 1930s, in Palermo, when my sister, Mariuccia, and my brother, Dino, and I were children, to stay inside the house during the day in the winter meant to be silent or whisper. If we made noise of any kind or were disorderly, we were sent to our rooms. No one was allowed to speak at all during dinner, including my mother, because that is when my stepfather listened to symphonic music. His favorite symphony was Beethoven's Ninth, which he conducted while he ate. To get someone to pass the salt meant using hand signals.

When we had been very quiet and good, my mother, Elena, would reward us with one of our favorite dishes, Spezzatino di Vitello, to savor during one of the concerts.

This humble, robust stew represents our most simple style of cooking. The veal, onions, olive oil, and tomato paste are combined only with cool water, vegetables, a little sugar, and salt and pepper to taste. As the water heats up, it draws out the flavors of the ingredients, like in a soup. The addition of flour and a reduction of the water produce a thickened, nicely seasoned, creamy sauce. Each person will want a generous portion, I promise you. The recipe can be doubled to serve 8 to 10. —w.t.

Serves 4

Put the olive oil, veal, and onion into a large, heavy-bottomed saucepan. Sprinkle with salt and pepper, mix together, and turn the heat to high. Cook for 5 minutes, stirring often.

Add the tomato paste, vegetable bouillon cubes, and sugar, and mix very well. Pour enough cool water into the pan to almost cover the top of the veal. Bring the stew to a boil. Sprinkle the flour over the top of the veal. Immediately reduce the heat to a low simmer and cook, partially covered, for about 30 minutes without stirring. After 30 minutes, remove the cover, stir, and simmer uncovered for 1 hour, stirring occasionally.

Transfer the *spezzatino* to a warmed serving dish and serve with mashed potatoes. If you want to include a green vegetable, green peas cooked in butter with a little onion would be a good choice.

Spiedini di Vitello

(Veal Kebabs)

1½ cups freshly grated dried
    bread crumbs
Olive oil
1 large egg yolk
Salt and freshly ground pepper
¼ cup grated pecorino
¼ cup currants, soaked in hot
    water for 10 minutes and
    drained
¼ cup pine nuts
2 tablespoons freshly chopped
    Italian parsley
2½ pounds veal scallops, cut
    into very thin pieces about 2
    inches wide by 6 inches long
3 medium onions, quartered, or
    enough to make 24 pieces of
    onion
24 small bay leaves, or 12 large
    ones broken in half crosswise

*I*n the summertime all over Sicily, you can smell the aroma of meat kebabs, usually grilled over wood-burning fires.

Serves 6

Set out six 8-inch metal or wooden skewers. (If wooden, soak them in water for 30 minutes.)

Put the bread crumbs into a frying pan and turn on the heat. Sprinkle with about ¼ cup olive oil and stir. Add the egg yolk and season well with salt and pepper, stirring constantly, and cook until golden. The mixture should be nice and moist but not wet. Add a little more oil, if necessary. Transfer to a bowl and add the pecorino, currants, pine nuts, and parsley, and mix together well.

Spread the veal scallops out on a work surface. Spoon equal amounts of the stuffing across the center of each piece of veal, lightly patting it down. Roll up each.

Make all 18 kebabs in the following manner: Force a metal or dampened wooden skewer through the center of an onion slice, 1 bay leaf, and a veal roll. Repeat, in the same order, two more times. Add a bay leaf and an onion slice at the end. The ingredients must fit snugly together. Prepare the remaining kebabs.

Brush the kebabs with olive oil and cook over a preheated grill or under the broiler until tender and golden brown, about 5 minutes per side.

Serve the kebabs with Patate ad Insalata (page 254).

Lacerto

(Braised Veal with Puréed Vegetable Sauce)

Serves 8

½ cup olive oil
One 3-pound boneless veal
    roast, tied
2 tablespoons sweet butter
2 carrots, scraped and sliced
1 large red onion, chopped
1 large potato, cut into quarters
2 tablespoons fresh rosemary
Salt and freshly ground pepper
Flour

Heat the olive oil in a deep, oval casserole as close to the shape of the meat as possible. Brown the meat on all sides. Add the butter, vegetables, rosemary, and season well with salt and pepper. Add enough water to almost cover the top of the veal. Stir the mixture together and sprinkle the top of the veal with flour. Bring the water to a boil. Reduce the heat and simmer, partially covered, for 2 to 2½ hours, turning the meat occasionally after the first 15 minutes of cooking time.

Remove the meat and let it cool. Remove the strings and carve into thin slices and place on a warmed serving platter.

Pass the liquid and vegetables in the pan through a food mill. Reheat the sauce and taste for salt and pepper. Lacerto can be served hot or cold.

I Giorni del Mercato a Gangi: Passato e Presente

(Past and Present Market Days in Gangi)

Gangi is a majestic town of 8600 inhabitants, about two miles east of Gangivecchio over hilly terrain.

Because it is our habit to visit this pleasant village at least once a day to food-shop; collect the mail and the daily newspaper, *Giornale di Sicilia;* enjoy a gelato while strolling through the ancient, winding streets; or attend to any personal need or errand, we sometimes forget what a spectacular place it is. Built on Monte Marone, at an altitude of nearly 3500 feet, the old part of Gangi covers the entire top of this unique dome-shaped mountain. Newer buildings have spread out along the lower perimeter of the town, but they are modern and less interesting. Still, when approaching Gangi from any direction, as you curve around the turn of a hill, the old hill town appears out of nowhere like an apparition—a fantastical, symmetrical architectural confection.

An old street in Gangi is named via Tornabene, after my great-grandfather's brother, Gaetano, who was a doctor. Unfortunately, we don't know the circumstances under which this honor was bestowed upon him.

Every Tuesday, one of Gangi's streets is host to dozens of vendors and local farmers who come to set up shop on portable tables under umbrellas or awnings and offer foods and wares. Like any Sicilian street market, it is a confusion of merchandise from handbags, sweaters, dresses, coats, fabrics, shoes, jeans, and underwear to cooking equipment, toys, bird cages, planters, potted herbs, flowering plants, small trees, and seeds. Most important for us is the mobile butcher's fine selection of meat, and the fresh seasonal vegetables and fruit and cheeses. We have noticed during the last year that the produce selection has been growing smaller and smaller because there are fewer farmers. Even so, we never miss our weekly market.

This market, at its best, is a pale imitation of the old traditional, rustic street fairs of the past. Of these, the most extraordinary one was held every year on August 14. It was the important animal fair. My father used to tell us amazing stories about this event.

Imagine a commotion of horses, pigs, sheep, goats, cows, and mule caravans, all heading toward Gangi, accompanied by herdsmen, dogs, and sellers, who had begun their journey during the night or even a day before. These men came from all around the Madonie region to reach Gangi's large valley at dawn—weary and hungry, but excited.

The clamor was enormous. Wailing, screeching animals, with their bells clanging, were accompanied by the happy voices of men greeting friends they hadn't seen since last year's fair. There was the exchange of stories about life's good and bad fortunes, about births and deaths and scandals. Add to this the sounds of anticipated friendly quarrels over prices, then loud shouts and clapping of hands at the conclusion of a deal. There was the usual screaming at the aggressive attempt of a bull trying to escape. Then cheers of approval as animals mated—proof of healthy animals and an advance dividend for the buyer. Finally, everyone returned home, exhausted but with filled pockets—the same route for the men, different paths for the animals.

It was absolutely forbidden for women to attend this or any animal fair. It was commonly thought that women would be troubled by the animals' coupling. And a woman present during her time of the month would trouble the animals. Also, perhaps, it was an occasion for the men to free themselves for a day—husbands from wives and vice versa.

Filetto in Casseruola con Cognac

(Fillet of Veal Cooked in a Casserole with Cognac)

*M*amma created this recipe one day when she couldn't resist a beautiful fillet of veal displayed at the meat vendor's truck in the market in Gangi. The tenderloin of veal was so magnificent, she wanted to cook it in a very special manner. Someone had given her a bottle of Cognac as a gift, so she brought it out of her private cabinet to use in the recipe.

One 5-pound fillet of veal, tied up
4 small onions, peeled and left whole
⅓ cup freshly chopped rosemary
¼ cup olive oil
¼ cup Cognac
Salt and freshly ground pepper

Serves 8

Put the veal in a deep, oblong or oval casserole pan or dish with high sides (as close in shape to the configuration of the veal as possible—Mamma uses a treasured old oblong copper pan) and add all the other ingredients through the Cognac. Pour in enough cool water to barely cover the veal, cover the pan, and put it into a cold oven. Turn the temperature to 425°F. After 15 minutes, reduce the heat to 350°F. Cook for 10 minutes and season to taste with salt and pepper. Uncover and cook about 45 minutes more, or until the meat is tender, turning the veal again after 10 minutes.

Transfer the veal to a carving board.

Meanwhile, pass the liquid and ingredients in the pan through a food mill.

Carve the veal into thin slices and arrange them across a warmed serving platter. Spoon the puréed sauce around and on top of the veal.

Polpette alla Wanda

(Wanda's Veal and Pork Meatballs)

1 pound ground veal
1½ pounds ground pork
2 eggs
⅓ cup freshly chopped parsley
⅓ cup freshly grated pecorino
¾ cup day-old bread, soaked in
    water and squeezed dry
½ cup diced mortadella
⅓ cup diced ham
Olive oil
1 medium onion, finely
    chopped
⅓ cup tomato paste
½ teaspoon sugar
Salt and freshly ground pepper
Flour

*M*amma's excellent meatballs are delicious as a main course on their own, but these tender spheres of mixed ground veal and pork are very versatile: crushed and combined with a fresh tomato sauce, they are splendid over pasta. If you like spaghetti with tomato sauce and meatballs, make small balls the size of walnuts with the meat mixture and cook them in the same manner.

The *polpette* are also a vital ingredient in Anelletti al Forno (a fantastic Baked Timbale of Anelletti with Veal and Vegetables, page 132).

Serves 8

Mix together all the ingredients from the veal through the ham in a large bowl. (Using your hands is the easiest method.) Shape into 8 equal-sized balls and flatten slightly into oval shapes about 1½ inches thick.

Cover the bottom of a large frying pan with ¼ inch of olive oil and fry the ovals until well browned on each side. Transfer to a heavy pot.

Add the onion, tomato paste, sugar, and 1 cup of water to the same frying pan, stirring to release any tasty particles sticking to the bottom, and cook for about 5 minutes. Season to taste with salt and pepper.

Pour the sauce over the meatballs and add enough cold water to almost cover them. Sprinkle the tops of the meatballs lightly with flour. Cover and simmer over low heat for 1 hour.

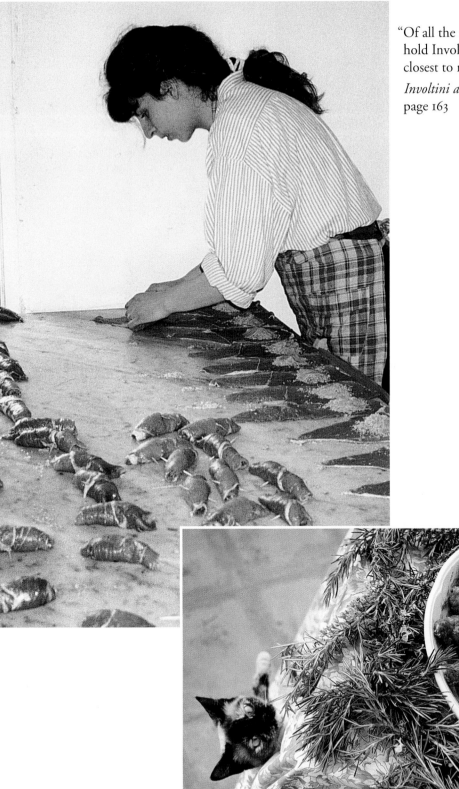

"Of all the recipes in this book, I hold Involtini alla Benedettina closest to my heart."

Involtini alla Benedettina,
page 163

"At Gangivecchio, our farmhand, Giovanni Salerno, is an expert cheesemaker. He creates superior caciocavallo, a mild but fragrant semisoft cheese made from cow's milk."

"Anna and Gaetano Mazzola,
a family of shepherds who live on
a small farm in the countryside
near Gangi, provide us with
superb sheep's cheese."

"Mamma's excellent meatballs are delicious as a main course or crushed and combined with tomato sauce over pasta."

Polpette alla Wanda, page 172

"Mamma created this recipe one day when she couldn't resist a beautiful fillet of veal displayed at the meat vendor's truck in the market in Gangi."

Filetto in Casseruola con Cognac, page 171

Carne ad Antipasto

(Veal and Pumpkin Stew)

My father's mother, Giovanna, invented this unusual dish, which, in consistency, is almost like a creamy veal and pumpkin risotto, but without the rice. (Rice goes very well with the stew, by the way.) No one in the family knows why Granny Giovanna called the dish antipasto, but we wanted to retain the name she gave to it in the old family recipe exercise book. —G.T.

Serves 4 to 6

1 tablespoon sweet butter
1 tablespoon olive oil
1 large onion, finely chopped
1½ cups fresh tomatoes, skinned and chopped
1¾ pounds ground veal
Salt and freshly ground pepper
1½ cups pumpkin, peeled and cubed

Heat the butter and olive oil in a large saucepan. Cook the onion over medium heat for 5 minutes, stirring often. Add the tomatoes and veal, season well with salt and pepper, and combine. Cook over low heat for 30 minutes.

Add the pumpkin and simmer for 20 minutes more, or until it is tender. Add a little water, if necessary.

Serve hot or cold.

Carne alle Cipolline alla Giovanna

(Giovanna's Veal Scallops Braised with Pearl Onions)

This was the first recipe Mamma's mother-in-law, Giovanna, taught her to cook at Gangivecchio. Mamma was surprised that it was so easy. Granny called the dish *carne* instead of veal because it could be made with veal, beef, pork, or chicken.

Serves 4

4 tablespoons sweet butter
2 tablespoons flour
Salt and freshly ground pepper
8 flattened veal scallops, about 2 ounces each
1 cup pearl onions, blanched, skinned, and left whole
Juice of 1 lemon
1 large egg yolk

Melt the butter in a saucepan over low heat. Whisk in the flour and season lightly with salt and pepper. Stirring constantly, cook until the color of honey. Whisk in a little water to thicken to a light cream consistency.

Add the veal and turn to coat evenly with the sauce. Stir in the onions and a little water, if necessary.

Cook over medium heat for about 30 minutes, until tender. Transfer the veal to a warmed serving dish.

Add the lemon juice and the egg yolk to the sauce in the pan and stir constantly over medium-low heat until the sauce has thickened. Season to taste with salt and pepper.

Spoon the sauce over the veal and serve.

Tritato alla Pizzaiola

*(Baked Chopped Veal Steaks
with Pizza Sauce)*

Serves 6

1 cup day-old crumbled bread
2¼ pounds ground veal
2 large eggs
½ cup freshly chopped Italian
    parsley
⅓ cup grated pecorino or
    Parmesan cheese
Salt and freshly ground pepper
1 cup diced tomatoes
Dried oregano
6 slices pecorino or provolone

Soak the bread in cold water for a few minutes until thoroughly moist. Squeeze out the water.

Put the bread, veal, eggs, parsley, and pecorino or Parmesan cheese into a large bowl. Season with salt and pepper and mix well.

Preheat the oven to 350°F.

Line a baking pan with aluminum foil and turn up the edges, making a little 1-inch collar.

Shape the veal mixture into 6 round steaks about 1½ inches thick. Place them on top of the foil, side by side, but not touching each other. Spread equal portions of the tomatoes on each steak, about a rounded tablespoonful placed across the center. Lightly sprinkle with salt, pepper, and oregano, and cover with a slice of cheese. Cook for 35 to 40 minutes, until done.

MAIALE *(Pork)*

Costolette di Maiale con Marsala, Aglio ed Erbe

Serves 4

(Pork Chops with Marsala, Garlic, and Herbs)

Preheat the oven to 350°F.

Lightly grease an ovenproof medium-sized frying pan with butter and put the chops in it.

Combine the herbs and garlic in a small bowl and season well with salt and pepper. Spread equal amounts over each chop and top each with ½ teaspoon butter. Pour the chicken stock or broth into the side of the pan and bake in the preheated oven for 30 minutes.

Remove the pan to a burner on top of the stove. Turn the heat to low and pour in the Marsala. Simmer for 5 minutes. Serve immediately.

Sweet butter
4 pork chops, 1 inch thick
1 teaspoon freshly chopped
    rosemary
4 fresh sage leaves, finely
    chopped
⅓ cup freshly chopped basil
2 garlic cloves, minced
Salt and freshly ground pepper
¾ cup chicken stock or broth,
    homemade or canned
½ cup Marsala wine

Costate di Maiale con Rosmarino e Vino

(Sautéed Pork Chops with Rosemary and Wine)

*A*n easier recipe for pork chops would be hard to find, but we think you will enjoy the combined flavors of the pork, white wine, and rosemary.

Serves 6

Season the pork chops well with salt and pepper.

Cover the bottom of a large frying pan with olive oil and heat the oil. Add the pork chops and sauté over low heat until golden brown on each side and thoroughly cooked, about 45 minutes.

6 loin pork chops, 1¼ inches
    thick, with the bones
Salt and freshly ground pepper
Olive oil
½ cup dry white wine
1 teaspoon freshly chopped
    rosemary

Transfer the chops to a warmed serving platter.

Add the wine and rosemary to the pan and bring to a boil, stirring. Cook for 3 minutes over high heat, stirring often. Taste for seasoning, then pour the mixture over the pork chops and serve immediately. Mashed potatoes and Zucchine Trifolate (Sautéed Baby Zucchini, page 224) go very well with the pork chops.

Salsiccia con Patate e Pomodori di Paolo

*(Paolo's Baked Pork Sausages
with Potatoes and Tomatoes)*

1½ pounds sweet Italian
    sausages, cut into 2-inch
    lengths
3 bell peppers—1 yellow, 1 red,
    and 1 green, seeded and cut
    into thin strips
1 large onion, thinly sliced
1½ pounds baking potatoes,
    peeled and cut into ¼-inch-
    thick slices
Salt and freshly ground pepper
⅓ cup olive oil
1¾ cups fresh peeled or canned
    tomatoes, chopped
1 cup cubed pecorino or pro-
    volone
⅓ cup freshly chopped Italian
    oregano
Crusty Italian bread

At home, we call this dish *pitanzedda* in Sicilian. In Italian, a main course or dish is called *pietanza*. This word comes from Latin *pietas,* meaning "compassion." In the mountains of Sicily people gave food out of compassion, so *pitanzedda* means "a little compassion."

Paolo invented this wonderful sausage dish, which includes potatoes, one of his favorite foods.

Serves 6

Put the ingredients from the sausages through the potatoes into an oiled baking dish or pan. Season well with salt and pepper, and drizzle with the olive oil.

Turn the oven on to 350°F and cook for 40 minutes, stirring occasionally.

Add the tomatoes, pecorino or provolone, and parsley, stir, and cook for about 10 minutes. Serve hot with bread.

Iudisco al Latte

(Pork Loin Braised in Milk)

This is not an old Madonie recipe, but a truly delicious dish that my mother and our neighbor Santina like to cook. They are always competing over who makes the best milk-braised pork. Both are excellent, but naturally I prefer Mamma's.

Serves 6 to 8

One 4-pound boneless loin of
  pork, tied
3 garlic cloves, quartered
½ cup olive oil
1 quart milk, heated to scalding
1 tablespoon chopped fresh
  rosemary
Salt and freshly ground pepper

Make 1-inch-deep incisions in the pork in about 16 places at various distances apart, and insert a piece of garlic into each.

Heat the olive oil in a deep, oval or round, heavy casserole pan as close to the shape of the roast as possible. Add the pork and brown it on all sides over high heat.

Off the heat, stir in the hot milk, a little at a time. Add the rosemary and season lightly with salt and pepper. Bring the milk to a boil and immediately reduce the heat to medium-low. Partially cover the pot and cook for about 2 to 2½ hours, stirring often and turning the roast every 30 minutes.

As the milk evaporates, little pieces of coagulated milk form on the bottom of the pan and begin to turn golden. These crumbly pieces are delicious and are always served with the pork. Depending on the amount of fat on the pork, you will need to spoon some off, especially toward the end of the cooking time.

When the pork is done, transfer to a cutting board, discard the string, and let rest for 10 minutes. Carve the pork into thin slices and place on a warmed serving platter with the little browned pieces from the pan.

Formaggi Locali e il Caciocavallo di Gangivecchio

(Gangivecchio's Caciocavallo and Local Cheese Production)

Since the Madonie Mountain region is renowned for its rich soil and sweet grazing pastures, our cheese production is highly esteemed. Cow's and sheep's milk provide the nectar for a small but delectable variety of cheeses.

At Gangivecchio, our farmhand, Giovanni Salerno, is an expert cheesemaker. He creates superior caciocavallo, a mild but fragrant semisoft cheese made from cow's milk. The method is uncomplicated yet precise, time-consuming, and strenuous work. The end product is formed into a pear-shaped gourd with a knot fashioned at the top. Giovanni smokes a small amount of caciocavallo because some Sicilians appreciate the taste. We use caciocavallo at home, in the restaurants, and we also sell it to our guests.

Anna and Gaetano Mazzola, a family of shepherds who live on a small farm in the countryside near Gangi, provide us with superb sheep's cheese. They continue a long family tradition of sheep raising and cheese production that has remained untouched by modern methods. Unfortunately, their son is not interested in carrying on this noble tradition, preferring a career in town. We often worry about who will make these beautiful fresh cheeses in the coming decades.

Gaetano tends the sheep with his dog, taking them to the pasture every day of the year, rain or shine, his weathered face reflecting a life spent outdoors. Anna is the cheese artisan, practicing her craft of extracting what the shepherd's call "*il frutto*" (the fruit) of the milk.

Anna's studio is a tiny, cramped dark room, with a single bare light bulb hanging from the low ceiling. Dressed in black, Anna stands for hours every day, tirelessly stirring the milk with a long paddle, her back a permanent curve that arches over the simmering copper pot set over a gas burner a few inches off the floor. She is accompanied by her well-nourished cat, who gazes lovingly at her, waiting for the inevitable ladle of warm milk, curds, or whey to be tossed into the cracked plate on the floor. Anna always whispers silent words to the milk as she stirs.

The first cheese produced from the sheep's milk is called *tuma*, a soft, supple, and rather bland unsalted cheese, with a subtle but decidedly earthy flavor. *Tuma* is pressed into various sizes of plastic or woven-reed basket strainers (called *fascedda* in

Sicilian). After a day or two, the *tuma* is salted and the next stage is *primo sale* (which means "first salting"). Aged for three months more and salted again, it turns into pecorino, which begins its life as a semisoft cheese that ages into a hard stage for grating. The taste develops from subtle *tuma* into a full-flavored, strong, aromatic pecorino grating cheese. Sometimes peppercorns are added to pecorino for a *piccante* cheese.

Ricotta (which means "recooked") is made from the whey that is left over from the *tuma* production. Its liquid simmers in the caldron until the ricotta forms at the surface. Anna ladles the ricotta into the basket strainers, where it drains briefly in a sloping wooden tray. When the cheesemaking process is finished, Anna makes the sign of the cross. Aged ricotta becomes ricotta salata, which also passes through stages from semisoft to grating quality.

Anna's ricotta is at its absolute best in the spring, when the Mazzolas' sheep enjoy a diet of rich greens. When we bring fresh ricotta home, we unmold the soft cheese, then cut it into slices with a string and eat it with bread—a fantastic treat. Of course, this is the time of the year when we make hundreds and hundreds of Mamma's Cannoli (page 281).

Agnello della Nonna Giovanna

(Grandmother Giovanna's Lamb Stew with Rosemary and Red Wine)

Serves 6

3 tablespoons olive oil
One 4-pound lamb shank and
    shoulder, cut into 1½-inch
    pieces, lightly salted
1 large onion, finely chopped
1 cup dry red wine
1 tablespoon finely chopped
    rosemary
Salt and freshly ground pepper

Heat the olive oil in a large frying pan and brown the lamb in batches over medium high heat. Transfer to a heavy casserole.

Add the onion to the frying pan and cook for 5 minutes, stirring often. Stir in the red wine and bring to a boil. Pour the onion-and-wine mixture over the lamb and sprinkle with rosemary. Add 1 cup of water, stir, and cover. Season with salt and pepper. Cook over medium-low heat for 1 hour, stirring occasionally. As the water evaporates, add ½ cup water at a time, as needed.

Serve the stew with boiled new potatoes tossed in butter.

Fricassea di Agnello di Bruna

(Bruna's Lamb Fricassee au Gratin)

1 cup olive oil
1¼ pounds onions, chopped,
    plus 1 small onion
3½ pounds lamb shoulder, cut
    into 1½-inch pieces
½ cup dry red wine
1½ cups green peas
Salt and freshly ground pepper
2 large eggs
⅔ cup freshly grated pecorino

Betty's mother, Bruna, gave us this unusual and beautiful lamb recipe. Guests like it so much that we often include it in our wedding party menus.

Serves 6

Heat the olive oil in a large frying pan and add the onions. Cook over medium heat for 5 minutes, stirring often. Add the lamb, red wine, and water to barely cover the lamb, and simmer for one hour or until very tender, stirring occasionally.

Meanwhile, in a small saucepan, cover the peas and the small onion with water and bring to a boil. Season lightly with salt and pepper. Cook about 8 minutes, until done. Discard the onion.

Preheat the oven to 350°F.

Beat the eggs in a bowl with a pinch of salt. Add the pecorino and parsley and let rest.

Drain the peas and add the lamb pieces, reserving the liquid the lamb is cooked in. Transfer the combined peas and lamb to an au gratin dish. Add 2 cups of the lamb-cooking liquid to the dish. Pour the egg-and-cheese mixture over the top. Bake in the preheated oven for 20 minutes. Serve with cooked and cooled green beans dressed like a salad, with oil and vinegar and seasoned with salt and pepper.

Interiora d'Agnello

(Lamb Kidneys Braised in Red Wine Sauce)

Serves 6

Heat the olive oil in a heavy saucepan. Add the onion and lamb kidneys, and season well with salt and pepper. Cook over high heat until the kidneys are almost sticking to the bottom of the pan, stirring often.

Pour the red wine into the pan, and cook for a few minutes until the liquid has almost evaporated. Stir in the tomato paste and sugar, and cook for 5 minutes. Add ½ cup of water or a little more—just enough for a small amount of sauce—stir, and simmer, covered, for about 20 minutes, or just until the kidneys are tender.

Two minutes before removing the lamb from the heat, sprinkle with parsley and stir. Serve with grilled or toasted bread slices.

VARIATION: The dish can also be puréed in a food processor and served as a pâté.

½ cup freshly chopped Italian parsley

½ cup olive oil
1 medium onion, chopped
2¼ pounds lamb kidneys, cleaned and diced
Salt and freshly ground pepper
⅓ cup dry red wine
1 teaspoon tomato paste
¼ teaspoon sugar
⅓ cup freshly chopped Italian parsley
Grilled or toasted Italian bread slices

Un Principe Viene a Pranzo a Gangivecchio

(A Prince Comes to Lunch at Gangivecchio)

It's not every day that we have the company of a royal highness, and some friends of ours, Marquise Anna Lanza and Barone Giovanni Carpinello, were bringing Prince Charles for lunch. So you can imagine what occurred in our household: people running around cleaning all spaces, like the drawing room, even the stables. Suddenly we realized that none of us had anything proper to wear, and on and on.

One of the biggest decisions to be made was selecting the right place to eat: On the terrace? It might be too hot. In our home dining room? The table is too small. In the restaurant? Too big. In the end, we decided that the spacious dining room off the main restaurant dining room was perfect.

The most important issue for us, of course, was the menu. Our friends hosting the Prince notified us in advance that he preferred light foods, no pasta, and not too many courses. Anna Lanza suggested chicken.

Mamma planned a menu of roast chicken flavored with onions and rosemary (recipe on page 184), beautiful fresh fava beans, Panzerotti con Ricotta (page 40), green salad, strawberry tart, Cannoli (page 281), and Sofficini (page 294).

On May 5, 1990, at precisely 12:30 p.m., the entourage arrived: our friends, the Prince, and his bodyguards—a party of twelve.

We were all standing and talking together in Gangivecchio's large courtyard when Prince Charles remarked what a pity it was that we couldn't dine right there in the outdoors—the one location we had not considered. But his wish was our command. Giovanni, Peppe, and Lucia scurried away to bring the tables and tablecloths and chairs, plates, cutlery, and glasses down into the courtyard. Mamma and I were concerned about threatening clouds, but nevertheless the meal began. Just as the main course was served, it began to sprinkle. Everyone, including Prince Charles, stood with their plate and began picking up chairs and moving swiftly to the stairway entranceway to the restaurant. Giovanni ran to help the Prince and began tugging at the chair he was holding and trying to take his plate away. "No, no," Prince Charles insisted, and he proceeded to carry his own things upstairs.

To our great relief, everyone ate happily and heartily, and dessert was about to be served when Lucia drew me aside, whispering excitedly into my ear, "What an appetite Principe Carlo has. He is still hungry and wants another bird. He just asked me for a *canarino* [canary]." What he had ordered, instead of tea or coffee, was hot water with lemon, an infusion called a *canarino,* which Lucia had never heard of before. She will never forget what a *canarino* is, and we will never forget the Prince's visit, which had turned into a beautiful day without protocol.

Prince Charles struck us as a very kind, friendly man. He was curious about our life in the countryside, our restaurant, our work on the farm, and our animals. To Mamma and me, he seemed a very thoughtful man, a man in touch with nature.

We thanked Marquise Lanza and Barone Carpinello for selecting Gangivecchio. And we thanked Gangivecchio for being so beautiful.

POLLO *(Chicken)*

Polletti Arrosto al Rosmarino

(Roast Baby Chickens with Rosemary)

6 Cornish game hens, butterflied with backbones cut
   away and spread open, and
   wings tucked back
Salt and freshly ground pepper
3 medium onions, halved across
   the stem end and top, and
   cut into slivers
2 tablespoons freshly snipped
   rosemary, plus 3 or 4 sprigs
   for garnish
⅔ cup olive oil

*H*ere is the recipe for the roast chicken Mamma prepared for Prince Charles's lunch at Gangivecchio. Uncomplicated as it is, it has become a favorite and, for us, something we serve just for special occasions.

The combined flavors of the chicken, onions, rosemary, and olive oil roasting together release delicious aromas in the kitchen— fragrances that sneak out into the hallways, often reaching as far as the dining room. Whenever Lucia, who always walks in a big hurry, as if she is on her way to extinguishing a fire, smells the chicken cooking, she pauses briefly and, raising her eyebrows knowingly, says, *"Ah, i polletti alla Principe Carlo."* We think it tastes even better than it smells.

At Gangivecchio, small local chickens are used in the recipe, but Mamma tested the recipe when we were in the United States with Cornish game hens, and she was very satisfied with the result. —G.T.

Serves 6 to 8

Preheat the oven to 350°F.

Season the hens with salt and pepper on both sides and arrange them in a large roasting pan, skin side down, in a single layer. The hens should fit snugly together, covering the bottom surface of the pan, or the onions will burn. Sprinkle with the onions and rosemary and drizzle with olive oil. Turn them over and spoon the oil-and-onion mixture over the tops. Cover loosely and refrigerate for 3 hours. Bring back to room temperature before cooking them.

Place the hens in the preheated oven and bake them, skin side up, with some of the onions and rosemary on top, for 50 minutes to 1 hour, or until tender, basting once midway through the cooking time. If necessary, pass briefly under the broiler so that the top is golden brown.

Remove the hens from the oven and transfer to a warm serving platter. Or, if you like, you can cut the hens in half through the breastbones, and arrange the halves in a circle in rows on the platter. This method makes a nice presentation, and many people like only small portions of meat these days. Season the hens lightly with salt and freshly ground pepper. Spoon any onions left in the pan around the hens and garnish with the fresh rosemary sprigs. Serve immediately.

Pollo alla Tornabene

Serves 6

(Baked Chicken Legs and Thighs with Tomatoes and Onions)

Heat the vegetable oil in a frying pan and brown the chicken well on each side over high heat. Transfer to a shallow baking dish, skin side down. Season with salt and pepper.

In a clean frying pan, heat the olive oil and cook the combined onion, tomatoes, sugar, and cayenne pepper, if you like, over high heat for 5 minutes, stirring often.

Spoon the sauce over the chicken and sprinkle with the parsley.

Put into a cold oven on the lower shelf and turn the heat on to 350°F. Cook for 45 minutes.

⅓ cup vegetable oil
6 chicken leg and thigh pieces, left intact
Salt and freshly ground pepper
¼ cup olive oil
1 medium onion, chopped
3 cups fresh or canned tomatoes, peeled and chopped
½ teaspoon sugar
Pinch of cayenne pepper (optional)
⅓ cup fresh Italian parsley, finely chopped

Scaloppine di Pollo con Spinaci

*(Sautéed Chicken Breasts
with Spinach)*

Serves 4

4 chicken breasts, boned,
    skinned, halved, and flat-
    tened
Olive oil
Salt and freshly ground pepper
Flour
5 tablespoons sweet butter
1½ tablespoons freshly chopped
    Italian parsley
Juice of ½ lemon
2 pounds fresh young spinach,
    washed and stemmed
2 tablespoons freshly grated
    Parmesan cheese

Place the chicken in a glass bowl and sprinkle lightly with olive oil, salt, and pepper. Turn so that each piece is flavored. Cover and refrigerate for 2 hours.

Pat the chicken pieces dry and coat with flour, shaking off any excess flour, and let rest for 5 minutes.

Heat 3 tablespoons of the butter with ½ cup olive oil in a frying pan. Add the chicken and season with salt and pepper. Cook until tender and golden brown on both sides, in batches, if necessary.

Transfer the chicken to a shallow baking dish, sprinkle with the parsley and lemon juice, and keep warm in a 300°F oven while you prepare the spinach.

Bring 1 cup of water to a boil in a large saucepan and add the spinach. Stir for about 2 minutes until wilted, then drain well.

In the pan the chicken cooked in, heat the remaining 2 table-spoons of butter and add the drained spinach. Toss and season to taste with salt and pepper. Sprinkle the spinach with the Parmesan cheese and mix thoroughly over low heat for 2 minutes.

Transfer the chicken to a serving platter and spoon the spinach around the chicken and serve at once.

Pollo della Nonna Elena

*(Grandmother Elena's Braised
Chicken with Potatoes)*

Serves 4

One 3½-pound chicken, quar-
    tered
1 herb bouquet (1 bay leaf, 4
    sprigs Italian parsley, and
    1 small branch rosemary tied
    together with string)

Cover the chicken quarters and herb bouquet with water in a large, heavy saucepan, and cook over medium heat for 20 minutes. Transfer the chicken to a plate, discard the bouquet of herbs, and strain the chicken broth and reserve it.

In a large saucepan, heat the olive oil with the onion and pota-toes, and season with salt and pepper. Cook over medium heat for 15 minutes, turning once halfway through cooking time. Add a lit-tle extra oil, if necessary. Turn the potatoes again, and add the chicken quarters (skinned, if desired) and ½ cup of the hot chicken broth. Gently combine the ingredients. Cook for 15 minutes. Taste for seasoning.

Transfer to a serving dish and sprinkle with the parsley.

⅓ cup olive oil, or as needed
1 medium onion, chopped
1½ pounds boiling potatoes, peeled and cubed
Salt and freshly ground pepper
½ cup freshly chopped Italian parsley

Involtini del Monastero

(Chicken Breasts Stuffed with Smoked Pancetta and Caciocavallo)

Serves 6

Put the chicken breasts on a work surface. Top each with a slice of pancetta and a slice of cheese. Roll up each breast.

On each of 6 metal or water-soaked 8-inch wooden skewers, place a chicken roll—skewered through the center—a slice of onion, and a piece of orange peel. Repeat with a chicken roll, slice of onion, and a piece of orange peel. Prepare the remaining 5 kebabs in the same manner.

Brush the kebabs liberally with olive oil and season with salt and pepper. Cook on a grilling pan under the broiler or on a grill, about 10 minutes on each side.

Serve with Insalata di Arance (Orange Salad with Black Olives, page 253).

6 large chicken breasts, skinned, boned, and halved and flattened
12 slices smoked pancetta
12 small slices caciocavallo or provolone cheese
2 medium onions, quartered
Peel of 1 orange, cut into 1 × 1½-inch pieces
Olive oil
Salt and freshly ground pepper

Lesso Misto

*(Turkey and Mixed Meat
Casserole with Vegetables)*

4½ pounds turkey legs, skinned
   and cut into several pieces
   each
1½ pounds veal, cubed
1½ pounds pork, cubed
3 large boiling potatoes, peeled
   and sliced
2 large onions, thinly sliced
1¼ pounds carrots, scraped and
   sliced
4 each, chicken legs and thighs
3 large tomatoes, peeled and
   chopped
Salt and freshly ground pepper
Salsa Verde (optional)

½ cup finely chopped Italian
   parsley
⅓ cup capers
4 anchovy fillets
3 large Sicilian green olives, or 6
   other oil-cured green olives
1½ cups olive oil, or as needed
Salt and freshly ground pepper

*L*esso Misto means "mixed boiled meats." It used to be prepared just in the winter to warm us up—it's delicious eaten hot with broth and croutons. Add some rice to the broth and you have a delicious soup. We serve it chilled now in the summertime, too, with Salsa Verde (recipe follows).

Serves 12

Put the turkey and all the ingredients through the carrots into a large pot, cover with water, and bring to a boil. Skim the top. Lower the heat and simmer for 1 hour. Add the chicken and tomatoes and cook 1 hour more. Remove the veal, pork, and chicken when tender. Add a little extra water, if needed.

When the turkey is cooked, return the veal, pork, and chicken to the pot, and season to taste with salt and pepper.

Transfer the meat to a large, shallow bowl with the other meat. Remove the skin from the chicken legs and thighs. Transfer the vegetables to another bowl and mash into a purée.

The meat and vegetables and broth can be served separately or combined in individual bowls.

Salsa Verde

Salsa Verde is traditionally served with boiled meats. It's delicious with Lesso Misto any time of the year. So it's up to you.

Makes about 2 cups

Put the parsley, capers, anchovies, olives, and ½ cup of the olive oil into the bowl of a food processor or blender. Turn on and add the remaining oil in a slow, steady stream through the lid opening. Season to taste with salt and pepper. The consistency should be thick and creamy. Add a little more oil, if necessary.

CONIGLIO *(Rabbit)*

Coniglio di Santina

(Santina's Stewed Rabbit)

Santina Consolo is a friend and neighbor who is famous for the terrific dinners she cooks. No one eats for three days before dining at the Consolos'. Santina and her husband, Luciano, are both extremely serious about their meals and food. Luciano is a lawyer by profession, so conversation at the dinner table always centers on a trial he is working on. Throughout dinner he and Santina debate back and forth about some fine points of the trial or personalities involved, as if no one else was present, but no one minds, because everyone is happily eating one of Santina's meals. Luciano makes a beautiful sweet wine called *sordo*, which he always generously serves at the end of dinner.

1 rabbit (wild, if possible), cut into 8 serving pieces
Salt
2 tablespoons red wine vinegar
½ cup olive oil
1 medium onion, chopped
2 tablespoons tomato paste
Freshly ground pepper
1 tablespoon freshly chopped Italian parsley

Serves 4

Season the rabbit pieces well with salt and put them into a bowl and cover with hot (not boiling) water. Add 2 tablespoons of vinegar and let rest for 5 minutes.

Heat the olive oil in a frying pan and stir in the onion, tomato paste, and ¼ cup of water. Mix this well. Add the drained rabbit and season well with salt and pepper. Turn and cook over low heat for 15 minutes. Turn the rabbit again and cook until tender, about another 15 minutes. Sprinkle with the parsley and serve.

Coniglio con Olive e Capperi

(Sautéed Rabbit with Olives and Capers)

½ cup olive oil
One 3½-pound rabbit, cut into
    serving pieces
½ cup pitted green olives, sliced
½ cup capers, drained
⅓ cup diced celery
Salt and freshly ground pepper
⅓ cup red wine vinegar

*T*his recipe is really a *cacciatore* ("hunter" in Italian) style dish that is sautéed and braised—the most common method of cooking rabbit. The rabbit in both our recipes can be replaced with chicken.

Serves 4

Heat the oil in a large frying pan and brown the rabbit over medium-high heat on each side. Transfer to a side dish.

Stir together the olives, capers, and celery in the same pan, and season with salt and pepper. Simmer over low heat for 15 minutes, stirring occasionally.

Return the rabbit to the pan and spoon some of the sauce over the top of each piece. Add vinegar and 1 cup of water, and bring to a boil. Reduce the heat and simmer for 30 minutes, turning the rabbit halfway through cooking time. We like the rabbit served with mashed potatoes.

Secondi di Pesce e Frutti di Mare

(Fish and Seafood Main-Course Dishes)

Ruota di Pesce Spada al Forno di Ginevra (*Ginevra's Roasted Round Swordfish Steak*) • Pesce Spada alla Ghiotta di Lisa (*Lisa's Swordfish with Piquant Tomato Sauce with Capers and Black Olives*) • Involtini di Pesce Spada (*Grilled or Baked Stuffed Swordfish Rolls*) • Pesce Spada alla Griglia in Due Maniere (*Grilled Swordfish—Two Ways*) • Pesce Spada in Umido (*Steamed Swordfish with Oregano and Garlic*) • L'ANIMA URLANTE DELLA VECCHIA PALERMO—LA VUCCIRIA (*The Screaming Soul of Old Palermo—La Vucciria*) • Ragù di Tonno di Maria-Angela (*Maria-Angela's Tuna Ragù with Fresh Tomato Sauce and Mint*) • Tonno con la Cipolla (*Cold Fried Tuna Marinated in Onion, Mint, and Vinegar Sauce*) • Cunigghiu di Lina (*Lina's Vegetable Stew with Salt Cod and Tuna*) • SARDE (*Sardines*) • Cernia al Forno (*Baked Grouper*) • Sarde Imbottite di Tanino (*Tanino's Sardines Stuffed with Fresh Bread and Cheese*) • Sarde a Beccafico (*Baked Sardines Stuffed with Pine Nuts and Currants*) • Sarde per Augusto (*Roasted Sardines with Garlic and Oregano*) • Baccalà (*Baked Salt Cod*) • Filetti di Baccalà all'Arancia (*Fillet of Salt Cod with Oranges and Black Olives*) • Fritto Misto (*Mixed Fried Seafood*) • Scampi Gratinati di Betty (*Betty's Stuffed Shrimp au Gratin*) • Cozze Gratinate (*Mussels au Gratin*) • ACCIUGHE (*Anchovies*) • Calamari Ripieni alla Siciliana (*Sicilian-Style Stuffed Squid*)

The island of Sicily, surrounded by three great seas—the Mediterranean, the Ionian, and the Tyrrhenian—is blessed with a splendid variety and abundance of fish and seafood delicacies. Of course, people residing in coastal areas enjoy the benefits most.

Living in the mountain countryside of the interior often deprives us of the great pleasure of eating fresh fish and seafood. In the neighboring town of Gangi, only a small quantity and a limited selection of fresh fish arrive at the little market. A recent new source has been provided by a seafood seller who makes several weekly stops at Gangi in a mobile van. We feel very unlucky if we happen to miss his brief visits.

We are seventy miles from the sparkling fish stalls of Palermo at La Vucciria market, where, depending on the time of the year, we can buy an incredible assortment of the freshest possible fish and seafood. There are said to be over 200 kinds, including delicate sea urchins, crayfish, mussels, crabs, clams, snails, and octopus ranging in size from 2-inch-long babies to giant adults. We have superb swordfish, tuna, sturgeon, pike, grouper, skate, bream, turbot, red mullet, scorpion fish, eels, sardines, anchovies, and herring. Tiny fish, which we only know as *cicireddu* in Sicilian dialect, are dusted with flour, deep-fried, and eaten whole. Of course, each Sicilian seaport city or village has lively, bountiful fish markets and restaurants, especially in the vicinities of Messina, on the northeastern tip of the coast, where swordfish is caught in the Messina Strait; and from there going south to Taormina, Catania, and Siracusa. On the northwest coast, Trapani is famous for its extraordinary tuna. (Read more about fish and seafood in the information box on La Vucciria on page 202.)

My mother would rather browse and shop in a fish market than a jewelry store. "These are life's true gems, and with prices to match," she likes to say. Her preferred fish is swordfish, but it has a very steep price. For a long time swordfish was known as a fish of the rich. It is a pity that so delicious and healthy a food can't be on every table. When my mother has an urge to splurge on something, she usually buys fish. If good-quality fresh swordfish appears at the fishmonger's or by van in Gangi, my mother purchases an enormous quantity and cooks it all immediately to satisfy her craving. She eats so much she usually becomes ill. But most of the time she must wait for visits to Palermo, where we always dine at our favorite seafood restaurant, La Trattoria Cambusa. At Cambusa, Mamma knows we will have the freshest and best grilled swordfish available, which fortunately is served in reasonable portions.

At landlocked Gangivecchio, most of the time, we must satisfy ourselves with more humble fish, such as sardines, mackerel, anchovies, salt cod, and canned or preserved tuna fish (page 69). These are fish whose flavors we also admire, so we have learned to prepare them in some very tasty dishes.

We normally serve fresh fish only in our family dining room at home

because it is rare for guests in the restaurant to want or ask for it. Sicilians are always suspicious when fresh fish is offered anywhere in the countryside. Regardless of how fresh it is, they are convinced that it's been frozen.

Our recipes include a stupendous swordfish dish—a 2-inch-thick cross-section of swordfish steak, flavored with olive oil, lemon juice, and oregano, roasted on bay leaves, and crowned with a golden bread-crumb topping. This is an impressive dish for a dinner party for an important celebration (the recipe appears on page 196). But we warn you in advance to just close your eyes and hand the fishmonger your wallet.

Also, here are our versions of several Sicilian fish classics like Sarde a Beccafico (Baked Sardines Stuffed with Pine Nuts and Currants, page 208) and Ragù di Tonno di Maria-Angela (a savory tuna fish ragout, page 204). Other wonderful fish and seafood recipes can be found in the Antipasti and Pasta chapters, and the Pesce in Brodo con Pasta (page 86) among the Minestre recipes.

Ruota di Pesce Spada al Forno di Ginevra

*(Ginevra's Roasted Round
Swordfish Steak)*

One 5-pound cross-section slice
    swordfish, 2 inches thick,
    10–11 inches in diameter,
    cut from the tail end of a
    large fish, just below the cav-
    ity opening
Olive oil
12 bay leaves
Juice of 1 lemon, plus 2 lemons,
    cut into wedges and seeded
Salt and freshly ground pepper
Dried bread crumbs
1 teaspoon chopped dried
    oregano

*I*n Sicily, we have superb swordfish, most of which comes from the Strait of Messina. In the realm of fish, swordfish reigns supreme.

Ginevra Carapezza gave a dinner party for us and Michele one fall evening in her lovely home on a high floor in an apartment building in a residential neighborhood on the fringe of Palermo. As a main course, she presented this spectacular swordfish dish, surrounded with cooked green beans and boiled potatoes. For a first course, we had a pasta timbale and, for dessert, creamy rice pudding with chocolate sauce, followed by fresh figs that we had brought from Gangivecchio. Ginevra's son, Marco, poured small glasses of Moscato di Pantelleria. Just as we finished dinner, fireworks exploded over Palermo's harbor, which everyone attending thought an appropriate finale to Ginevra's beautiful meal.

The magnificent swordfish is remarkably easy to make and perfect for a special dinner party for 8 to 10.

We normally serve just lemon wedges with portions of the swordfish. However, when there is any leftover fish, the next day we make a sauce called Salmorigano to spoon over the chilled fish (recipe follows).

Serves 8 to 10

You will have to specially order the swordfish from your fishmonger. Be sure to leave the skin on.

Preheat the oven to 450°F.

Brush the bottom of a large, shallow baking dish, round if possible, with olive oil. Place the bay leaves in the bottom of the dish in a 10-inch circle. Put the swordfish steak on top of the bay leaves.

Alternately, lightly sprinkle olive oil and lemon juice over the surface of the fish, while piercing deep into the flesh across the top of the fish with the tines of a fork, making about 20 incisions.

Lightly sprinkle the top of the fish with salt and pepper, bread crumbs, and the oregano, and drizzle again with olive oil.

Roast the fish in the preheated oven for 10 minutes. Reduce

the heat to 350°F and cook for about 30 minutes, or until the fish is done. Remove and let the swordfish rest 10 minutes.

Transfer the fish with 3 or 4 large spatulas—two people are usually required for this task—to a warmed serving platter, round if possible. Surround the fish with cooked green beans and small boiled potatoes tossed in butter and Italian parsley, if desired. Cut the fish into wedges. Serve with the lemon wedges.

Salmorigano

*T*his simple sauce also tastes good with roasted chicken or veal.

Makes about 1½ cups

Off the heat, combine ½ cup of lukewarm water and ½ cup of the olive oil in a small saucepan. Whisk in the lemon juice, parsley, garlic, and oregano, and season to taste with salt and pepper. Cook over medium heat for 5 minutes, stirring often, without letting the sauce boil.

1 cup olive oil
⅓ cup freshly squeezed lemon juice, or to taste
⅓ cup finely chopped Italian parsley
2 garlic cloves, minced
1½ teaspoons dried oregano
Salt and freshly ground pepper

Pesce Spada alla Ghiotta di Lisa

*(Lisa's Swordfish with
Piquant Tomato Sauce with
Capers and Green Olives)*

5 garlic cloves, chopped
2 tablespoons chopped Italian
   parsley, plus extra for garnish
1 cup fresh tomatoes, peeled
   and diced
¼ cup diced celery hearts
1 medium onion, minced
1 cup tomato sauce (Salsa di
   Pomodoro, page 93)
¼ cup capers
¾ cup green olives, pitted and
   halved
½ cup olive oil
Salt and freshly ground pepper
2 pounds swordfish steaks, ¾
   inch thick, cut into bite-size
   pieces

*G*hiotto in Italian means "appetizing," which appropriately describes this traditional Sicilian dish from Messina.

Serves 6

Put all the ingredients except the swordfish into a large frying pan and cook over medium heat for 10 minutes, stirring often.

Season to taste with salt and pepper. Add the fish, partially cover the pan, and simmer for 15 minutes, or until the fish is cooked. Serve hot.

NOTE: The sauce is excellent served over pasta, especially spaghetti or penne. Small diced potatoes can be added to the dish with the other ingredients in the first step of the recipe.

Involtini di Pesce Spada

Serves 4

(Grilled or Baked Stuffed Swordfish Rolls)

If grilling the swordfish *involtini,* use small metal skewers or soak eight 8-inch wooden skewers in water, and heat up the grill. (The *involtini* can also be broiled.) If baking the *involtini,* preheat the oven to 350°F.

First, prepare the stuffing, and note that before you can begin, the currants must be soaked in warm water and be well drained. In a bowl, combine 3 tablespoons olive oil with the garlic and 1 cup of the bread crumbs. Stir in the parsley, pine nuts, and currants, and season with salt and pepper. Turn onto a work surface and chop everything together finely. Add a little more olive oil, if necessary. The mixture should be moist but not wet.

Arrange the 12 swordfish slices in a row in front of you and spoon the filling evenly across the top in equal portions. Press down lightly with your fingertips. Carefully roll up each piece of fish and rest it on the open seam end.

If grilling or broiling the *involtini,* place 3 rolls next to one another and put a bay leaf in between and on the outer sides of the rolls. Force one of the metal or dampened wooden skewers, about 1 inch from one outer end of the swordfish rolls, through the bay leaves, to the other end. Add a bay leaf at the end. The rolls and bay leaves should fit snugly together. Pass another metal or wooden skewer through the three rolls and bay leaves 1 inch from the opposite side so that 2 skewers are securing the 3 rolls. Prepare the remaining 3 skewers of *involtinis* in the same manner. Brush them on each side lightly with olive oil and coat with bread crumbs.

Grill or broil for about 4 minutes on each side. (If broiling them, use a lightly oiled or shallow, nonstick pan with a ridged bottom to cook them in.) Serve each grilled *involtini* with half a lemon.

If baking the *involtini,* prepare as directed above and place in an oiled, shallow baking dish, side by side, in 2 rows. The dish should be just large enough to hold them snugly, about 9 × 12 inches. Put a bay leaf between each roll and bake in the preheated oven for about 15 minutes, or until done. Let rest 5 minutes before serving. Serve each *involtini* with half a lemon.

Twelve ⅛-inch-thick swordfish slices, 6 inches long and 4 inches wide*

STUFFING

¼ cup currants, soaked in warm water and drained
Olive oil
4 garlic cloves, minced
1 cup fresh bread crumbs, plus extra for coating
⅓ cup freshly chopped Italian parsley
¼ cup pine nuts
Salt and freshly ground pepper
16–18 bay leaves (fresh, if possible)
2 lemons, cut in half and seeded

*A fishmonger must cut these slices for you. The best manner is to have him cut 6 extra-thin slices from the entire cross-section of the tail end of a large swordfish, no more than 10 inches in diameter. At home, you simply cut the slices in half, carefully remove the center bone cartilage, and trim off the skin and pointed tip ends of each slice.

Pesce Spada alla Griglia in Due Maniere

(Grilled Swordfish—Two Ways)

For us, one of the secrets of successfully grilling swordfish lies in the thickness of the fish, which should be cut into thin slices— no more than ½ inch thick, perhaps a little less. Another suggestion for grilling swordfish well is to use only olive oil, a spray of lemon juice, and salt and pepper as flavorings. Nothing more is needed. The idea is to taste the swordfish.

The first method we propose is simply grilling thin swordfish steaks brushed with olive oil and seasoned lightly with salt and pepper. Serve each portion with a lemon wedge.

The second method includes the addition of bread crumbs. This method adds an interesting dimension to the texture of the fish, but the bread crumbs don't detract from the flavor. Brush the swordfish steaks lightly with olive oil and season them with salt and pepper. Coat the seasoned fish lightly with dried bread crumbs on each side. Grill the swordfish until done and serve each with a lemon wedge.

Here are two ancient Sicilian sauces to serve with either method of grilled swordfish.

Agliata *(Garlic and Mint Sauce)*

Makes about 1¼ cups

1 cup olive oil
10 garlic cloves, finely chopped
½ cup red wine vinegar
Salt and freshly ground pepper
3 tablespoons chopped fresh
    mint leaves

Heat the olive oil in a small saucepan until the oil is very hot but not smoking. Reduce the heat to low and stir in the garlic and red wine vinegar. Cook for 1 minute, then season to taste with salt and pepper.

Add the mint and cook 2 minutes more. Remove from the heat and let cool.

Agrodolce *(Sweet and Sour Sauce)*

Makes about 3 cups

Heat the olive oil in a large frying pan. Add the onion and cook for 5 minutes over medium heat, stirring often.

Meanwhile, mix the flour with enough water to make a smooth paste.

Add the tomato sauce to the onions and stir in the flour paste. Simmer for 15 minutes, stirring often.

Stir in the remaining ingredients and simmer for 10 minutes. Discard the hot pepper. Cool the sauce. We like this sauce served at room temperature over grilled swordfish or cold poached fish.

1 cup olive oil
1 large onion, finely chopped
2 tablespoons flour
1 cup tomato sauce (Salsa di Pomodoro, page 93)
1 tablespoon capers
10 Sicilian green olives, pitted and chopped
½ cup red wine vinegar
2 tablespoons sugar, or to taste
⅔ cup toasted almonds, finely chopped
1 small whole hot red pepper

Pesce Spada in Umido

(Steamed Swordfish with Oregano and Garlic)

Serves 4

Arrange the fish in one layer in the top pan of a steaming pan. Sprinkle lightly with olive oil, salt and pepper, the oregano, and sliced garlic. Place the pan over another pan of lightly boiling water and steam until done, about 15 minutes.

Transfer the fish to a serving dish and sprinkle with lemon juice.

Serve with small boiled potatoes and cooked asparagus.

Four 6-ounce swordfish steaks, about 1 inch thick
Olive oil
Salt and freshly ground pepper
1½ teaspoons dried oregano
4 garlic cloves, thinly sliced
Juice of 1 lemon

L'Anima Urlante della Vecchia Palermo— La Vucciria

(The Screaming Soul of Old Palermo— La Vucciria)

Sicily's most fascinating and popular market, Palermo's La Vucciria, takes its name from a butcher's shop that existed in the very same location in the early eighth century. The Sicilian word for butcher is *vuccere* (from the ancient French for butcher). To "make Vucciria" means to cause a noisy disturbance or racket, just what it sounds like at this market. To promote their products, dozens of vendors shout out comments—sometimes quite rude—to people passing by. Shoppers bargain and argue loudly, taste samples, squeeze fruit, sniff suspiciously, and make purchases as they bustle through the meandering labyrinth of narrow little streets and passageways. On a recent visit a squawking rooster ran right past our feet—an amazing spectacle, even for us.

The vendor's *bancarelle* (stalls), positioned under colorful red and pastel awnings, display a tempting array of foods that are lit by hanging bare light bulbs. The artificial light and flickering sunlight in the changing shadows of surrounding buildings cast an unusual pinkish-red lumination on everything. The theatrical lighting and commotion of activity resemble lively street theater. What lures people here, of course, is the splendid cornucopia of food. There are enormous bags of fresh and dried herbs, spices, fruits, and nuts, as well as artfully presented seasonal vegetables and fruits: tied-up bunches of wild fennel, crates of shiny eggplants of all sizes, long green squash, sweet and hot peppers, gigantic wedges of tangerine-colored pumpkins, braids of fresh garlic heads, plump Zibibbo grapes, and exquisite piles of blood oranges and figs—a few of each cut open to expose succulent interiors. Adding to the array are huge mounds and jars of olives of every description, little packages or heaps of salted capers, plastic bags of *estratto casareccio* (homemade tomato extract), fresh baked breads, and chickens and lambs hanging from racks above other meats neatly exhibited in butchers' refrigerated showcases.

Most remarkable, though, are the fabulous fresh fish and seafood stalls, with glistening nautical still lifes of perfectly filleted sardines, anchovies, rows of red mullet, whole salmons, dentrix, tuna steaks, massive slabs of swordfish, plus mussels, clams, squid, lobsters, and shrimp, and on and on.

It's possible to catch your breath and rest in La Vucciria at Piazza Garrafello, a small square at the center of the maze of souklike alleyways where the fish stalls are located. You can sample a plate of fresh steaming octopus or try excellent hot, just-out-of-the-frying-pan snacks of Sicily's famous street food, like delicious *panelle* (chick-pea fritters, page 48) eaten in a soft bun, *arancine* (rice croquettes, page 145), and *crocchè di patate* (Sicilian potato croquettes, page 46). Perhaps the most esteemed Palermo street fare are little sandwiches called *guastelle*—thin slices of spleen cooked in lard and stuffed into soft round buns, topped with ricotta and shredded caciocavallo. (We never cook these at Gangivecchio.) The cooks here are experts, the food fresh and perfectly safe to eat.

Vendors at La Vucciria also sell a profusion of merchandise from socks, underwear, handbags, sweaters, and jeans to cheese graters, pots and pans, fabrics, aprons, and tablecloths. Apart from food, we always find useful, reasonably priced items here. People scurry into La Vucciria empty-handed and leave with overflowing shopping bags. We are always sorry Peppe isn't along to help carry the bundles.

It's rare if we don't run into friends here—not just from Palermo, but from all over Sicily. Anyone visiting Palermo should not miss the special light, sights, smells, and tastes of this fantastic market—the screaming soul of Old Palermo.

Ragù di Tonno di Maria-Angela

(Maria-Angela's Tuna Ragù with Fresh Tomato Sauce and Mint)

One 2½-pound tuna steak in 1 piece, about 1½ inches thick
1 medium onion, cut into slivers
4 garlic cloves, cut into slivers
6 black peppercorns
⅓ cup mint leaves, plus 2 tablespoons chopped mint
Salt and freshly ground pepper
½ cup olive oil
4 scallions, white and 2 inches of green tops, cut into julienne strips
3½ cups fresh tomato sauce (Salsa di Pomodoro, page 93)
1 teaspoon sugar

*M*arsala is a city on the west coast, renowned for Marsala wine and superb tuna fish. It is hardly surprising that there are many excellent tuna fish dishes unique to the western region of Sicily.

Maria-Angela Ucelli, from Marsala, stayed in Tenuta Gangivecchio for a week soon after it opened, and she came for a Sunday lunch at Gangivecchio. During her visit, after several long, enjoyable conversations, we became friends. One of the great advantages of owning a restaurant, and now a hotel, is making happy new relationships, especially if we share common interests, like food. People from Sicily and all over the world, whom we would never, ever meet under normal circumstances because we are so isolated, appear right at our door.

Maria-Angela cooked this special tuna dish during that first visit. It was as delicious as she promised.

Serves 6

Cover the tuna steak with cold water in a shallow glass bowl and let rest 5 minutes. Change the water and let it rest another 5 minutes. Pat tuna dry with paper towels.

With the sharp point of a small knife, make 1-inch-deep incisions along the sides of the tuna steak. Insert slivers of onion and garlic, the black peppercorns, and mint leaves in alternating incisions. Tie the circumference of the tuna with string. Season both sides with salt and pepper.

Pour ¼ cup of the olive oil into a large frying pan and brown the tuna quickly on both sides over high heat. (Use 2 wide spatulas to turn the fish.) Set aside.

Put the remaining ¼ cup of olive oil into a large saucepan and cook the scallions over low heat for 5 minutes. Stir in the tomato sauce, chopped mint, and sugar, and season to taste with salt and pepper. Carefully place the tuna into the sauce and simmer for about 1 hour over low heat. Discard the string.

Serve each portion of the tuna, cut into wedges, with a little of the sauce spooned on top. The remainder of the sauce can be tossed with pasta and served with the fish, or the sauce can be saved and used on pasta, with or without fish, for another time.

Tonno con la Cipolla

(Cold Fried Tuna Marinated in Onion, Mint, and Vinegar Sauce)

Serves 8

Combine the onions, ½ cup of the olive oil, and 1 cup of water in a large frying pan. Bring to a boil and cook until the water has evaporated, stirring often, 15 to 20 minutes.

Add the sugar, a pinch of salt, and the vinegar. Simmer for 5 minutes.

Meanwhile, in a separate frying pan, heat the remaining ½ cup of olive oil. Brown the tuna on each side.

Transfer the fish to the onion mixture, spooning some over the tuna, and simmer for 10 minutes.

Transfer to a casserole dish, cover, and refrigerate for at least 2 hours. Serve cold and garnish each serving with a mint sprig. Accompany the dish with cooked spinach.

4 large onions, thinly sliced
1 cup olive oil
1 teaspoon sugar
Salt
½ cup red wine vinegar
One 2½-pound fresh tuna
    steak, 1 inch thick, cut into
    8 pieces
8 fresh mint sprigs

Cunigghiu di Lina

(Lina's Vegetable Stew with Salt Cod and Tuna)

2¼ pounds salt cod
8 artichoke hearts, sliced
3 celery stalks, sliced
1 large cauliflower, florets only, chopped
1 pound fennel, sliced
3 pounds potatoes, peeled, cubed, boiled, and drained
Salt
Olive oil
2 large onions, chopped
1½ pounds fresh tuna, cut into 1-inch cubes
¾ cup green Sicilian olives, pitted and halved
¾ cup black Gaeta olives, pitted and halved
⅓ cup capers
½ cup finely chopped onions
¾ cup red wine vinegar
2 tablespoons sugar, or to taste

*C*unigghiu originated in the Madonie village of Polizzi, where the dish was and still is traditionally prepared for Christmas dinner. *Cunigghiu* is Sicilian dialect for rabbit, but no rabbit exists in the dish. The name was given to the sweet-and-sour fish stew by poor people who couldn't afford rabbit but had a wealth of humor.

The stew takes extra time to prepare, so we cook a big amount for up to 12 people, but we often serve it two days in a row for two meals. Of course, the recipe can be cut in half.

This unusual version of *cunigghiu* was given to us by our friend Lina Alberti.

Serves 10 to 12

Soak the salt cod overnight in cool water that has been changed several times. Rinse the cod pieces and pat them dry. Remove the skins and bones and cut the cod into small pieces.

Cook the vegetables from the artichoke hearts through the potatoes separately in lightly salted, boiling water until tender, about 8 minutes. Drain.

Put ½ cup of the olive oil into a frying pan and fry the onions for 5 minutes. Add the cooked vegetables and simmer for 5 minutes.

Put the tuna in a saucepan and just cover it with lightly salted, boiling water. Simmer for about 10 minutes, or until cooked. Drain.

Add ½ inch of olive oil to another frying pan and fry the cod pieces for about 10 minutes. Drain.

Combine all the ingredients together with the olives and capers in a large pot with enough olive oil to moisten the dish. Add the finely chopped onion. Stir and cook for 5 minutes.

Add the vinegar, sugar, and salt to taste, and simmer for 10 minutes.

$\mathcal{S}$arde

(Sardines)

Sardines are extremely popular in Sicily. We like them best of all when they are glistening fresh, and must cook them right away—simply fried or grilled, or stuffed and baked, or featured in our fabulous pasta dish, Bucatini con le Sarde Come la Faccio Io (page 124). Fresh sardines have a distinct, delicious, bold flavor of the essence of the sea. Those preserved in salt are also admired in Sicily. These come packed in big tins and must be rinsed and soaked. The canned variety, though also tasty, can't compete in flavor with the fresh. At Gangivecchio, we use only fresh sardines. At our markets they are displayed over ice in perfect rows, like pieces of silver jewelry.

In America, fresh sardines (also known as Atlantic or sea herring, pilchard, or sprat) are occasionally available at fish markets and sometimes at Oriental markets. They can also be obtained frozen and whole. Thawed and cleaned, these are very good substitutes for the fresh sardines in our recipes.

Cernia al Forno

(Baked Grouper)

Serves 4

Four 8-ounce grouper fillets
Salt and freshly ground pepper
½ cup olive oil
2 garlic cloves, minced
4 fresh tomatoes, peeled, seeded, and chopped
⅓ cup capers, washed and drained
⅓ cup finely chopped fresh Italian parsley

Preheat the oven to 350°F.

Season the grouper fillets with salt and pepper.

In a shallow baking pan or dish, combine the olive oil, garlic, tomatoes, capers, and parsley. Arrange the grouper over the top and turn each to coat both sides. Bake for 30 minutes. Let rest 15 minutes before serving.

Serve with small boiled potatoes tossed in butter and finely chopped Italian parsley.

Sarde Imbottite di Tanino

(Tanino's Sardines Stuffed with Fresh Bread and Cheese)

1 cup fresh bread crumbs
Olive oil
2 large egg yolks, lightly beaten
2 tablespoons grated pecorino
⅓ cup caciocavallo or Parmesan cheese, finely diced
½ cup freshly chopped Italian parsley
Salt and freshly ground pepper
12 large fresh sardines, about 6 inches in length without the heads, or use 18 smaller sardines, cleaned and boned but left whole (do not separate into 2 fillets)
Flour
½ cup vegetable oil
2 lemons, cut into wedges and seeded

*W*hen my father was alive, he had a doctor friend named Tanino who loved good food and liked to cook. Whenever Tanino planned to make dinner at Gangivecchio, he would invariably appear late and end up making a big mess in the kitchen. My mother always forgave him, however, because he was my father's friend and such a talent in the kitchen.

Serves 6

Toast the bread crumbs in about 1½ tablespoons of olive oil, stirring constantly with a wooden spoon until golden. Cool 10 minutes. Stir in the egg yolks, cheeses, and parsley, and season with salt and pepper. Add a little olive oil to the mixture to make it moist but not wet. Transfer to a bowl and cool completely.

Stuff the filling in equal amounts on the center of each sardine and gently press each side together, closing the fish. Coat each sardine with flour.

Heat the vegetable oil in a large skillet and slowly sauté the sardines, in batches, using a little more oil, if necessary, until golden on each side. Serve hot or cold with the lemon wedges.

Sarde a Beccafico

(Baked Sardines Stuffed with Pine Nuts and Currants)

24 fresh sardines (about 3 pounds), approximately 6 inches long, without the heads (thawed frozen sardines can be used)
1 cup dried bread crumbs

*S*arde a Beccafico is a famous and delicious sardine dish, popular in Palermo, composed of individual stuffed fillets rolled up into little *involtini*. The sardines, placed snugly together in rows with their tails left intact, stand upright at attention and produce an enchanting effect. The sardines are meant to resemble the little birds for which they are named, *beccafichi.*

The recipe given below is our favorite version of the dish. Variations, however, include sprinkling a little vinegar, lemon or orange juice, and extra toasted bread crumbs on top before baking. And a tablespoon of freshly chopped Italian parsley can be added to the stuffing mixture.

Excellent as a main course when served with a vegetable and salad, Sarde a Beccafico can also play a significant role as a dish on an antipasti table.

Serves 6

Scale and gut the sardines, but leave the tails intact.*

Preheat the oven to 375°F.

Put the bread crumbs into a large frying pan and sprinkle with ¼ cup olive oil. Combine thoroughly over medium-high heat with a wooden spoon, stirring constantly, until lightly toasted. Transfer to a bowl and cool for 10 minutes, stirring occasionally.

Combine the egg yolk, pecorino, currants, and pine nuts in a bowl. Season with salt and pepper and the sugar.

Spoon equal amounts of the filling onto the sardines; smooth and pat down gently. Roll up each sardine, starting at the head end. Place the rolled sardines onto a lightly oiled and lightly salted rectangular or square-shaped shallow baking dish, just large enough to hold them, side by side, in rows, with tails sticking up into the air. Place a bay leaf and a slice of onion between each sardine. The curved, concave side of the onion slice should fit behind the bay leaf and tail end of each sardine, acting as a brace.

Drizzle a little olive oil over the sardines and bake in the preheated oven for 30 minutes on the middle shelf.

Serve at room temperature or cold with lemon wedges.

Olive oil
1 large egg yolk
⅓ cup freshly grated pecorino
¼ cup currants, soaked in warm water for 10 minutes
¼ cup pine nuts
Salt and freshly ground pepper
½ teaspoon sugar
24 small bay leaves, or 12 large leaves, halved
24 onion pieces, about 1½ inches long and ¾ inch wide
2 lemons, cut into wedges and seeded

*Remove center bone and tiny dorsal fins from the sides and snip off the fin on the top of the back of each sardine with a pair of kitchen scissors. Spread out the butterflied sardines on a work surface, skin side down.

Sarde per Augusto

(Roasted Sardines with Garlic and Oregano)

Serves 4

16 small fresh sardines, thoroughly cleaned, boned, with heads removed
Olive oil
3 garlic cloves, sliced
Salt and freshly ground pepper
1 teaspoon dried oregano
Juice of 1 lemon
2 tablespoons freshly chopped Italian parsley

Prepare the sardines and be sure they are left whole with the tails intact. Each sardine should be about 6 inches long.

Preheat the oven to 375°F.

Cover the bottom of a shallow baking pan or dish with olive oil and arrange the sardines in one layer, skin side up. Sprinkle with the garlic, salt and pepper, oregano, lemon juice, and parsley. Drizzle generously with olive oil and let rest for 10 minutes.

Bake in the preheated oven for about 15 minutes, or until done. Serve immediately with plenty of Italian bread.

VARIATION: Mackerel can be substituted for the sardines in the recipe.

Baccalà

(Baked Salt Cod)

2 pounds salt cod pieces
Olive oil
2 cups freshly chopped tomatoes
1 small onion, thinly sliced
½ cup pitted black olives, Gaeta, if possible
⅓ cup capers, washed and drained
Freshly ground pepper
Italian crusty bread

*T*his recipe is typical of Sicilian salt cod dishes served in the mountain countryside, especially for those craving unobtainable seafood.

Serves 6

Soak the salt cod for 24 hours in enough cool water to cover, rinsing the cod and changing the water several times.

Preheat the oven to 350°F.

Rinse the cod pieces and pat them dry. Discard all skin and bones. Chop the cod into small pieces.

Cover the bottom of a baking dish or pan liberally with olive oil. Spread the cod across the pan and top with the tomatoes, onion, olives, and capers, and season to taste with pepper. Bake in the preheated oven for 30 to 40 minutes.

Serve with Italian crusty bread.

Filetti di Baccalà all'Arancia

(Fillet of Salt Cod with Oranges and Black Olives)

*T*his noble recipe, made with humble salt cod, comes from the Trapani region of Sicily. The recipe calls for sour oranges, but a little lemon juice can be added to regular orange juice as a substitute.

Serves 6

Soak the salt cod for 24 hours in enough cool water to cover, rinsing the cod and changing the water several times.

Drain and press the water out of each piece of salt cod in a dishcloth. Dust the cod with flour and fry in ½ cup of the olive oil until golden brown.

Meanwhile, in another saucepan, heat the remaining ½ cup of olive oil. Add the onion and cook until lightly browned. Mix in the grated rind of 2 oranges and the olives. Season to taste with salt and pepper.

Place the fried fish on top of the mixture and spoon some over each piece of fish. Pour the juice of 2 sour oranges (or the juice of 2 navel oranges mixed with the juice of a lemon) over the fish. Simmer the dish for 5 minutes. Turn the fried cod and cook another 5 minutes. Serve the dish hot and garnish with the remaining orange slice.

6 salt cod pieces
Flour
1 cup olive oil, or as needed
1 large onion, chopped
Grated rind of 2 oranges
12 black olives, pitted and left whole
Salt and freshly ground pepper
Juice of 2 sour oranges or juice of 2 navel oranges and 1 lemon

Fritto Misto

(Mixed Fried Seafood)

*W*e give a combination of seafood for our Fritto Misto—calamari, shrimp, octopus—but you can cook and serve only one or two of these delicious seafoods. Sadly, baby octopuses are not easy to find. A platter of either fried shrimp or calamari is an exquisite feast. The seafood must be extra fresh to produce a light *fritto misto*.

Serves 6

Coat the shrimp, calamari rings, and octopuses lightly with flour. Shake off any extra flour from each piece of seafood and place on a

1 pound medium shrimp, shelled and deveined
1 pound calamari rings
1 pound baby octopuses (optional)
Flour
Sunflower or vegetable oil, for deep-frying

Fritto Misto *(cont.)*
Salt
3 lemons, cut in half and
seeded

baking sheet next to the stove. Let the seafood rest for 10 minutes.

Heat 3 inches of sunflower or vegetable oil in a large, deep-sided frying pan or saucepan until the oil is hot but not smoking. Cook the seafood in small batches so that each piece can be turned easily in the pan. Cook only a few minutes, until golden brown all over. Drain on paper towels in a single layer. If you drain the seafood in a pile, it will become soggy. Cook the remaining seafood in batches and sprinkle lightly with salt when done.

Transfer the drained seafood to a serving platter, garnish it with lemon wedges, and serve immediately while it's still very hot.

Scampi Gratinati di Betty

(Betty's Stuffed Shrimp au Gratin)

24 extra-large shrimp, with
shells intact
1½ cups dried bread crumbs
3 garlic cloves, finely minced
¼ cup freshly chopped Italian
parsley
Salt and freshly ground pepper
Olive oil
1 lemon, cut into wedges and
seeded

*H*ere is Betty's beautiful broiled shrimp recipe in which the garlic-and-parsley-flavored stuffing cradles each shrimp inside its own shell.

Serves 4 to 6

To prepare the shrimp, remove the underside feathery fins but leave the shells and tails intact. With a pair of scissors or the point of a small, sharp knife, detach the shells from each side of the shrimp all around until the meat is uncovered, but leave the shell attached at the back.

Combine the bread crumbs, garlic, and parsley, and season well with salt and pepper. Add enough olive oil, about ⅓ cup, to moisten the mixture. The stuffing should be nice and damp but not wet. Spoon into the little shell pockets on each side of each shrimp, leaving the meat exposed. Put the stuffed shrimp into a large baking dish or pan, shell side down, side by side, and drizzle the tops lightly with olive oil.

Broil for about 10 minutes until the tops are golden brown. Serve hot and pass the lemon wedges.

Cozze Gratinate

(Mussels au Gratin)

etty serves this dish for dinner at Tenuta Gangivecchio when she has returned from Palermo with fresh mussels.

Serves 4

Steam the mussels in a large pot in 2 cups of water or dry white wine, if you like, over high heat, tossing the mussels often until the shells open. Transfer to a bowl. Strain and reserve the liquid.

Preheat the oven to 350°F.

When the mussels are cool enough to handle, remove and discard the empty halves of the mussel shells. Place the shells with mussels in one layer in a lightly oiled au gratin dish.

Heat the olive oil in a large frying pan and cook the remaining ingredients for 5 minutes, adding a little mussel water to moisten. Spoon the stuffing over each mussel in equal amounts and drizzle with oil. Bake in the preheated oven for 15 minutes.

3½ pounds mussels, scrubbed, debearded, and washed
2 cups dry white wine (optional)
½ cup olive oil, plus more for drizzling on top
1 medium onion, chopped
1 cup dried bread crumbs
½ cup freshly grated pecorino or provolone piccante (a spicy cheese is required)
½ cup freshly chopped Italian parsley
2 medium-sized fresh tomatoes, peeled and chopped
2 garlic cloves, minced
Salt and freshly ground pepper

Secondi di Pesce e Frutti di Mare / 213

Acciughe
(Anchovies)

Sicilians love the taste of anchovies, so we use these flavor-filled little fish in a great many dishes. Fresh anchovies are a great delicacy but not easy to find.

There are two kinds of preserved anchovies—those packed in salt in cans or those filleted and preserved in olive oil in little glass jars or flat cans.

Salt-preserved anchovies are larger and fleshier than those that come in cans or jars. Salted anchovies are usually sold whole and must be beheaded, skinned, and boned. Then the excess salt must be soaked and washed off. Since these anchovies aren't easily found in America, our recipes use flat anchovy fillets packed in oil. In the Italian food markets in New York, we discovered small jars and cans of flat anchovy fillets in oil from Sciacca, a seaport city on the southwest coast of Sicily. Try these if you can find them.

Even anchovies packed in oil have been salted, so use salt sparingly.

Anchovies are featured in dishes like our Spaghetti con Acciughe e Mollica Rossa (Spaghetti with Anchovy and Fresh Tomato Sauce and Toasted Bread Crumbs, page 129) or Insalata Siciliana (page 254), a fragrant tomato salad. Or anchovies can play only a minor role, adding just a suggestion of their special flavor to recipes like Calamari Ripieni alla Siciliana (page 215).

If using only a few anchovies from a small can—this often happens—transfer the remaining ones to a small glass container and cover them with olive oil. Secure with a tight-fitting lid and store in the refrigerator. If using anchovies from jars, after taking out the required amount, it is sometimes necessary to add a little olive oil to the jar to completely cover them. In either instance, use the anchovies within the next couple of days for the best taste.

We never use anchovy paste in tubes, because the true flavor is missing.

Calamari Ripieni alla Siciliana

(Sicilian-Style Stuffed Squid)

*D*elicious stuffed squid is served at seaside restaurants all over Sicily. There is always great competition over who makes the best. Here is our entry.

Serves 4

Remove the head and tentacles of the squid and chop fine. Be sure to leave the body intact.

Heat 3 tablespoons of olive oil in a frying pan and cook the chopped squid over low heat for 5 minutes. Add the garlic and cook for 5 minutes, stirring often.

Meanwhile, preheat the oven to 350°F.

Add the ingredients from the bread crumbs through the parsley to the pan. Season to taste with salt and pepper, and transfer to a bowl to cool.

When cool enough to handle, fill each squid body cavity with equal amounts of the stuffing. Close the ends with toothpicks.

Place the stuffed squid side by side in an oiled shallow baking pan or dish. Season lightly with salt and pepper, and drizzle a little olive oil over the top. Bake in the preheated oven for 20 minutes.

Pass under the broiler for about 5 minutes, turning the stuffed squid so that each is lightly browned.

Serve the squid with an arugula and tomato salad.

8 medium-sized squid, cleaned
Olive oil
1 garlic clove, minced
2½ cups toasted bread crumbs
    (page 121)
2 anchovy fillets, finely chopped
⅓ cup capers, washed and
    drained
⅓ cup pine nuts
⅓ cup currants
⅓ cup chopped Italian parsley
Salt and freshly ground pepper

Verdure

(Vegetables)

Many of our delicious vegetable dishes are also located in the Antipasti chapter.

Gli Orti di Gangivecchio *(The Gardens of Gangivecchio)* • Canazzo *("Big Dog"—Mixed Vegetable Top-of-the-Stove Casserole)* • Fricassea di Melanzane *(Eggplant Fricassee)* • Melanzane in Agrodolce *(Sweet and Sour Eggplant)* • Le Nostre Melanzane alla Parmigiana *(Our Baked Eggplant Parmigiana)* • Zucchine Ripiene *(Baked Stuffed Zucchini)* • Zucchine Trifolate *(Sautéed Baby Zucchini)* • Zucchine Gratinate *(Zucchini with Ham and Cheese au Gratin)* • Finocchi Gratinati *(Fennel au Gratin)* • Carciofi alla Villanella *(Peasant-Style Artichokes)* • Broccoli Gratinati *(Au Gratin of Cauliflower)* • Brasato di Sparacelli *(Braised Broccoli with Black Olives and Anchovies)* • Patate a Sfincione *(Baked Potato Casserole with Tomatoes and Anchovies)* • Patate di Peppe *(Peppe's Sautéed Potatoes with Black Pepper)* • Pasticcio di Patate con Cinque Formaggi *(Baked Potato Pie with Five Cheeses)* • Gatto' di Patate *(Mashed Potato Cake)* • Patate Novelle in Umido *(Stewed New Potatoes)* • Le Orribili Patate di Vincenzo *(Vincenzo's Horrible Potatoes—Sautéed with Onions, Peppers, and Herbs)* • Pomodori Ripieni *(Baked Stuffed Tomatoes)* • Pomodori Ripieni alla Marsalese *(Marsala-Style Baked Stuffed Tomatoes with Shrimp and Green Olives)* • Funghi Trifolati *(Sautéed Mushrooms with Garlic and Onions)* • Un Segreto Tesoro Siciliano—Funghi Ferla *(A Secret Sicilian Treasure—Ferla Mushrooms)* • Funghi Gratinati *(Gratin of Mushrooms with Ham and Parmesan and Pecorino Cheeses)* • Peperoni Picchio Pacchio *(Sautéed Peppers with Picchio Pacchio Sauce)* • Peperoni con Capperi e Olive Nere al Forno *(Baked Peppers with Capers and Black Olives)* • Peperoni a Cotoletta *(Fried Breaded Red and Yellow Peppers)* • Peperoni Saltati *(Sautéed Peppers with Bread Crumbs and Garlic)* • Fave Stufate delle Quacelle *(Quacelle-Style Fava Bean and Potato Casserole)*

• FAVE *(Fava Beans)* • Fave Alla Ghiotta *(Stewed Fava Beans with Tomatoes)* •
Purè di Fave con Cicoria della Famiglia Loiacono *(The Loiacono Family's Puréed Fava Beans with Chicory)* • Frittella *(Mixed Spring Vegetables)* •
Zucca in Agrodolce *(Sweet and Sour Pumpkin)*

Vegetables are considerable, yet fundamental, pleasures in our menus at home and in the restaurant, for they add wonderful, satisfying flavors, textures, and colors. In Sicily, a meal without vegetables, raw or cooked, is unthinkable as in all Mediterranean countries.

We love each spring because that is when the earth's bountiful parade of vegetables begins. Here, land is king and we are the loyal subjects. In spring we eat fresh, tender fava beans raw, out of the pod, up until the time when they develop hard skins and must be shelled and well cooked. (In the winter we have the dried variety.) Spring's harvest in Sicily also brings glorious, delicate-flavored artichokes and tender green peas, which we celebrate with Frittella (page 242), a fragrant dish that also includes artichokes.

In the summer we have an abundance of eggplant to transform into dozens of dishes—Melanzane in Agrodolce (page 222), a delicious sweet-and-sour eggplant, and Fricassea di Melanzane (page 221), a wonderful eggplant fricassee. Eggplant, of course, is featured in many of our pasta sauces.

Summer also brings tomatoes, peppers, and the many vegetables you will read about in *Gli Orti di Gangivecchio* (The Gardens of Gangivecchio) on page 219.

Zucchini is a significant crop from June into late September or early October. We cultivate many meters of zucchini so we can make Mamma's exquisite zucchini flower fritters (Frittelle di Fiori di Zucca, page 54), as well as countless tasty vegetable dishes and soups.

We eat lots of wild asparagus, wild fennel, and wild greens that we buy or forage for in the fields. In our recipes here, we substitute Swiss chard, escarole, and spinach for wild greens. Mustard greens, beet tops, and kale can also be used. In Sicily, we have two kinds of greens—wild and cultivated. The wild greens are slightly bitter-tasting. Cultivated greens resemble spinach in flavor. Bulb fennel's dark green feathery tops are mild yet satisfactory replacements for our wild fennel, but there really is no substitute for wild asparagus.

For a very short time in the spring and fall we enjoy great ferla mushrooms at Gangivecchio. Read about these treasures on page 234.

At the Sicilian table we often eat vegetables as part of an *antipasti* or as a course on their own as a light meal. At the restaurant green vegetables are always featured in one of our two pasta courses, and a vegetable side dish is served with the meat course as well.

Some Sicilian vegetable vendors offer, along with their choice raw produce, cooked seasonal vegetables, such as roasted peppers, grilled artichokes, or boiled potatoes, green beans, and onions. They are sold from big copper caldrons and trays. Hard to resist, they disappear quickly.

Gli Orti di Gangivecchio
(The Gardens of Gangivecchio)

There has always been a home garden at Gangivecchio during my lifetime, but when my mother arrived, in the late '40s, it was larger and grander—everything from tomatoes, peppers, carrots, cauliflower, cabbages, zucchini, and broccoli to cucumbers, watermelons, yellow melons, eggplants, potatoes, radishes, fava beans, and too many other things to list, plus a tremendous amount of herbs. Mamma remembers Zu Vicé, the old man who lovingly cared for that garden. When you have a garden in Sicily, we say, "*Orto, uomo morto*," which means "Home garden, dead man." As anyone who looks after a garden knows, it is arduous, tedious, unending work, but few occupations are as rewarding—like having a child, after the labor, the miracle appears.

Eventually, Peppe, our farmhand, became the keeper of the garden. Because he had so many other chores, the garden was reduced in size (no more fava beans, potatoes, or other demanding crops). We also had a big cutting garden, with roses, daisies, and many other beautiful flowers that we have since let go wild.

In the late '70s our farm production went into serious decline when the area's agricultural economy began deteriorating. Happily, our garden remained healthy, so we, like so many others, sold what we didn't eat. Peppe filled boxes with whatever extra vegetables there were and took them off to the market, where he was transformed into a proud vendor. People in Gangi came to recognize the high quality of Gangivecchio's vegetables and would look for Peppe's vegetable stand. Judging from the enormous amount of green beans and hot peppers that Peppe plants every year now, we suspect that he's still selling vegetables on the side.

Back when we opened the restaurant in 1978, Peppe was brought inside to help with the kitchen work—learning to prepare foods and cook, also serving and cleaning. Peppe still had the garden to run, as well as all his other farm duties, like feeding the animals, collecting the nuts and fruits, and so on. I remember him running into the garden to work outdoors for a short time—pulling weeds, planting seeds, watering them, and picking the foods Mamma needed in the kitchen. In the middle of this work my mother would call out through the upstairs balcony doors for him to come back inside to shell some pine nuts, lift a heavy pot, or do any of a hundred other things. So he would dutifully return to the house and begin working as instructed. All of a sudden Mamma would remember that she needed four more eggplants, seven sprigs of fresh rosemary, and a big branch of bay leaves. *Presto! Presto!* Out poor Peppe ran to fetch these things. He still works hard, but not like back then. We say our gardens are sprinkled half by water and half by Peppe's sweat, so we hope he is selling plenty of green beans and hot peppers.

We have two gardens at Gangivecchio now. The large one is near the abbey, and a smaller one is outside the hotel. This year both gardens produced big crops of arugula, peppers, tomatoes, eggplants, zucchini, and herbs. Betty and Paolo are expanding their garden. Paolo plowed several acres for fava beans and potatoes, so next year we will again have these prized vegetables at Gangivecchio.

Canazzo

Serves 6 to 8

Heat 1 cup of the olive oil in a large saucepan and add the onion.
Cook for 5 minutes over medium heat, stirring often. Add the
tomatoes, a pinch of salt and cayenne pepper, if you like, and simmer for 15 minutes.

Meanwhile, heat the remaining cup of olive oil in a large frying pan and cook the eggplant cubes, in batches, until golden
brown. Drain on paper towels.

Add the red and yellow peppers to the pan and cook for 5 minutes over medium-high heat, adding a little more oil, if necessary.
Transfer to a side dish.

Add the potatoes to the frying pan and season well with salt
and pepper. Sauté over medium heat until golden, turning a few
times.

Put the eggplant, peppers, and tomatoes in the pan with the
potatoes. Gently combine the ingredients. Simmer over low heat
for about 10 minutes. Cool and serve at room temperature, or
refrigerate and serve thoroughly chilled.

2 cups olive oil
1 large onion, chopped
1 cup fresh or canned tomatoes,
    peeled and chopped
Salt
Cayenne pepper (optional)
2 medium eggplants, cut into
    1-inch cubes
2 red bell peppers, cored,
    seeded, and sliced
2 yellow bell peppers, cored,
    seeded, and sliced
1½ pounds yellow potatoes,
    peeled and cubed
Freshly ground pepper

Fricassea di Melanzane

(Eggplant Fricassee)

Serves 6

Heat ½ cup olive oil in a large frying pan. Cook the eggplant slices,
in batches, until lightly browned on each side. Drain on paper towels. Cook remaining eggplant slices in the same manner, adding a
little olive oil, as needed.

Heat the tomato sauce with the garlic cloves in a saucepan and
simmer for 10 minutes. Discard the garlic.

Preheat the oven to 350°F.

Grease the interior of a shallow, rectangular or oval-shaped
baking dish, about 9 × 14 inches. Sprinkle the bread crumbs on the
bottom and sides of the dish. Make a layer of eggplant. Season

½ cup olive oil, and more as
    needed
2 large eggplants, cut lengthwise
    into ½-inch-thick slices
3⅓ cups fresh tomato sauce
    (Salsa di Pomodoro,
    page 93)
4 garlic cloves, peeled
¼ cup dried bread crumbs
Salt and freshly ground pepper

Fricassea di Melanzane *(cont.)*

1 pound fresh Italian hot (or
   sweet) sausage, crumbled
   and sautéed until no longer
   pink, and drained
4 hard-boiled eggs, shelled and
   thinly sliced crosswise
1 cup diced caciocavallo or provolone cheese
½ cup freshly grated pecorino
12 fresh basil leaves
2 large eggs, lightly beaten

lightly with salt and pepper. Spoon half the sauce over the eggplant. Making layers, top with half the sausage, half the eggs, half
the cheeses, and arrange 6 basil leaves across the top. Make another
layer of eggplant and season it to taste with salt and pepper. Spoon
on the remaining sauce, then repeat the layers as before, this time
putting the basil leaves on top of the sliced eggs.

Bake in the preheated oven for 20 minutes. Then pour the
beaten eggs over the top of the dish, and continue baking until the
eggs are cooked, about 10 minutes more. Serve hot.

Melanzane in Agrodolce

(Sweet and Sour Eggplant)

Serves 6

Olive oil
2 medium eggplants, cubed
4 garlic cloves, peeled and cut
   into slivers
½ cup red wine vinegar
3 tablespoons sugar, or to taste
1 cup freshly chopped celery,
   with leaves
½ cup capers, rinsed and
   drained
Salt and freshly ground pepper
⅓ cup chopped pine nuts

Heat 2 inches of olive oil in a large saucepan or deep-sided frying
pan until the oil is hot but not smoking. Fry the eggplant cubes, in
batches, until just golden. Drain the cooked eggplant on paper
towels.

Heat ½ cup olive oil in a large saucepan and cook the garlic for
2 minutes, stirring often. Add the vinegar, sugar, celery, capers,
fried eggplant, and salt and pepper to taste. Bring to a boil. Immediately reduce the heat and simmer for 20 minutes, stirring often
to keep the eggplant mixture from burning on the bottom—
remember, sugar is included.

Remove from the heat and let rest 1 hour. Mix again and sprinkle with pine nuts just before serving. Serve cool or well chilled. It
will keep for about a week.

Le Nostre Melanzane alla Parmigiana

Serves 8 to 10

(*Our Baked Eggplant Parmigiana*)

Heat ½ inch sunflower or vegetable oil in a large frying pan and fry the eggplant, in batches, until golden brown, adding extra oil as needed. Drain the cooked eggplant on paper towels and let rest at room temperature for 30 minutes.

Preheat the oven to 350°F.

Season the eggplant to taste with salt and pepper.

Ladle a small amount of tomato sauce on the bottom of a 9 × 12–inch shallow baking dish. Line the dish with a layer of eggplant slices, dot with small pieces of butter, sprinkle a little basil and Parmesan cheese on top. Repeat the same sequence of ingredients, making two more layers. Spoon the remaining sauce over the top and sprinkle with Parmesan cheese.

Bake in the preheated oven for 30 minutes. Let rest 10 minutes before serving.

Sunflower or vegetable oil, for frying
4 medium to large eggplants, cut lengthwise into ⅓-inch-thick slices
Salt and freshly ground pepper
3 cups tomato sauce (Salsa di Pomodoro, page 93)
Sweet butter
⅓ cup chopped fresh basil leaves
Freshly grated Parmesan cheese

Zucchine Ripiene

Serves 8 to 10

(*Baked Stuffed Zucchini*)

With the very thin blade of a sharp knife, remove the center pulp from each zucchini, working from both ends, leaving an unbroken zucchini shell about ⅓ inch thick.

Put the bread crumbs into a large bowl and add the ingredients through the tomatoes. Season to taste with salt and pepper, and blend well. Add enough olive oil and a little water to make a stuffing that holds together but is not wet.

Stuff each zucchini with equal amounts of the stuffing by pushing it inside with your fingers or forcing it inside with the stick end of a wooden spoon. Replace the end pieces, securing them with toothpicks—two at each end.

Pour enough olive oil into a large frying pan to just cover the bottom. Heat the oil and add the zucchini. Gently cook and roll the zucchini until golden brown all over.

3 large zucchini, about 3–4 inches wide and 10–12 inches long, scrubbed and washed, with stem ends cut off and saved
1½ cups fresh bread crumbs
½ cup finely chopped boiled ham
¼ cup freshly grated pecorino
¼ cup freshly grated Parmesan cheese
2 slices salami, finely minced
½ cup diced provolone

½ cup freshly chopped Italian
   parsley
¼ cup finely chopped pine nuts
¼ cup chopped currants, soaked
   in water for 10 minutes and
   drained
3 medium tomatoes, chopped,
   peeled, and seeded
Salt and freshly ground pepper
Olive oil
1 medium onion, thinly sliced
½ cup dry white wine
1 tablespoon sweet butter

Carefully transfer to a lightly oiled, shallow baking dish.

In the same frying pan, cook the onion until golden. Add the wine and ½ cup of water, the butter, and salt and pepper to taste. Stir and cook for 1 minute. Pour over the zucchini and put the dish into a cold oven. Turn the heat to 350°F and bake for 45 minutes.

Remove the stuffed zucchini and let cool completely. Cover and refrigerate for several hours.

When ready to serve the dish, preheat the oven to 350°F. Remove the toothpicks and end pieces and discard them. Cut each stuffed zucchini into ⅓-inch slices and arrange them in a clean, greased baking dish. Spoon the sauce from the original baking dish over the zucchini. Bake in the preheated oven for 10 minutes and serve immediately.

Zucchine Trifolate

(Sautéed Baby Zucchini)

Serves 6

½ cup olive oil
2 pounds baby zucchini, thinly
   sliced crosswise
4 whole garlic cloves, peeled
Salt and freshly ground pepper
¼ cup fresh Italian parsley,
   finely chopped
¼ cup fresh mint, finely
   chopped

Heat the olive oil in a large frying pan and add the zucchini and garlic. Season to taste with salt and pepper and toss. Cover the pan and cook over medium heat for 5 minutes. Toss again and cook, uncovered, for 2 minutes.

Sprinkle with the parsley and mint, and gently toss to blend. Cook 1 minute, discard the garlic, and serve immediately.

Zucchine Gratinate

(Zucchini with Ham and Cheese au Gratin)

Serves 8

Preheat the oven to 350°F.

In a large bowl, mix together the ingredients from the bread crumbs through the cayenne pepper, if you are using it.

Lightly grease the bottom of a shallow baking dish or pan about 9 × 14 inches with olive oil. Arrange one layer of half of the zucchini slices across the bottom of the dish. Sprinkle half the bread-crumb mixture over the zucchini. Pat down lightly. Add another layer of zucchini and top with the remaining bread crumbs, spreading evenly and patting down slightly. Dot with the butter and bake in the preheated oven for 30 minutes, or until golden brown on top.

1½ cups fresh bread crumbs
¼ cup grated pecorino or Parmesan cheese
¼ cup diced caciocavallo or provolone cheese
¼ cup pine nuts
¼ cup currants, soaked in water for 10 minutes and drained
½ cup finely chopped boiled ham
⅓ cup freshly chopped basil
1 medium onion, finely chopped
1 medium tomato, peeled, diced, seeded, and well drained
Salt and freshly ground pepper
Pinch of cayenne pepper (optional)
Olive oil
2½ pounds medium-sized zucchini, washed, scrubbed, and cut into ¼-inch-thick slices
1½ tablespoons sweet butter

Finocchi Gratinati

(Fennel au Gratin)

Serves 6

6 medium white fennel bulbs, with the stem ends and tops cut off and the tough outer stalks discarded, sliced into ¼-inch-thick slices
1 medium onion, thinly sliced
Salt and freshly ground pepper
Butter
1½ cups Salsa Besciamella Morbida (page 96)
Freshly grated Parmesan cheese

Bring 6 cups of water to a rolling boil in a saucepan. Add the fennel and onion and ½ teaspoon salt. Cook at a low boil for about 12 minutes, or until the fennel is tender. Drain well, return the vegetables to the pan, and season to taste with salt and pepper.

Generously butter the bottom and sides of an 8 × 10–inch shallow baking dish. Put half the fennel-and-onion mixture into the bottom of the dish and spoon ½ cup of the Salsa Besciamella Morbida over it, sprinkling lightly with Parmesan cheese. Repeat for a second layer.

Place under an unheated broiler. Turn it to high and broil until the top is golden brown. Serve immediately.

Carciofi alla Villanella

(Peasant-Style Artichokes)

Serves 4

1 cup olive oil
3 whole garlic cloves, peeled
16 small, young, fresh artichokes, cleaned (page 58)
Salt and freshly ground pepper
½ cup freshly chopped Italian parsley
Toasted Italian bread slices

Heat the olive oil and garlic cloves in a large saucepan. Add the artichokes and season well with salt and pepper. Stir in 1 cup of water and cook, covered, over medium-low heat about 15 minutes, or until the artichokes are tender.

Add the parsley, toss, and taste for seasoning. Serve immediately with toasted bread slices to soak up the delicious liquid.

Broccoli Gratinati

(Au Gratin of Cauliflower)

Serves 6

Bring 2 quarts of water to a rolling boil. Add the cauliflower and stir in ½ teaspoon of salt. Reduce the heat to medium and cook until the cauliflower is tender, about 10 minutes. Drain the cauliflower well and transfer to a large bowl.

Preheat the oven to 375°F.

Add the ham, cheeses, 2 tablespoons of melted butter, parsley, olive oil, and ½ cup of the Salsa Besciamella Morbida and season lightly with salt and pepper. Mash coarsely with a potato masher. Taste again for seasoning.

Grease a shallow baking dish with olive oil. Spoon the cauliflower into the dish and gently pat down evenly. Spoon the remaining Salsa Besciamella over the top and sprinkle lightly with bread crumbs and dot with butter. Bake in the preheated oven for about 25 minutes. If the top isn't golden brown, pass the dish briefly under the broiler. Cool for 10 minutes before serving. The cauliflower can also be served at room temperature.

1 large cauliflower, cored and cut into florets
Salt
¾ cup diced boiled or cooked ham
½ cup diced caciocavallo or provolone cheese
¼ cup freshly grated pecorino
¼ cup freshly grated Parmesan cheese
3 tablespoons butter, melted, plus 1 tablespoon for topping
⅓ cup fresh Italian parsley, finely chopped
2 tablespoons olive oil, plus extra for the pan
1¼ cups Salsa Besciamella Morbida (page 96)
Salt and freshly ground pepper
Dried bread crumbs
Sweet butter

Brasato di Sparacelli

(Braised Broccoli with Black Olives and Anchovies)

½ cup olive oil
2 pounds broccoli, chopped
¼ cup diced caciocavallo or provolone cheese
2 medium onions, finely
  chopped
4 anchovy fillets, chopped
1 cup Gaeta black olives, pitted
  and halved
Salt and freshly ground pepper
½ cup dry red wine

Serves 6 to 8

Pour 2 tablespoons of the olive oil into a large, heavy-bottomed saucepan. Put in half the broccoli and top with layers of half the cheese, onions, anchovies, and olives, and season with salt and pepper. Make another layer, beginning with the broccoli. Drizzle with the remaining olive oil and red wine, and cook over low heat, without stirring, for about 25 minutes.

Patate a Sfincione

(Baked Potato Casserole with Tomatoes and Anchovies)

5 pounds baking potatoes,
  unpeeled and washed
Olive oil
Fresh bread crumbs
12 anchovy fillets, patted dry
  and chopped
1½ pounds fresh tomatoes,
  peeled and chopped, or one
  28-ounce can Italian plum
  tomatoes, drained and
  chopped
1 large yellow onion, thinly
  sliced
Salt and freshly ground pepper

Serves 10

Put the potatoes into a large pot and cover with cold water. Bring to a boil and cook until tender.

Drain and cool under cold running water. Let rest at room temperature for 1 hour.

Preheat the oven to 375°F.

Peel the potatoes and cut them into ¼-inch-thick slices.

Generously rub olive oil over the bottom and sides of a rectangular baking dish, approximately 9 × 14 inches, and sprinkle lightly with bread crumbs. Arrange ¼ of the potato slices, anchovies, tomatoes, and onion in layers. Sprinkle the top lightly with olive oil and salt and pepper. Repeat the same procedure, making three more layers. Sprinkle bread crumbs on top and drizzle lightly with olive oil. Bake in the preheated oven for about 30 minutes, or until the top is golden.

Let the potatoes rest 10 minutes before serving.

Patate di Peppe

(Peppe's Sautéed Potatoes with Black Pepper)

Olive, sunflower, or vegetable
  oil
3 pounds small yellow-skinned
  potatoes, peeled and cut into
  ½-inch-thick wedges, and
  patted dry
3 whole garlic cloves (optional)
1 tablespoon freshly chopped
  rosemary (optional)
Salt and freshly ground pepper
Freshly chopped Italian parsley

eppe Bevacqua, our houseman, farmer, cook, and do-everything man, whom we consider a family member, has been at Gangivecchio for thirty years. He often cooks his recipe for us on cold winter evenings. In the very lean times of the past, a plate of cooked potatoes was often all his shepherd family had for dinner in the one-room hut they shared. Each person would eat half a kilo, and be grateful and happy. It's certainly a humble dish, seasoned only with olive oil, salt, and pepper (we added the parsley). We often serve this dish with fried eggs for a simple lunch, or with roasted meats. Sicilians love potatoes cooked in any manner—boiled, mashed, fried, sautéed, baked, roasted, or turned into little croquettes (page 46).

Occasionally, at any time of the year, we find Peppe in the kitchen in the evening cooking himself a mountain of his potatoes, which he consumes with only a glass of red wine for dinner, saying softly with a smile and shrug, "*Come ieri* [Like yesterday]." Then he sleeps like a baby.

If you like, you can add 3 whole garlic cloves and a tablespoon of chopped fresh rosemary to the potatoes at the beginning of cooking time.

One serving for Peppe, or serves 4 to 6 with normal appetites

Heat ½ inch of olive, sunflower, or vegetable oil in a large frying pan. Add the potatoes and stir them with a wooden spoon. (Add garlic cloves and rosemary, if desired.) Season the potatoes with salt and lots of freshly ground pepper. Cook over high heat, stirring occasionally, until they begin to brown. Turn the potatoes and lower the heat to medium, cover, and simmer for 10 minutes.

Increase the heat, turn the potatoes again, and cook until golden brown. Taste for seasoning, sprinkle with the parsley, and serve immediately.

Pasticcio di Patate con Cinque Formaggi

(Baked Potato Pie with Five Cheeses)

3½ pounds boiling potatoes, peeled and quartered
Salt and freshly ground pepper
2 large eggs
¼ cup freshly grated Parmesan cheese, plus extra for topping
⅓ cup freshly chopped Italian parsley
¼ cup freshly grated provolone
½ cup diced Swiss cheese
½ cup diced Gouda cheese
½ cup diced Italian Fontina cheese
1 cup hot milk
6 tablespoons sweet butter, melted, plus extra for greasing the pan
Dried bread crumbs

Serves 8

Cook the potatoes in boiling water until very tender.

Preheat the oven to 400°F.

Drain the potatoes. Pass them through a food mill or ricer into a large bowl. Season them well with salt and pepper, add the eggs, half the Parmesan cheese, the remaining ingredients through the milk, and 4 tablespoons of the melted butter. Mash together until creamy. Add a little extra butter and milk, if necessary. Taste for seasoning.

Grease the bottom and sides of a 10-inch round baking dish with at least 3-inch sides with butter. Coat with bread crumbs. Turn the potatoes into the pan and smooth the top. Sprinkle lightly with bread crumbs and the remaining 2 tablespoons of Parmesan cheese, and drizzle with the remaining 2 tablespoons of melted butter.

Place in the preheated oven on a baking sheet and bake for about 30 minutes, or until the top is golden brown. If necessary, pass under the broiler.

Gatto' di Patate

(Mashed Potato Cake)

4 pounds potatoes, peeled and quartered
4 large eggs, lightly beaten
1 cup milk
6 tablespoons sweet butter, plus extra for greasing the pan
½ cup freshly grated pecorino

*T*here are many variations of this potato cake, but this is our favorite one. We serve this dish at picnics in the countryside, accompanied by fruit and, of course, red wine.

Serves 8 to 10

Cook the potatoes in lightly salted, boiling water until very tender, about 15 minutes. Drain.

Preheat the oven to 375°F.

Pass the potatoes through a food mill or ricer into a large bowl. Cool for 5 minutes. Add the eggs, milk, and other ingredients through the parsley. Season well with salt and pepper, and mash together until creamy.

Grease the bottom and sides of a 10-inch round baking pan with at least 3-inch sides with butter. Coat with bread crumbs.

Turn the potatoes into the pan and smooth down evenly. Sprinkle lightly with bread crumbs and gently press into the potato mixture.

Bake in the preheated oven for 45 minutes.

Let rest for 5 minutes. Pass the thin blade of a knife along the sides of the pan. Put a round plate several inches larger than the pan over it and, holding both securely, invert the pan. Serve hot, at room temperature, or cold.

1 cup chopped boiled ham
4 slices Napoli salami, chopped
½ cup diced caciocavallo or provolone cheese
⅔ cup diced mozzarella
½ cup freshly chopped Italian parsley
Salt and freshly ground pepper
Dried bread crumbs

Patate Novelle in Umido

Serves 6

(Stewed New Potatoes)

Cook the potatoes in boiling water for 10 minutes. Drain and, when cool enough to handle, peel.

Heat the olive oil and onion in a large frying pan. Cook about 2 minutes over medium heat. Stir in the chicken stock or broth, Parmesan cheese rind, the potatoes, and season lightly with salt and pepper. Cook for 10 minutes, or until done. Taste for seasoning.

Remove the potatoes from the heat. Discard any remaining piece of cheese rind and sprinkle with the parsley. Gently toss and let rest in the pan for 15 minutes. Serve the potatoes at room temperature with grilled or roasted meat or chicken.

2 pounds small new potatoes, as similar in shape as possible
¼ cup olive oil
1 medium onion, chopped
1 cup homemade chicken stock, canned broth, or 1 cup of water and 1 chicken bouillon cube
One 2-ounce piece Parmesan cheese rind (page 82)
Salt and freshly ground pepper
⅓ cup freshly chopped Italian parsley

Le Orribili Patate di Vincenzo

(Vincenzo's Horrible Potatoes—Sautéed with Onions, Peppers, and Herbs)

Olive oil

2½ pounds potatoes, peeled and cut into bite-size pieces

3 medium-sized red or yellow onions

1 small red bell pepper, cored, seeded, and cut into small pieces

1 teaspoon fresh rosemary or ½ teaspoon dried

4 sage leaves, chopped, or ½ teaspoon dried sage

1 small fresh hot pepper, chopped, or hot pepper flakes (optional)

Salt and freshly ground pepper

*W*e think our good friend Vincenzo Mollica's potatoes are wonderful—spicy and filled with a bouquet of flavors, but his neighbor Elisa D'Arpa always teases him because he adds so many ingredients. She eats a big portion of these delicious potatoes—even though she always calls them *orribili*—whenever Vincenzo prepares them. He usually cooks them outdoors over a wood-burning fire, but the potatoes are tasty when made inside the house, too, of course.

Serves 6

Pour ¼ inch of olive oil into a large frying pan. Add the potatoes, onions, red bell pepper, herbs, and hot fresh pepper, if used, and toss over high heat. Cook until lightly browned on the bottom. Turn and season well with salt and pepper to taste. Add a little more oil, if necessary. Lower the heat to medium and cook for about 10 minutes.

Turn the potatoes again, season with salt and pepper, and sprinkle with a pinch or more of hot pepper flakes, if you are not using the fresh hot pepper. When the potatoes are done, serve immediately.

Pomodori Ripieni

(Baked Stuffed Tomatoes)

Serves 8

16 medium-sized firm, ripe tomatoes, cut in half, cross-wise

6 garlic cloves, minced

1¾ cups fresh dried bread crumbs

Preheat the oven to 350°F.

Cut ½ inch off the tops (opposite the stem ends) of each tomato. Scoop out a little but not all of the center seeds and pulp. Set each tomato cut side up on a work surface. Put equal amounts of minced garlic into each tomato.

Mix the bread crumbs, parsley, cheese, and about ¼ cup of olive oil into a light, but moist mixture. Season well with salt and pepper. Put a rounded tablespoonful into the center of each tomato.

Grease a shallow baking pan with olive oil and arrange the tomatoes side by side. Sprinkle the breaded tops with a little olive oil.

Cook for about 20 minutes, or until the skins begin to wrinkle. Remove from the oven and cool. Serve at room temperature.

½ cup freshly chopped Italian parsley
3 tablespoons grated cacio-cavallo or pecorino cheese
Olive oil
Salt and freshly ground pepper

Pomodori Ripieni alla Marsalese

(Marsala-Style Baked Stuffed Tomatoes with Shrimp and Green Olives)

*T*he port city of Marsala on the southwestern coast of Sicily is famous for Marsala wine, but it is also a town that lives on fish. The shrimp and olive filling in this recipe can be eaten in uncooked tomatoes or in baked tomatoes, as it is normally served.

Serves 6

Preheat the oven to 400°F.

Cut about ½ inch off the tops (opposite the stem ends) of each tomato. Remove the tomato pulp and seeds with a small spoon and discard.

In a large bowl, combine the shrimp, anchovies, and olives. Whisk together the olive oil and lemon juice, and season to taste well with salt and pepper. Pour over the shrimp and toss well.

Spoon equal amounts of the shrimp mixture into the cavity of each tomato. (The dish can be eaten at this stage as a salad. Garnish each tomato with a basil leaf.)

Put the tomatoes into a lightly greased, shallow baking dish and cook for 15 minutes.

Serve the tomatoes warm or cold with a basil leaf stuck in the top of each tomato.

6 large ripe, firm tomatoes
1½ pounds boiled small shrimp, shelled and deveined
2 anchovy fillets, finely chopped
¾ cup chopped green olives, Sicilian, if possible
½ cup olive oil
1 tablespoon freshly squeezed lemon juice
Salt and freshly ground pepper
6 fresh basil leaves

Funghi Trifolati

*(Sautéed Mushrooms with
Garlic and Onions)*

⅔ cup olive oil
4 garlic cloves, minced
1 small onion, thinly sliced
1 pound Portobello mush-
    rooms, thinly sliced
Salt and freshly ground pepper
¼ cup freshly chopped Italian
    parsley
¼ cup freshly chopped arugula

Serves 4

Heat the olive oil in a large frying pan. Add the garlic and onion
and cook for 2 minutes, stirring often.

Add the mushrooms and season to taste with salt and pepper.
Toss and cook over medium-high heat for 5 minutes. Turn the
mushrooms and cook about 3 minutes more.

Remove the pan from heat and sprinkle the parsley and
arugula over the mushrooms. Toss and serve immediately.

Un Segreto Tesoro Siciliano—Funghi Ferla

*(A Secret Sicilian Treasure—
Ferla Mushrooms)*

In the Madonie region of Sicily there are at least forty species of mush-rooms. At Gangivecchio, the most representative and prized mushroom is the ferla (*pleurotus eringi, varietà ferula*). This exquisite mushroom is so rare that most Sicilians are unaware it exists, especially those who live in coastal cities. Ferlas are sold in very few local markets and for only very short periods of time in the spring and fall. Everyone wants to keep their precious ferlas to enjoy for themselves.

In the autumn it is a tradition for us to invite our friends to Gangivecchio to go foraging in the fields and woods. We search for ferlas as seriously as Tuscans hunt for porcini. The porcini is, of course, the king of Italian mushrooms. For us, the ferla is the heir apparent.

A member of the fennel family, the ferla (which the mushroom takes its name from) is a wild plant that grows only in Sicily and on a few surrounding islands. The mushrooms appear at the base of the young ferla plant, which grows out of the center of the previous one in spring. The mushroom's nourishment comes from the rotted roots of the dead ferla plant.

There are two ferla mushroom harvests. In the spring they appear ten days after the first good rain that is followed by strong Sicilian sunshine. The spring ferla mushrooms are smaller in size than those that are harvested in the fall. In the autumn, when the new plant has died, and ten days after the first rain, usually in late September or early October, the mushrooms—tremendous in size—appear, producing a much larger yield.

Aromatic ferla mushrooms are cream to warm tan in color, with smooth-surfaced caps. The thick, fleshy, round to wavy caps have underside gills descending down to short, thick, stocky stems. Ferlas have a distinct woodsy flavor and have the amazing capacity to grow up to five pounds—the cap sometimes reaches beyond 12 inches in diameter.

The ferla plant itself is extremely versatile. In the spring it bursts into bright yellow flower clusters on gangly, reedy stalks that resemble a giant fennel plant. The plant can reach a height of over ten feet. Standing like proud sentinels dotting the countryside, ferla plants are very easy to recognize. When one withers and dies, the stalks fall to the ground, like a broken skeleton. The sturdy stalks are cut away and crafted into charming little square stools called *furrizzi*. Peppe makes our *furrizzi*. In Sicily, you may see them on sale in shops and markets in the Madonie and all over the country.

During Michele's first visit to Gangivecchio in May, Peppe arrived in the kitchen one morning with a basket filled with beautiful ferlas. He grilled some over a wood fire for lunch. We also cooked our recipe for Funghi Trifolati (page 234)—mushrooms sautéed in olive oil and garlic with a small amount of onion and parsley. Like porcini, ferlas are wonderful in risotto.

Substituting any other mushroom for ferlas would only produce a poor imitation of the original. Ferla is not as fragile as porcini or as firm as Portobello. They have a smooth texture and unique flavor. If you come to Sicily in the fall and are in the Madonie, ask farmers or the owners of local vegetable markets if there are any ferlas. They will be astonished that you know about this secret mushroom. If we have any at Gangivecchio, we will be happy to cook them for you.

Funghi Gratinati

(Gratin of Mushrooms with Ham and Parmesan and Pecorino Cheeses)

Olive oil
3 tablespoons sweet butter,
  softened
2 pounds Portobello mush-
  rooms, cut into thick slices
⅓ cup grated Parmesan cheese
⅓ cup pecorino
½ cup chopped boiled or
  cooked ham
1 large tomato, peeled, seeded,
  and chopped
2 medium onions, thinly sliced,
  with the rings separated
¼ cup freshly chopped Italian
  parsley
¾ cup fresh bread crumbs
Salt and freshly ground pepper

Serves 8

Preheat the oven to 350°F.

Grease a shallow baking dish or pan about 9 × 14 inches with 1 tablespoon of olive oil and 1 tablespoon of the softened butter. Arrange half the mushrooms over the bottom of the dish. In layers, sprinkle half the cheeses, ham, chopped tomato, onions, parsley, and bread crumbs on top. Season to taste with salt and pepper and dot with 1 tablespoon of the butter. Make one more layer in the same manner. Drizzle generously with olive oil and bake in the preheated oven for 30 minutes.

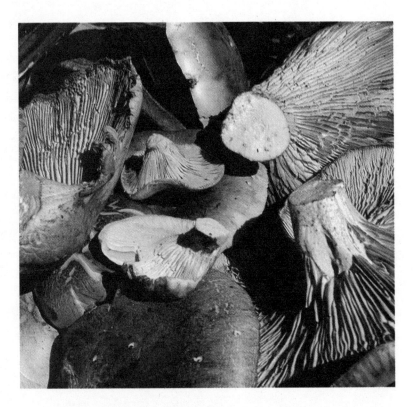

"If good-quality fresh swordfish appears at the fishmonger's or by van in Gangi, my mother purchases an enormous quantity."

Ruota di Pesce Spada al Forno di Ginevra, page 196

Fresh fish for sale in Palermo

"The sardines are meant to resemble the little birds for which they are
named, *beccafichi*."
Sarde a Beccafico, page 208

Steamed fresh octopus at Palermo's *La Vucciria*

The ferla and its mushroom (*clockwise from left*): Giovanna with Cetta Teresi, a friend, surrounded by flowering yellow ferla plants; *Funghi Trifolati*, page 234; *furrizzi*, stools fashioned by Peppe from ferla stalks; a basket of fresh-picked ferla mushrooms; a giant mushroom growing at the base of the plant from which its name comes

"Sicilians love potatoes cooked
 in any manner."
Patate di Peppe, page 229

"The most desired stage
of fava beans is when
they are very young and
can be eaten raw."

Peperoni Picchio Pacchio

Serves 6

Heat the olive oil in a large frying pan until the oil is hot but not smoking. Add the peppers and zucchini, and cook over medium-high heat for 5 minutes, stirring often. Add Salsa Picchio Pacchio and reduce the heat to low. Simmer for 30 minutes, partially covered, stirring occasionally. Season to taste with salt and pepper.

Transfer to a serving bowl and sprinkle with parsley.

⅓ cup olive oil
2 large red bell peppers, cored, seeded, and cut into ¼-inch-thick strips
2 large yellow bell peppers, cored, seeded, and cut into ¼-inch-thick strips
2 medium zucchini, scrubbed clean and cut into ¼-inch-thick, 2-inch-long strips
1½ cups Salsa Picchio Pacchio (page 122)
Salt and freshly ground pepper
1 tablespoon freshly chopped Italian parsley

Peperoni con Capperi e Olive Nere al Forno

Serves 6 to 8

(Baked Peppers with Capers and Black Olives)

Preheat the oven to 350°F.

Cut the peppers in half. Remove the stem ends, seeds, and white membranes. Cut the peppers into squares a little bigger than 1 inch.

Coat the bottom and sides of a shallow 9 × 12–inch baking dish with olive oil. Put the peppers into the dish and sprinkle with the capers, olives, garlic, basil, parsley, bread crumbs, and a drizzle of olive oil. Season lightly with salt and pepper. Toss the ingredients and smooth evenly.

Bake in the preheated oven for 45 minutes. Serve at room temperature.

2 large yellow bell peppers
2 large green bell peppers
2 large red bell peppers
Olive oil
¼ cup capers
1 cup pitted Gaeta black olives
5 garlic cloves, chopped
6 fresh basil leaves, finely chopped
1 tablespoon freshly chopped Italian parsley
1 cup dried bread crumbs
Salt and freshly ground pepper

Peperoni a Cotoletta

*(Fried Breaded Red and
Yellow Peppers)*

3 large red bell peppers, quartered, with stem ends cut off
and seeds and membrane
removed
3 large yellow bell peppers,
quartered, with stem ends
cut off and seeds and membrane removed
Flour
4 large eggs
Salt and freshly ground pepper
Dried bread crumbs
Olive oil

Serves 6

Wash the pepper quarters and coat them with flour.

Beat the eggs lightly in a medium-sized bowl and season them
well with salt and pepper. Coat each piece of pepper with the egg,
and coat with bread crumbs. Let rest a few minutes.

Heat 2½ inches of olive oil in a large, heavy-bottomed
saucepan or fryer and cook the breaded peppers, in batches, until
golden brown all over. Drain them as cooked. Season with salt and
serve immediately.

Peperoni Saltati

*(Sautéed Peppers with Bread
Crumbs and Garlic)*

3 large yellow bell peppers
3 large red bell peppers
⅓ cup olive oil
3 tablespoons dried bread
crumbs
3 garlic cloves
1 teaspoon sugar
Salt and freshly ground pepper

Serves 6 to 8

Put the whole peppers on a grill pan under a broiler and cook
them, turning, until the skins brown and char on all sides. Remove
the peppers and, with the help of the tip of a small, sharp knife,
peel off all the skins. Cut the peppers in half and remove the stem
ends, seeds, and white membrane. Cut the peppers into ⅓-inch-
thick strips.

Heat the olive oil in a large frying pan and add the bread
crumbs and garlic cloves. Toss the bread crumbs and garlic around
in the pan for 1 minute. Add the peppers and sugar, and season
them to taste with salt and pepper. Toss them well and cook over
medium heat for about 10 minutes, until tender, mixing often.
Add a little extra olive oil, if desired. When done, discard the garlic. Eat hot, at room temperature, or well chilled.

Fave Stufate delle Quacelle

(Quacelle-Style Fava Bean and Potato Casserole)

Quacelle is the ancient name of a small region high in the Madonie Mountains. This dish is very representative of a typical peasant casserole from the area and is made with dried fava beans, potatoes, and onions.

Serves 8

Drain the fava beans. Remove the skins and the dark sprout on each bean. Drop into a large pot of boiling water and cook for about 1½ hours, until tender. Drain and season with salt.

Pour half the olive oil into a 6-quart casserole dish and add half the cooked fava beans, flattening evenly. Top with a layer of half the potatoes and chopped onion, salt to taste, and sprinkle with oregano, a few red pepper flakes, and half the pecorino. Make one more layer in the same manner. Drizzle with the remaining olive oil.

Simmer on top of the stove for about 45 minutes, partially covered. Add a little water, if necessary. Serve hot with grilled bread slices.

2 pounds dried fava beans, soaked in water overnight
Salt
¼ cup olive oil
1¼ pounds small baking potatoes, peeled and cut into thin slices
1 medium onion, finely chopped
Dried oregano
Red pepper flakes
½ cup shaved pecorino
Grilled bread slices

Fave
(Fava Beans)

Fava beans are highly appreciated in the Sicilian kitchen. The most desired stage of fava beans is when they are very young and can be eaten raw, or steamed for just 1 minute, and served in a bowl along with sweet pecorino cheese, bread, and wine. This is a humble yet elegant meal—the favas have the taste of the earth, the sun, and springtime.

Fresh fava beans are light green—the size and color of lima beans—and as they mature, they grow into large kidney-bean shapes. The fresh fava beans we use in the following recipes are the latter variety because the young ones are almost impossible to find except during their brief season.

Fava beans are quite a finicky crop to cultivate. The soil surrounding the rows of leafy plants must be kept completely free of weeds in order for the favas to thrive. Still, Sicily produces enormous quantities.

Dried, shelled favas are a pale wheat color. Cooked after an overnight soaking, these favas have a delicious, more pronounced earthy flavor. The dried variety we use are *fave sgusciate,* which have been shelled and skinned. Dried favas last forever—certainly for up to a year—and provide food for both people and animals in Sicily, especially for sheep during the winter when there is no pasture for them to graze in.

Aside from the recipes given here, we have included two other important fava bean dishes. A typical and ancient Sicilian recipe uses fava beans for a thick, hearty peasant soup called *u'maccu* (see our own recipe on page 75). A bowl of steaming *u'maccu* in the winter will instantly warm your body and soul. And last year Paolo invented a wonderful, aromatic pasta dish, Pennette alla Crema di Fave Fresche (Pasta with Fresh Fava Bean Cream Sauce, page 108).

NOTE: To reduce the unpleasant aftereffects of digesting beans, especially dried ones, add ½ to 1 teaspoon of baking soda to the water you cook them in.

Fave alla Ghiotta

(Stewed Fava Beans with Tomatoes)

Serves 8

Drain the fava beans. Add the beans to a large pot of boiling water. Stir in 1 tablespoon of salt. Cook for about 1½ hours, until tender.

Meanwhile, heat the olive oil in a large saucepan. Cook the onion until golden but not brown, about 15 minutes. Add the tomatoes, basil, and salt and pepper to taste. Drain the fava beans, reserving ½ cup of the cooking water. Mix the favas into the saucepan, then add the cooking water. Simmer for about 20 minutes, stirring often. Taste for seasoning.

Serve hot in individual bowls and drizzle with a little olive oil. Pass fried bread cubes or croutons.

2 pounds dried fava beans, soaked in water overnight
Salt
¾ cup olive oil, plus more for drizzling on top
1 large onion, chopped
One 28-ounce can imported Italian plum tomatoes, drained and chopped
6 fresh basil leaves, torn into pieces
Freshly ground pepper
Fried bread cubes or croutons

Purè di Fave con Cicoria della Famiglia Loiacono

(The Loiacono Family's Puréed Fava Beans with Chicory)

*B*etty's family recipe for puréed fava beans with chicory is a traditional and well-loved dish from Apulia, where her father was born. When you are served the dish in a restaurant, the waiter arrives with a big steaming bowl and plops a large spoonful onto your plate. Many Apulians ask for second helpings—not after they've eaten the first serving, but right then, when they are first being served.

Serves 8

Drain the beans. Skin them, removing the little dark sprouts from each bean. Put them into a large, heavy pot and add enough water to just cover. Bring the water to a rolling boil. Reduce the heat to a simmer and cook until very tender, approximately 1 hour.

1½ pounds dried fava beans, soaked overnight
Salt
1 head chicory, shredded, with the stem end and outer tough leaves removed
Olive oil

Meanwhile, heat 2 tablespoons of olive oil in a large pot. Add 2 cups of water and ½ teaspoon of salt and bring to a boil. Stir in the chicory and cook until tender, about 5 minutes. Drain well and transfer to a bowl. Season with a little olive oil and salt. Set aside.

Pass the fava beans through a food mill, food processor, or blender—in batches. Turn into a large bowl, add ½ cup olive oil and season to taste with salt. Beat together very well. Taste for seasoning again. You may want to add more salt and oil. The cooked chicory is normally served on the side, but you can also stir it into the purée. Put a bottle of olive oil on the table for those who might like to drizzle more over the top.

Frittella

(Mixed Spring Vegetables)

Serves 6

Olive oil
1 medium onion, chopped
12 small fresh artichokes, cleaned (page 58)
⅓ cup freshly chopped Italian parsley
1 pound fresh (shelled) or frozen (thawed) green peas
1 tablespoon butter
2 pounds fresh fava beans, removed from pods and skinned
Salt and freshly ground pepper
2 tablespoons white wine vinegar
1 teaspoon sugar, or to taste

Heat ¼ cup of olive oil in a large saucepan and cook the onion for 2 minutes, stirring often. Add the artichokes and ½ cup of water and simmer, covered, until tender, about 6 minutes. Add the parsley, mix, and turn into a bowl.

Cook the peas until tender in a quart of lightly salted, boiling water. Remove with a slotted spoon and add to the artichokes. Add the butter and toss.

In the same water in which the peas were cooked, drop in the fava beans. Cook until tender, about 5 minutes. Drain the beans and transfer to a large frying pan and add the artichokes and peas. Sprinkle with a little olive oil, vinegar, and sugar. Toss to combine well. Cook over high heat for 1 minute. Turn the vegetables into a bowl and let rest for 30 minutes before serving, or refrigerate until well chilled.

Zucca in Agrodolce

(Sweet and Sour Pumpkin)

Serves 6 to 8

Pour enough olive oil in a large frying pan to generously cover the bottom. Fry the pumpkin or squash slices, in batches, in a single layer, until golden on each side. Drain the pumpkin on paper towels as it is cooked, then season with salt and pepper. Add more olive oil to the pan as needed.

Add 3 tablespoons of water to the pan, stir in the onion, and cook 5 minutes.

Lightly grease a shallow ceramic or glass dish, about 9 × 14 inches, and arrange the pumpkin or squash slices, in layers, in the dish.

Stir in the vinegar, 2 tablespoons of water, and the sugar. Cook over high heat for 2 minutes. Taste for seasoning. Spoon the sweet and sour sauce over the pumpkin. Cool the pumpkin to room temperature, cover, and refrigerate. Serve cold the next day, if possible. Garnish with fresh mint sprigs.

Olive oil
2 pounds fresh pumpkin (or West Indian calabaza), butternut or acorn squash, peeled and cut into ⅓-inch-thick slices, about 1 inch wide and 3–4 inches long
Salt and freshly ground pepper
1 medium onion, finely chopped
¼ cup red wine vinegar
2 tablespoons sugar
2 fresh mint sprigs

Insalate

(Salads)

Insalata Tricolore *(Green Bean, Potato, and Tomato Salad)* • Verdure
Mediterranee in Insalata *(Mediterranean Mixed Vegetable Salad)* • Insalata di
Gina *(Gina's Spinach, Arugula, and Walnut Salad)* • Rucola con Pinoli e
Melograno *(Arugula with Pine Nuts and Pomegranate)* • MELOGRANI
(Pomegranates) • Insalata Mista con Pecorino di Betty *(Betty's Mixed Green Salad
with Pecorino)* • ORIGANO *(Oregano)* • Insalata di Pomodori Freschi con
Origano *(Fresh Tomato Salad with Oregano)* • Insalata di Arance *(Orange Salad
with Black Olives)* • Insalata Siciliana *(Tomato Salad with Anchovies, Olives, and
Peppers)* • Patate ad Insalata *(Potato Salad with Oregano)* • Insalata di Broccoli
con Succo di Limone *(Cold Cauliflower Salad with Lemon Juice)* • Insalata di
Mare di Cefalù *(Cefalù Seafood Salad)* • Insalata Casareccia di Olive di Gangivec-
chio *(Gangivecchio's Homemade Mixed Olive Salad)* • Insalata di Penne e Tonno
di Ferruccio *(Ferruccio's Penne and Tuna Salad with Peppers and Mint)* •
Conchiglie ad Insalata di Betty *(Betty's Shell Pasta and Tuna Salad with Black
Olives)* • FACENDO IL PANE ALLA MANIERA ANTICA *(Old-Fashioned Bread
Making)* • PANE RIMACINATO DELLE MADONIE *(Madonie Mountain Country
Bread)* • Gamberi con Rucola e Pompelmo Rosa *(Shrimp with Arugula and
Pink Grapefruit)* • Aringhe in Compagnia *("In Good Company"—Herring
and Egg Salad)* • Insalata di Pollo Primavera *(Spring Chicken Salad)* •
Insalata di Natale I *(Christmas Salad I)* • Insalata di Natale II
(Christmas Salad with Oranges, Olives, and Capers)

Before Betty entered our lives through my brother's love, at Gangivecchio we
thought of salads primarily as a single garden green seasoned with olive oil, vine-

gar, salt, and pepper. Once in a while, for a change, we added sliced tomatoes, cucumbers, red onions, grated carrots, or other fresh vegetables to the greens for a mixed salad, but salads have never played an important role in our kitchen or, indeed, in Sicily's cuisine.

There are many dishes we have always eaten that are classified as salads, yet we regard them more as dishes featuring certain ingredients, usually vegetables. For instance, if Mamma suggests tomatoes with oregano for lunch, I know she means one of our favorite tomato dishes—wedges of plump ripe tomatoes showered lightly with olive oil, dried oregano, and salt. The flavor of the vine-ripened tomatoes explodes in your mouth. Other salads we enjoy highlight potatoes, such as Insalata Tricolore (page 248), a lovely mixture of boiled potatoes and green beans with fresh tomatoes. Both of these salads are only lightly dressed with oil and vinegar because, first and foremost, it's the earthy taste of the potatoes we want to savor.

Along the entire coast of Sicily, superb seafood salads are prepared, and every wife here makes her own blend of mixed olive salad. Sicily's well-known orange-and-black-olive-and-lemon salads are considered light, refreshing dishes. The most unusual salads we admire from the past are special multi-ingredient creations, like our colorful Insalata di Natale II (page 269).

But back to Betty, our newest family member. She is what my father would have called *una capruzza* (meaning "a little goat" in Sicilian). Since her first day at Gangivecchio she has insisted on having some type of salad as part of her daily diet. Betty learned to recognize the healthful value of salads from her uncle Ferruccio, a nutritionist in Palermo.

Eager to educate Mamma, Paolo, and me on the big subject of salads, Betty began giving us serious, boring lectures during dinner on the healthy aspects of spinach, arugula, peppers, broccoli, cauliflower, pumpkin, zucchini, celery, carrots, and an abundance of other vegetables, fruits, and foods, both raw and cooked. She was constantly instructing us on the important issues of fiber and vitamin and mineral content. Betty is a schoolteacher by profession, and she must be very good because she finally captured our attention by tempting us with a variety of delectable examples that go beyond greens and raw vegetables, like delicious Insalata di Penne e Tonno di Ferruccio (Ferruccio's Penne and Tuna Salad with Peppers and Mint, page 257) and Gamberi con Rucola e Pompelmo Rosa (Shrimp with Arugula and Pink Grapefruit, page 265).

Little by little, we began regarding salads not only as unpleasant-sounding nutritional elements but also as wonderful-tasting, satisfying dishes.

Mamma and I, secretly at first, to keep any disastrous failures to ourselves, started experimenting on our own and soon discovered that there were limitless varieties of salad possibilities when we started creatively combining seasonal produce and other foods—like meat, fish, and seafood, nuts, herbs, spices, cheeses, beans, and pasta—with tasty dressings. For us, this discovery was incredible.

Well, in the end, we passed our exams. Today a good salad is rarely missing from our table, whether it be a composition of simple greens or more exotic mixtures of contrasting, complementing ingredients and textures.

Sometimes I surprise myself when I hear myself telling guests at the restaurant that they are going to like the special salad we are serving today—composed of arugula, pine nuts, and pomegranate seeds—and have the extra benefit of all the vitamins and minerals it contains. Although I never liked school, I have always been a good student.

In Gangivecchio's restaurant, of course, we primarily serve traditional Sicilian foods, but Mamma and I are enthusiastically developing new salad dishes that embrace the seasonal vegetables, fruits, nuts, and cheeses produced here on the farm. (You can read about our gardens on page 219.) For a few weeks in the spring, when we have fresh young fava beans, we serve a classic simple Sicilian salad of fresh fava beans, diced pecorino cheese, and chopped parsley, dressed with olive oil, salt and pepper, with delicious country bread. (The bread recipe is on page 263.)

Among the recipes that follow are our favorite traditional Sicilian salads and some of our more recent inventions, along with a few contributed by salad-loving friends, and, of course, Betty.

Insalata Tricolore

(Green Bean, Potato, and Tomato Salad)

18 small new or red boiling
    potatoes, peeled and cut into
    ¾-inch cubes
1 pound fresh cooked green
    beans, with the stem ends
    cut off
4 medium-sized fresh, firm but
    ripe tomatoes, cut into
    wedges
Salt and freshly ground pepper
Olive oil
White wine vinegar

The *tricolore* (three colors)—green, white, and red—of this beautiful-looking and beautiful-tasting salad represent the vivid colors of the Italian flag. Although a basic salad, the green beans, potatoes, and tomatoes produce a harmonious blend of flavors.

Serves 6

Put the vegetables into a large bowl and season to taste with salt and pepper. Sprinkle lightly with olive oil and vinegar. Gently toss, cover, and chill thoroughly. Toss again before serving and taste for seasoning. Add a little more oil and vinegar, if desired.

Verdure Mediterranee in Insalata

(Mediterranean Mixed Vegetable Salad)

his is a Mediterranean rather than a strictly Sicilian compo-sition. We began preparing the salad with only tomatoes, peppers, and cucumbers, but every now and then, for a change and when our *orto* (vegetable garden) provides inspiration, we add a new ingredient. Here's our most recent combination.

Serves 4

To make the dressing, whisk together the lemon juice, vinegar, thyme, and salt and pepper to taste. Drop by drop, whisk in the olive oil. Add the mayonnaise and whisk until very well combined, and set aside.

Meanwhile, gently combine the salad ingredients in a large bowl. Pour the dressing over the salad, gently toss, and let rest for 10 minutes. Taste for seasoning and toss again. Serve with grilled or toasted Italian bread slices.

DRESSING

1 tablespoon freshly squeezed lemon juice
1 tablespoon white wine vinegar
1 tablespoon fresh thyme or 1 teaspoon dried
Salt and freshly ground pepper
½ cup olive oil
¼ cup mayonnaise

4 large tomatoes, cut into ¾-inch cubes
1 yellow bell pepper, cored, seeded, and cut into julienne strips
1 red bell pepper, cored, seeded, and cut into julienne strips
1 medium cucumber, peeled and diced
2 carrots, scraped and grated
20 cured black olives in oil, cut into slivers
1 small bunch young arugula, washed and dried
4 anchovy fillets, minced
¾ cup diced smoked pancetta or slab bacon, cooked
3½ ounces shaved Parmesan cheese pieces
Salt and freshly ground pepper
Grilled or toasted Italian bread slices

Insalata di Gina

(Gina's Spinach, Arugula, and Walnut Salad)

DRESSING

1½ tablespoons green pepper-
 corn vinegar, or to taste (If
 unavailable, add ½ teaspoon
 jarred green peppercorns to
 1½ tablespoons white wine
 vinegar. Mash the peppercorns with the back of a
 spoon.)
⅛ teaspoon sugar
Salt and freshly ground pepper
½ cup olive oil

1 pound fresh spinach, washed,
 dried, and torn into small
 pieces
1 small bunch arugula, washed,
 dried, and torn into small
 pieces
1 small head radicchio, leaves
 washed, dried, and separated
1 red pepper, cored, seeded, and
 cut into thin strips
½ cup chopped walnuts
3 ounces pecorino, shaved into
 thin slices

Grissini (breadsticks)

Gina Degano is the newest member of our Madonie group of close friends. An accomplished equestrian, Gina was born in Udine, a city north of Venice. She lived there all her life, until she divorced. When an opportunity to teach riding in Sicily for one year presented itself, she accepted the position without hesitation, looking forward to a complete change of scenery.

As happens in this life, she met and fell in love with a Sicilian man, a dear friend of ours, Antonio Pucci. In Sicily for six years now, she has become a classical Sicilian countryside woman, look-ing after an ancient, beautiful villa and her gardens, horseback rid-ing daily and cooking wonderful meals for Antonio, their friends and their family.

We often exchange recipes with Gina during visits to each other's homes and over the telephone. Like Betty, Gina loves sal-ads, and she is constantly giving us delicious new ideas, usually strongly influenced by her northern Italian background.

Serves 4

Make the dressing by whisking together the vinegar, sugar, and salt and pepper to taste. Drop by drop, whisk in the olive oil and taste for seasoning. Add a little more vinegar, if desired. Set aside.

Combine all the salad ingredients, except for the pecorino, in a large salad bowl. Pour the sauce over the salad and toss. Add the cheese and gently toss. Serve with *grissini*.

Rucola con Pinoli e Melograno

Serves 4

(Arugula with Pine Nuts and Pomegranate)

Put the arugula into a large bowl.

Heat the 2 tablespoons of olive oil in a frying pan and add the pine nuts. Cook the nuts over medium-high heat, shaking the pan often, until golden brown. Drain on paper towels.

To make the dressing, put the vinegar, mustard, and minced shallot into a small bowl and whisk together. Add the olive oil, drop by drop. Season to taste with salt and pepper.

Sprinkle the toasted pine nuts and half the pomegranate seeds over the arugula and pour the dressing over the salad. Gently toss. Arrange the salad in equal portions on 4 salad plates. Sprinkle the top of each with equal amounts of the remaining pomegranate seeds.

2 bunches young arugula, washed and dried, with the stem ends cut off
2 tablespoons olive oil
¼ cup pine nuts
¼ cup fresh pomegranate seeds

DRESSING

2 tablespoons red wine vinegar
1 teaspoon Dijon mustard
1 shallot, minced
½ cup olive oil
Salt and freshly ground pepper

Melograni

(Pomegranates)

Pomegranates are a unique and beautiful fruit to look at and just as delicious to eat, but they are going to disappear because of people's laziness. It is a time-consuming procedure to pick the edible seeds from inside the fruit. The seeds are impacted like teeth in a white membrane. Each tiny tart and sweet, juicy, garnet-colored seed is encased in a thin-skinned transparent covering. They look like little jewels. Pomegranate seeds are delicious sprinkled onto salads, fruit dishes, and ice cream. We like to pass pomegranate seeds through a food mill and drink the refreshing liquid.

It is also easy, once the seeds are extracted, to make a wonderful thick pomegranate syrup with a quart of filtered juice. It is an ancient recipe. Put the juice into a saucepan with 3 cups of sugar and cook it over medium-low heat until it begins to boil and the sugar has dissolved. Cool this mixture and store it in a covered bottle in the refrigerator. Pomegranate syrup is fantastic served over ice cream and other confections.

Insalata Mista con Pecorino di Betty

(Betty's Mixed Green Salad with Pecorino)

Serves 6

12 small romaine leaves, washed, dried, and torn into bite-size pieces

½ pound fresh young spinach, washed, dried, and torn into bite-size pieces

2 cups curly endive, washed, dried, and torn into bite-size pieces

1 medium head radicchio, leaves separated, washed, and dried

1 small bunch arugula, washed and dried

½ cup chopped sun-dried tomatoes, packed in oil

¼ pound pecorino, shaved into very thin slices

DRESSING

2 tablespoons red wine vinegar
Salt and freshly ground pepper
⅔ cup olive oil

Combine the salad ingredients, except for the pecorino, in a large salad bowl.

To make the dressing, put the vinegar into a small bowl and season it with salt and pepper to taste. Drop by drop, whisk in the olive oil. Pour the dressing over the salad and gently toss.

Arrange the salad on 6 salad plates in equal amounts and shave the pecorino cheese over the top with a vegetable peeler in equal amounts.

Origano
(Oregano)

In Sicily, we have superb mountain-grown oregano, but we only use it dried. Oregano is the only herb that we don't use fresh, because it tends to overwhelm any dish it is used in and also brings a slightly bitter taste to the mouth.

Our dried oregano is magnificent. If you visit Sicily, bring a big bag of our dried oregano home with you. Stored in a tightly sealed jar in a cool, dark place, it will last for months. When you open the jar, the sunny smell of Sicily will be released.

Insalata di Pomodori Freschi con Origano

(Fresh Tomato Salad with Oregano)

*T*his plain, wonderful salad, composed of vine-ripened tomatoes seasoned only with olive oil, dried oregano, and a little salt—no vinegar or pepper—permits you to taste the pure flavors of the sun and earth.

For variety we sometimes use different herbs and, occasionally, canned or our own preserved tuna fish (page 69) with the fresh tomatoes. The variations follow the recipe.

Serves 6

6 medium-sized garden-fresh
    ripe tomatoes, at room tem-
    perature, cut into wedges,
    with the stem ends removed
Olive oil
Salt
1 teaspoon dried oregano, or to
    taste

Put the tomato wedges into a bowl and sprinkle lightly with olive oil, salt, and oregano. Gently toss. Let rest 5 minutes before serving.

VARIATIONS: The oregano can be substituted with freshly chopped basil or mint. A few drops of Olio Santo (Hot Oil, page 76) can also be added. Preserved or canned white-meat tuna, drained and flaked, added to the tomatoes, with either the dried oregano or fresh basil or mint, is delicious.

Insalata di Arance

(Orange Salad with Black Olives)

*T*his *Palermitana* recipe normally accompanies Sarde a Beccafico (Baked Sardines Stuffed with Pine Nuts and Currants, page 208), but it's also splendid with any roasted or fried seafood dish.

Orange groves and olive groves surround Palermo's countryside, so it's no wonder that local cooks unite these two fine ingredients. The sweetness of the oranges and saltiness of the olives produce a refreshing, simple salad.

Serves 6

3 large navel oranges, in
    sections, peel and white pith
    removed
18 pitted black olives, Gaeta, if
    possible, cut into slivers
Salt and freshly ground pepper
Olive oil
Lettuce greens, for garnish

Combine the orange sections with the black olives in a bowl. Sprinkle lightly with salt, pepper, and olive oil. Let rest for 10 minutes before serving on crisp lettuce greens.

Insalata Siciliana

*(Tomato Salad with
Anchovies, Olives, and
Peppers)*

5 medium-sized ripe tomatoes,
   cut into wedges, with the
   stem ends removed
1 medium onion, thinly sliced
1 dozen pitted green Sicilian
   olives
18 black olives, Gaeta, if possible, pitted and halved
6 anchovy fillets, finely chopped
6 romaine lettuce leaves, cut
   crosswise into thin strips
1 red bell pepper, cored, seeded,
   and cut into julienne strips
Salt and freshly ground pepper
Olive oil
½ teaspoon oregano

Serves 6

Combine the ingredients in a bowl and let rest for at least 15 minutes before serving. Or cover and refrigerate for several hours. Toss
again before serving.

Patate ad Insalata

(Potato Salad with Oregano)

1½ pounds small new or boiling
   potatoes, unpeeled
Olive oil
White wine vinegar
1 teaspoon dried oregano
1 tablespoon freshly chopped
   Italian parsley
Salt and freshly grated pepper

Serves 4

Bring 2 quarts of water to a boil. Add the potatoes and cook just
until tender, about 15 minutes. Drain and cool until you can handle them. Carefully remove the skins.

    Cut the potatoes into ¾-inch cubes and transfer to a bowl.
Sprinkle with a small amount of olive oil and vinegar, the oregano,
parsley, and salt and pepper to taste.

    Gently toss and let rest at room temperature for 30 minutes.
Toss and taste again for seasoning before serving.

Insalata di Broccoli con Succo di Limone

(Cold Cauliflower Salad with
Lemon Juice)

*T*his is an old Sicilian recipe that we enjoy at Gangivecchio
in fall and winter. The crisp, flavorful cauliflower is so light. It's a
nice contrasting dish when served with roasted or fried meats.
Sometimes we have the salad as a course by itself after the pasta.
The meal ends with some caciocavallo cheese and fruit.

1 small head cauliflower, sepa-
    rated and cut into small flo-
    rets
Salt and freshly ground pepper
Olive oil
Juice of 1 lemon, seeds removed

Serves 6

Cook the cauliflower in lightly salted, boiling water until al dente,
or just tender, about 6 minutes. Drain and cool.

Sprinkle lightly with salt and pepper, olive oil, and lemon
juice. Gently toss. Cover and chill for several hours in the refrigerator before serving.

VARIATION: Add 2 cups washed and dried spinach, cut into thin
strips, and 3 tablespoons toasted pine nuts (cooked in a little olive
oil in a small frying pan until lightly browned) to the salad before
dressing.

Insalata di Mare di Cefalù

(Cefalù Seafood Salad)

½ pound baby octopuses (if
    unavailable, double the
    amount of squid below)
½ pound squid, cleaned and
    chopped
½ pound shrimp, shelled and
    deveined
1 pound mussels
1 pound cherrystone clams
2 lemons
10 bay leaves

DRESSING

⅔ cup olive oil
1½ tablespoons freshly squeezed
    lemon juice, or as needed
1 cup thinly sliced celery
2 carrots, scraped and cut into
    julienne strips
¼ cup freshly chopped Italian
    parsley
Salt and freshly ground pepper

Cefalù is a beautiful seaside resort about sixty kilometers north of Gangivecchio on the Tyrrhenian Sea on Sicily's north coast. It has justifiably become a popular holiday retreat for Sicilians and foreigners throughout the year. All of the many seafront restaurants in the area serve their own version of *insalata di mare*. Here is one that we particularly admire.

This salad is an exquisite first course, but it can also be served as a main course. Just double the recipe.

Serves 4

Cook each of the 5 seafoods separately in a frying pan with 2 cups of water, a lemon peel, and 2 bay leaves, just until tender. This method insures that the individual flavors are retained. Drain and cool. Shell the mussels and clams.

Put the seafood in a large bowl. Mix the dressing ingredients together and pour over the seafood. Toss the salad and taste for seasoning. Serve immediately or well chilled.

Insalata Casareccia di Olive di Gangivecchio

Makes about 6 cups

Toss the green olives with the olive oil in a bowl. Add the remaining ingredients and mix very well. Let rest in a cool room for half a day.

NOTE: Any leftover olive salad can be puréed in the food processor like a pesto, then spread on grilled bread slices for *bruschetta*.

(Gangivecchio's Homemade Mixed Olive Salad)

3 cups Sicilian green olives, pitted and quartered
½ cup olive oil
2 medium onions, thinly sliced
4 anchovy fillets, coarsely chopped
1 red or yellow bell pepper, cored, seeded, and cut into julienne strips
1 teaspoon dried oregano
2 tomatoes, diced and well drained
Freshly ground pepper

Insalata di Penne e Tonno di Ferruccio

Many people go to Betty's nutritionist uncle, Ferruccio, to get slimmer. He likes to invent interesting light recipes for his patients so they can escape the boredom of ordinary diet foods like radishes, celery, carrots, and boiled fish. We always think of him when we eat this salad, not only because it's his recipe but because when he gave the recipe to Betty, he told her this story. A very fat lady had been coming to see him for two weeks and hadn't lost half a kilogram, yet she claimed to be rigidly following the regimen he had prescribed for her. She told him that each day she ate only 300 grams of one of the salad recipes he had given her, plus fruits and vegetables and vitamin pills. After she left his office, he took a

(Ferruccio's Penne and Tuna Salad with Peppers and Mint)

1 large green bell pepper
1 large red bell pepper
3 garlic cloves, cut into slivers
One 6⅛-ounce can tuna fish
½ cup freshly chopped mint, plus 1 mint sprig
Salt and freshly ground pepper
Olive oil
1 pound penne

break and went across the street to a *tavola calda* for a cup of espresso and found himself standing face to face with this woman patient who was holding a large *arancina* in each hand. Neither of them spoke, but her face reddened and her eyes filled with tears. In spite of her tears, back in his office, Ferruccio told his secretary to cancel her next appointment.

Whenever Betty puts Ferruccio's penne and tuna salad on the menu at Tenuta Gangivecchio, Mamma calls and tells her, "I'll bring the *arancine*."

Serves 4 as a main course or 6 as a first course

Roast the peppers under the broiler until the skin is blackened all over. Remove the skins and seeds and cut into strips.

Put the peppers in a bowl with the garlic, tuna fish, and chopped mint, and season to taste with salt and pepper. Add about ¾ cup of olive oil. Let rest for 30 minutes.

Bring 4 quarts of water to a rolling boil in a large pot. Stir in 1½ tablespoons of salt, add the penne, and cook until al dente, or just tender.

Drain the pasta and turn into a bowl. Immediately add the sauce (which has been brought back to room temperature) and toss well. Let the salad rest for 10 minutes. Toss again and taste for seasonings. Garnish with the mint sprig. Serve warm or cold.

Conchiglie ad Insalata di Betty

(Betty's Shell Pasta and Tuna Salad with Black Olives)

Serves 6 as a main course

3 medium tomatoes, diced
½ cup (about 4 ounces) diced
    caciocavallo or provolone
    cheese
Two 6⅛-ounce cans white-meat
    tuna fish
¾ cup black olives, pitted and
    coarsely chopped
1 tablespoon freshly chopped
    basil or 1 teaspoon dried
1 teaspoon dried oregano
Salt and freshly ground pepper
1 cup olive oil
1 pound conchiglie (shell pasta)

Combine ingredients from the tomatoes through the olive oil. Let rest in a cool place, covered, for several hours.

Bring 4 quarts of water to a rolling boil in a large pot. Stir in 1½ tablespoons of salt, stir, and add the pasta. Cook until al dente, or just tender.

Drain the pasta and turn it into a large bowl. Immediately add the sauce and toss well. Let the salad rest for 15 minutes before serving.

FACENDO IL PANE ALLA MANIERA ANTICA
(Old-Fashioned Bread Making)

Near us, in the town of Gangi, we have several excellent bakeries, where we buy bread for home use and for the restaurant. It has been many years since we've made bread at Gangivecchio. Bread is rarely made at home anymore in all of Sicily, unless it is done out of love and devotion.

Since we wanted to include the recipe in the book for our outstanding local country bread, *pane rimacinato delle Madonie,* I organized a "bread day" at a friend's home high up in the Madonie Mountains, half an hour's drive from Gangivecchio. We enlisted the help of Elisa D'Arpa, whose mother passed on her love of homemade old-fashioned country-style breadmaking to her daughter. Elisa still enjoys the formidable task. Too busy with work in my own kitchen, Giovanna took Michele to observe this simple, but unusual method, so she could photograph the process and record Elisa's unwritten recipe.

W.T.

Our friends Vincenzo Mollica and Elisa D'Arpa and her sister, Maria, often gather together with their friends who live in neighboring mountain houses in the Madonie for companionship. The area is a desolate wilderness, over 5,000 feet above sea level, with magnificent views of the countryside and the world's clearest, sweetest air. This particular part of the Madonie Mountains, at Piano Battaglia, is a national park now, so no more private homes can be built. Vincenzo and Elisa and Maria and their friends, who've had homes here for many years, consider themselves very fortunate.

It is customary for our Madonie friends to cook their favorite traditional Sicilian dishes on weekends—men and women all contribute, even if it's just to criticize.

Early on a cool and windy October morning, Michele and I drove through thick mist and low-lying clouds along the mountainside roads. Soon the sun broke through and continued to shine all day.

Vincenzo, a retired doctor, who was my father's best friend, has a lovely garden with vegetables, herbs, and flowers—his greatest pride and joy are his beautiful mountain peonies. His property has a traditional small home and, a few meters away, a simple log cabin. In between the two houses, there is a long table situated outdoors under a covering next to an old brick oven. Not many of these ovens exist any longer in Sicily.

Vincenzo calls his home "The Place of the Fox" because for some years now a small red fox has befriended him. At night the fox comes up to the window of the cabin and, standing on his hind legs, peers inside. Vincenzo opens the window and offers the fox little pieces of raw meat, which the fox gently accepts, then runs off with them into the darkness of the wild, only to reappear the next night. There is a carved wooden sign in Vincenzo's garden that reads WE THINK THIS PLACE IS MAGIC. LOVE AND RESPECT IT.

For our "bread day" we brought along some bottles of Maschio Chardonnay wine, a *frizzante*. I know that these friends need wine like cars need gasoline to work. When we arrived at Vincenzo's "magic place," Elisa, the master breadmaker, was telling everyone that she had had to make up a story to tell her business partner to get the day off. "I told him I was going to a funeral in Palermo, and put on

a very sad face, like this," she said, demon-
strating a mournful expression, followed
by an explosion of laughter.

Elisa brought along several loaves of
bread for us to eat while we were making
the fresh bread. There must always be
bread in a Sicilian's home.

Elisa began to work 5 kilograms of
flour sprinkled with warm water in a huge
wooden *maidda,* the traditional breadmaking trough, moving her hands like a
magician. Meanwhile, Vincenzo roasted
eggplant slices over the grill outside, while
Maria and her cousin Filippo prepared the
sliced red onions and grated cheese for
the topping of the pizza to be made with
the extra bread dough. Maria also cooked a
ragù sauce. Everyone tasted samples and
complained that one or the other needed
more salt, less garlic, or more olive oil. All the time, Maria stirred, humming happily, paying no attention to anyone, because she is quite deaf.

A total of fourteen people joined in the work that day. Massimo Accascina,
another neighbor, and Vincenzo fed the waist-high, dome-shaped brick-lined
oven with dried cypress branches that would impart the best possible flavor to the
bread. When the bricks inside the oven turn white, the desired temperature for
baking the bread has been reached. The ashes and burning-hot red wood coals are
scooped out of the oven into metal buckets, and the coal is used later in the stove
to warm the house.

This ancient recipe for country bread uses only superior hard durum wheat
flour, water, fresh yeast, and a little salt. Sesame seeds top it. The dough is kneaded
by pressing with the fists and folding it over and over for about 30 minutes, until
it is perfectly silky. Vincenzo suggested, "It would not be wise for a man to con-
tradict a woman with arms as strong as Elisa's."

When the dough was ready, it was put into an immense bowl to rise. After
the first rise, Elisa cut the dough into pieces and formed them into three different
shapes—round, braided, and long—for nine loaves of bread. Extra dough was
saved for the pizza. The idea, like in the old days, is to make enough bread to last

for one week. The shaped loaves of bread, blessed with a cut sign of the cross, were put onto cotton cloths and covered with another. A wool blanket went on top to warm the dough. We all watched the bread as if it were a sleeping baby, even whispering as we passed the table on which it was resting. The exact process is described in the following recipe. Elisa topped the loaves with sesame seeds for the second rising. Then she released them, one by one, off a long-handled wooden paddle onto the floor of the white-hot oven.

To celebrate this moment, Vincenzo offered us his famous Orribili Patate (Horrible Potatoes), a tremendous mixture of potatoes, bell peppers, onions, rosemary, sage, and hot pepper sautéed in olive oil (page 232), making poor Elisa's eyes water—"How can you use my beautiful onions in these horrible potatoes?" They were delicious, though, and we hungrily devoured them all.

Momentarily fortified, we returned inside to the kitchen, for there was much more food preparation to be done for our feast. Elisa issued instructions to all of us to grate some bread for crumbs and to season and roll up the *spiedini*. But first, Elisa made a toast, "To the mamma of the veal, we thank you, and to the male cow for being so masculine, bravo!" I brought in branches of fresh-cut bay leaves from Gangivecchio for the *spiedini*. "These must be washed; they are covered with dust," Maria shouted, as she mashed hot boiled potatoes for the potato cake.

The day's menu included Vincenzo's grilled eggplant and horrible potatoes, beautiful grilled veal *involtini,* a mashed potato cake filled with ragout, and slices of yellow melon to clear our palates before Elisa's fantastic, yeast-flavored fresh bread, which we ate plain and also cut into slices and grilled. We sprinkled olive oil, oregano, mint, and salt and pepper on the grilled bread. We call this Pane Consato (page 264). Finally, when other friends arrived with their children, we consumed the big square red onion and pecorino pizza, sizzling hot from the oven.

Elisa divided the remaining loaves of bread among us all and announced that she and Maria were departing. After a day of making bread the ancient way, these two modern Sicilian women had appointments to keep at the beauty salon.

We concluded our feast with espresso. Finding no grappa in the house, we tried to make our own with the help of an old distillery. After one hour we produced just three little drops of a terrible liquid, but, anyway, it was our grappa.

G. T.

$\mathcal{P}$ane Rimacinato delle Madonie

(Madonie Mountain Country Bread)

To make our wonderful Madonie country bread, you must have the time to knead it for 30 minutes or more, plus the two risings and baking time.

Pane Rimacinato delle Madonie is made with hard semolina, so the flavor and texture are superb. Firm and dense, but still soft and chewy, this true country bread is best when cooked in a wood-burning oven, but the result is quite good when made in a home gas or electric oven.

The bread's ancient method is distinct, allowing the dough to be made by first combining only the flour and salted warm water, so that the flour fills itself. Then the yeast is added later.

Makes 3 loaves

Warm water
3 envelopes dry active yeast
3 pounds semolina (fine-ground hard durum flour)
Olive oil
Sesame seeds

We used an enormous *maidda* (an old-fashioned rectangular bread tray/trough) to make the bread on our special day. You can use a very large bowl or even a rectangular plastic tray with at least 5-inch sides.

Put the yeast into a bowl with 2 cups of warm water (about 110°F). Stir and let rest until it dissolves and proofs, about 10 minutes.

Meanwhile, put the flour into a large bowl. Pour about 1½ cups of warm water into the side of the bowl. Hand-mix until it almost forms into a dough; turn the dough over and over, pressing with your knuckles. Remove the dough. Sprinkle 1½ teaspoons of salt into the bowl and add about ½ cup of warm water. Stir the water around until the salt has dissolved. Pour all but ¼ cup of the salted water into a container and reserve. Return the dough to the bowl and continue working, turning over and over and pressing down with your knuckles and fists until the flour has absorbed the salted water. Add ¼ cup of the salted water and continue kneading. Continue adding the water, ¼ cup at a time, and working it into the dough until all the water is used. The dough becomes softer, but still firm. Now add the yeast and incorporate it into the dough, until smooth and silky. This will take about 10 minutes of constant turning and pressing.

Put some olive oil on your hands and coat the dough lightly. Let it rise in a large bowl until doubled in size, about 1½ hours.

Punch the dough down and knead it for a few seconds, turning it over and over. Divide into 3 equal portions. Shape the dough into any shape you desire. We suggest a round flat loaf (*guastedda*), then 1 portion divided into 2 ropes that are twisted together (*treccia*), and a long regular loaf of bread (*pistuluna*). Place on 1 or 2 baking sheets. Pat the top of each loaf with water and sprinkle lightly with sesame seeds. Cover with clean cloths. Let rise again. This time it will only take 35 to 40 minutes.

About 15 minutes before the end of the second rise, preheat the oven to 400°F.

Bake on the lower shelf of the oven for about 35 minutes, or until golden brown. If you have unglazed quarry tiles to put on the oven rack under the baking sheets, this will produce a crustier bread.

VARIATIONS

Pizza

You can make pizza with some of the dough, if you like, but you must add a little more water and a tablespoon or two of olive oil to the dough.

Pane Consato

With a loaf of the baked bread, you might want to try *pane consato,* which Sicilians have a passion for at any time of the day. *Pane consato* is made with a loaf of bread, hot from the oven (or reheated), usually a round loaf, cut open crosswise. The cut side of the bottom half is spread with an already prepared mixture of ground garlic, mint, basil, and olive oil seasoned with salt and pepper. It can be sprinkled with shredded pecorino cheese—sometimes pieces of sardines are added. Replace the top half over the filling quickly, so that the cheese will melt. If the mixture isn't moist enough, remove the top and drizzle some extra olive oil over the filling, then recover it. *Pane consato* can be served cut into wedges, quartered, or halved. A hungry man can eat the whole thing by himself with no trouble at all.

Gamberi con Rucola e Pompelmo Rosa

Serves 4

(Shrimp with Arugula and Pink Grapefruit)

Line 4 individual salad plates with equal amounts of the romaine and arugula. Arrange equal portions of the shrimp and grapefruit sections over the lettuce.

Combine the dressing ingredients well with a whisk, and spoon over the salads evenly.

1 quart romaine lettuce, thinly sliced
2 cups arugula, thinly sliced
1 pound shrimp, shelled, deveined, and cooked
2 pink grapefruits, with rind and piths cut off, separated into sections

PINK GRAPEFRUIT DRESSING

⅔ cup olive oil
2 tablespoons freshly squeezed pink grapefruit juice
1 tablespoon freshly squeezed lemon juice
Salt and freshly ground pepper

Aringhe in Compagnia

("In Good Company"—
Herring and Egg Salad)

Serves 4

4 hard-boiled eggs, shelled and
    sliced crosswise
3 smoked herring, chopped
1 large head romaine lettuce,
    shredded
20 green Sicilian olives, pitted
    and halved
½ pound cooked asparagus, cut
    into 1¼-inch lengths
Italian bread slices

DRESSING

½ cup olive oil
1 tablespoon freshly squeezed
    lemon juice
5 drops Tabasco sauce (or less)
½ teaspoon paprika
1 tablespoon heavy cream
Salt and freshly ground pepper

Italian bread slices

Combine all the salad ingredients, except for 1 sliced egg, in a large bowl. To make the dressing, mix all the ingredients together and pour over the salad. Garnish with the remaining egg slices. Serve with Italian bread slices.

Insalata di Pollo Primavera

(Spring Chicken Salad)

*T*his creamy chicken salad, filled with vegetables, is an excellent salad to serve in the spring, when the weather has warmed up and our appetites are longing for light meals. It's a dish we enjoy throughout the summer, too, of course.

Cooked shrimp can be substituted for the chicken in this recipe. For the shrimp salad, we change the garnish from lemon slices with capers to small ribs of celery hearts, with the leaves left intact.

Serves 4 to 6

Bring 2 quarts of water to a boil. Stir in 1 teaspoon of salt and add the chicken. Bring the water back to the boil. Reduce the heat to a simmer and cook for about 25 minutes, turning the chicken occasionally, until tender.

Meantime, prepare the dressing. Whisk the egg yolks, mustard, and lemon juice together in a medium-sized bowl. Drop by drop, whisk in the olive oil. Add the remaining ingredients, whisking after adding each. Taste for seasoning. Refrigerate until needed.

Drain the cooked chicken and cool. Shred the chicken breast into thin strips and transfer to a large bowl. Add the potatoes, green beans, and tomatoes, and gently combine. Turn the dressing over the salad and gently toss.

Line a serving platter or bowl with the romaine lettuce leaves and top with the salad. Garnish the platter with the lemon slices. Put 3 capers in the center of each lemon slice.

The salad can be served immediately or well chilled. If the day is very hot, the salad can be presented in the bowl over a larger bowl of shaved ice.

Salt
1¾ pounds chicken breasts, boned, skinned, and halved
2 cups boiled new potatoes, cubed and cooled
2 cups boiled green beans, cut into 1-inch lengths and cooled
2 medium-sized firm, ripe tomatoes, cubed
12 small romaine lettuce leaves
6 lemon slices, for garnish
Capers

MAYONNAISE DRESSING

3 large egg yolks
1 teaspoon dry mustard
2 teaspoons freshly squeezed lemon juice
1 cup olive oil
2 tablespoons ketchup
¼ teaspoon Angostura bitters
2 drops Tabasco sauce
¼ teaspoon Worcestershire sauce
1 tablespoon Cognac or brandy
Salt and freshly ground pepper

Insalata di Natale I

(Christmas Salad I)

1 large cauliflower, cooked,
    drained, and cut into florets
10 anchovy fillets, chopped
20 green Sicilian olives, pitted
    and halved
⅓ cup freshly chopped Italian
    parsley
2 tablespoons capers, washed
    and drained
Olive oil
White wine vinegar
Pinch of cayenne pepper
Salt and freshly ground pepper

*T*his salad has been on our table every Christmas I can remember. In the past, we always used red wine vinegar in the recipe because that was all we had. It turned the cauliflower pink, but we didn't mind, because it was a great vinegar that came from a big barrel started by my great-grandfather. Each year a piece of the mother—or vinegar starter—was taken from the barrel and put into a cleaned one, and my grandfather added wine. No one wants the chore of cleaning the barrel anymore, so we have sadly ended the tradition of vinegar-making.

Serves 8

Mix the cauliflower, anchovies, olives, parsley, and capers together in a large bowl. Sprinkle lightly with olive oil and white wine vinegar, and season to taste with cayenne pepper, salt, and pepper. Serve at room temperature.

"The three colors—green, white, and red—of this beautiful-looking and beautiful-tasting salad represent the vivid colors of the Italian flag."

Insalata Tricolore, page 248

Old-fashioned bread making (*clockwise from upper left*): Elisa works the dough in a huge wooden *maidda*; Elisa and Giovanna prepare the loaves for the oven; Vincenzo Mollica making his "horrible potatoes" to go with the bread; the different shapes of Sicilian bread; a special bread from Panificio lo Giudice."

"Pomegranate seeds are delicious sprinkled onto salads, fruit dishes, and ice cream."
Melograni, page 251

"Small watermelon jelly molds are ancient
Arabian sweets of Sicily. Mamma transforms
the delicious watermelon base into a beautiful tart."
Torta di Gelo di Mellone, page 278

"Cannoli are perhaps the most famous dessert of Sicily. I have tasted none better than my mother's."

Cannoli, page 281

Peppe preparing Mamma's secret (until now) recipe for *sofficini*, page 294.

"At Gangivecchio, we have two enormous green fig trees in the courtyard of the abbey."
Torta di Fichi, page 277

"There are never any *sofficini* left over." *Sofficini*, page 277

Insalata di Natale II

*H*ere is our adaptation of a very old, classic recipe that you'll find in every Sicilian cookbook. It's cheerful, colorful, and tasty. Of course, it can be served throughout the fall and winter as well as on Christmas Day.

Serves 8

Immerse the endive or escarole and celery in boiling water for 1 minute. Drain well.

Combine the endive or escarole and the celery with the olives, capers, and a little olive oil. Sprinkle lightly with salt and pepper to taste.

Oil a 1-quart bowl and spoon the mixture into the bowl. Press the top down gently and let rest for 15 minutes.

Invert the salad onto a serving dish and place the orange and lemon slices in overlapping, alternating rows over the entire top of the salad, which is now a delicious dome. Sprinkle with rosy-red pomegranate seeds.

2 quarts curly endive or escarole, torn into bite-size pieces

3 celery ribs with leaves, thinly sliced

½ cup green Sicilian olives, pitted and finely chopped

⅓ cup capers, washed and drained

Olive oil

Salt and freshly ground pepper

3 navel oranges, peeled, with white pith removed, and very thinly sliced

3 lemons, peeled, with white pith removed, and very thinly sliced (seeds discarded)

½ cup pomegranate seeds

Dolci

(Desserts)

Crema Pasticciera *(Basic Pastry Cream)* • Crema di Cioccolato *(Chocolate Pastry Cream)* • Crema di Ricotta *(Ricotta Cream)* • Pasta Frolla *(Pastry Dough)* • Pasta Frolla Piccante *(Pastry Dough for Vegetable Tarts)* • Cassata al Forno di Ricotta *(Ricotta Cake)* • Torta alla Frutta *(Fruit Tart)* • Torta di Fichi *(Fig Tart)* • Torta di Mandorle *(Almond Tart with Chocolate Cream)* • Torta di Gelo di Mellone *(Watermelon Tart)* • Torta ai Frutti di Bosco di Betty *(Betty's Wild Berry Tart)* • Cannoli • Canne per Cannoli *(Cannoli Forms)* • Frittelle di Ricotta *(Ricotta Fritters)* • Sfince *(Pastry Fritters Filled with Sweetened Ricotta)* • La Torta di Nozze di Betty e Paolo *(Betty and Paolo's Wedding Cake)* • Dolce di Cioccolato *(Unbaked Chocolate Cake)* • Budini di Sicilia *(Sicilian Puddings)* • Dolce al Cucchiaio *(Cream and Fruit Pudding)* • Budino di Ricotta *(Lemon and Ricotta Pudding)* • Crema di Bucce di Limone con Frutta *(Molded Lemon Peel Cream with Fruit)* • Prugne Secche di Betty *(Betty's Dried Spiced Prunes with Red Wine)* • Datteri con Pasta di Mandorle *(Dates Filled with Almond Paste)* • Bocconcini *(Coffee-Flavored Almond Balls)* • Croccante di Mandorle *(Almond Brittle)* • Gelato di Ricotta *(Ricotta Ice Cream)* • Semifreddo di Caffè *(Frozen Coffee Cream)* • Sofficini *(Fried Pastry Stuffed with Sweet Lemon Pastry Cream)*

Nella vita, quando qualche cosa finisce, di solito lascia un sapore amaro, ma non un pranzo . . . un dolce arriva.

(In life, when something ends, it usually leaves a bitter taste, but not a meal . . . a sweet arrives.)

—*Wanda Tornabene*

Mamma truly loves sweets of any kind, especially cakes. She will stop in front of a *pasticceria* and gaze in the window forever. Then, of course, she must go inside and almost always buy. There are many excellent *pasticcerie* in Sicily, but in Palermo we especially like one called I Peccatucci di Mamma Andrea, which means "the little sins of Mamma Andrea." I asked Mamma if she thought we should open our own *pasticceria* called I Peccatucci di Mamma Wanda—I believe she actually considered this for a few moments. When she can't sleep, and doesn't have dark thoughts, she invents her own dessert recipes, writing them down at three o'clock in the morning in her enormous copper-framed bed—and then, no doubt, dreams of a showcase for her creations.

We Sicilians all love our desserts. It is part of the rich culinary legacy we inherited from Arabian domination. Arabians were responsible for introducing us to extraordinary *gelati,* almonds, pistachios (and many other nuts that we use in our cuisine), as well as the fondness we have for all things made with sugar or honey. Our almond brittle—*croccante di mandorle*—half caramelized sugar and half almonds, is ambrosial. Sugar is almost as vital to Sicilian cooking as salt. We even insist on putting a little sugar in our pasta sauce, and very much admire *agrodolce* (sweet and sour) flavors in sauces.

Sicilians love to eat plain fruit for dessert, too. In restaurants or homes we will often have just a slice of melon—watermelon or perhaps our luscious yellow melon—or we may have one of our fantastic blood or sweet oranges. We have superb figs, persimmons, peaches, plums, pears, prickly pears, quince, blackberries, cherries, mulberries, kiwi fruit, and dates—all of which are cultivated here. In Sicily, we traditionally eat just one kind of fruit at a time. But in Mamma's recipe for Crema di Bucce di Limone con Frutta (page 289), a molded lemon-cream dessert, she surrounds the mold with mixed sliced fruit and berries. It is a delicious and beautiful dessert.

When my father was a child, he always went to bed with some kind of pastry on a little plate on his night table, left there by his mother. The pastry plate was always empty in the morning, not one crumb left.

Mamma liked this tradition, so she would place a small cannoli—Papa's favorite bedtime snack—and a little portion of her latest invention on his table before turning out the light. In the morning, if Papa said he'd had a bad dream, she would throw out the new recipe.

Crema Pasticciera

(Basic Pastry Cream)

*W*e use our basic pastry cream for many desserts, especially for tart and *sofficini* fillings. It is also the base for Mamma's delicious spoon pudding, Dolce al Cucchiaio (page 288). We also turn it into a chocolate pastry cream with Amaretto or coffee liqueur and cocoa. The directions are found below.

Crema Pasticciera keeps well in the refrigerator for one day.

Makes about 1½ quarts of pastry cream

1½ quarts milk
1 teaspoon vanilla extract
Peel of 2 large or 4 small lemons, cut in one long strip each
8 large egg yolks, at room temperature
2¼ cups sugar
⅔ cup cornstarch

Over low heat, slowly bring the milk, vanilla, and lemon peel to a boil in a large, heavy-bottomed saucepan, stirring occasionally.

Beat the egg yolks and sugar together in a large bowl until light and fluffy. Add the cornstarch and blend well.

Remove it from the heat and discard the lemon peels. Little by little, beat ¾ cup of the hot milk into the eggs.

Slowly stir the egg mixture into the remaining milk in the saucepan, constantly stirring. When it is thoroughly incorporated, return the pan to high heat and let the *crema* boil for 2 minutes, stirring constantly, until thick and creamy.

NOTE: The recipe is easily cut in half.

VARIATION:

Crema di Cioccolato
(Chocolate Pastry Cream)

Stir ¾ cup of unsweetened cocoa powder into the hot milk and vanilla. (Do not use the lemon peel.) Add 1 tablespoon of Amaretto (or coffee liqueur), then follow the recipe exactly as instructed above, using the same amounts of ingredients, but taste for the right sugar amount. You'll probably need a little more.

Crema di Ricotta

(Ricotta Cream)

4 cups whole milk ricotta,
    drained in refrigerator for
    one or two nights (see
    instructions on page 39)
1 cup sugar, or to taste
1 teaspoon vanilla extract

Ricotta cream is called for in several of our dessert recipes for cakes and tarts, and is the filling for Mamma's magnificent cannoli. In New York's Little Italy, we sampled some very good cannoli, but we discovered, as we'd been forewarned, that most commercially produced ricotta in the United States is quite different from ours in texture, with a watery consistency and rather bland taste. We have worked out a formula for a fairly close resemblance to Sicilian fresh sheep's ricotta. Take note that the ricotta must be drained one or two nights beforehand in the refrigerator. After sweetening the ricotta, it needs to rest in the refrigerator overnight again. So to make it, you must plan ahead.

Makes enough for 18–24 cannoli or two 9-inch tarts

Mix the well-drained ricotta and sugar together very well and let it rest at room temperature for 8 hours.

Pass the ricotta through a fine *setaccio* (sieve) into a large bowl. Do not use a food processor for this purpose, because the ricotta will have the consistency of glue. We use the bottom of a small, heavy glass jar to press the ricotta through the fine mesh. Add the vanilla to the strained ricotta and mix together well. Cover the bowl and refrigerate it overnight.

Pasta Frolla

(Pastry Dough)

4 cups all-purpose flour
2 cups sugar
2 tablespoons baking powder
Finely grated zest of 1 small
    lemon

The base for all our tarts—ricotta, fig, almond, and watermelon, or any fruit you like—is Pasta Frolla, a sweetened pastry that is extremely delicious and flaky. Simple to prepare, it shouldn't be handled too much or it will toughen. We have two types of Pasta Frolla—the sweet one with sugar, grated zest of a lemon and no salt, and a Pasta Frolla Piccante, used for vegetable tarts like

Sformato di Carciofi (Artichoke Tart, page 59). The Pasta Frolla Piccante contains a little salt, less sugar than Pasta Frolla, and no lemon zest. Directions can be found below. Betty uses her own version of Pasta Frolla in her recipe for Torta ai Frutti di Bosco (wild berry tart, page 280).

Makes two 8- or 9-inch tarts

6 large eggs, at room temperature
½ teaspoon vanilla extract
1⅓ cups sweet butter, melted, then brought to room temperature

Put the flour, sugar, and baking powder into a large bowl. Add the lemon zest, eggs, and vanilla, and mix together with a pastry blender or the blades of 2 knives. Little by little, incorporate the butter. Knead the dough, only enough so that the dough sticks together. Coat your hands with a little flour, but take care not to overwork the dough or it will toughen.

Pasta Frolla can also be made in a food processor. The procedure is as follows: Put the flour, sugar, baking powder, lemon zest, and butter into the bowl of the processor and blend until coarse-crumb consistency. With the machine running, add the eggs and vanilla through the feed tube. Process just a few seconds, until the dough is combined.

Form the dough into 2 balls, cover each with plastic wrap, and refrigerate them overnight, if possible. It must be refrigerated for at least 1 hour. The dough also freezes well for future use. Instructions for using the dough are given in individual recipes. The recipe is easily divided in half.

VARIATION:

Pasta Frolla Piccante
(Pastry Dough for Vegetable Tarts)

Pasta Frolla Piccante is made in exactly the same manner as regular Pasta Frolla, except that only 1¼ cups of sugar are used. Eliminate the zest of lemon from the recipe, but add 2 teaspoons of salt to the flour.

Cassata al Forno di Ricotta

(Ricotta Cake)

½ recipe Pasta Frolla (page 274)
Sweet butter and flour, for
    greasing and coating the pan
¼ cup candied citron, cut into
    ¼-inch cubes
¼ cup chocolate chip pieces
½ recipe Crema di Ricotta
    (page 274—the ricotta must
    be prepared one to two days
    in advance; see page 39 for
    directions)
Confectioners' sugar

*M*y grandmother Giovanna made a wonderful classic Sicilian cake prepared with a filling composed only of combined fresh ricotta and sugar baked inside the pastry shell. It is spectacular in its simplicity and always our personal favorite. The other famous *cassata* cake, *cassata alla Siciliana,* the one made with *pasta reale,* is such a big production that we never even attempt to make it.

Serves 8

Preheat the oven to 350°F.

Roll two thirds of the Pasta Frolla into an 11-inch circle (¼ inch thick) and fit into a 9-inch springform pan, lightly greased with butter and coated with flour.

Mix the candied citron and chocolate chips into the Crema di Ricotta. Spoon the mixture into the pastry shell, smoothing the top evenly.

Roll the leftover dough into little ropes about ⅓ inch thick and place across the top of the filling at about 1-inch intervals in two directions, making a lattice design.

Place the cake on a baking sheet and bake on the middle shelf of the preheated oven for about 45 minutes. Cool the cake for 10 minutes before serving, then sprinkle the top with confectioners' sugar.

Torta alla Frutta

(Fruit Tart)

½ recipe Pasta Frolla (page 274)
Sweet butter and flour, for greas-
    ing and coating the pan
½ recipe Crema Pasticciera, still
    warm, but not hot (page 273)

Serves 8

Preheat the oven to 350°F.

Roll the Pasta Frolla into a 10½-inch circle and fit into a 9-inch tart pan that has been lightly greased with butter and coated with flour.

Turn the Crema Pasticciera into the pastry shell. Bake on a baking sheet on the middle shelf of the preheated oven for 45 minutes. Cool the tart for 30 minutes, then refrigerate it for several hours.

Heat the apricot preserves in a small pan with 2 tablespoons of water and boil for 5 minutes. Strain the preserves and cool for 10 minutes. Stir the preserves and spread evenly over the top of the Crema Pasticciera.

Arrange the fruit across the top of the preserves. If using a mixture of fruit, make circles of each fruit, starting from the outside of the pastry. Serve chilled.

1 cup apricot preserves
2–3 cups of one fruit, like strawberries or raspberries, or a mixture like halved seedless green or red grapes, slices of pineapple, blueberries, blackberries, or any other berry

Torta di Fichi

(Fig Tart)

*A*t Gangivecchio, we have two enormous green fig trees in the courtyard of the abbey. Our harvest yields hundreds of figs, all ripening within a two-week period. Since figs are so perishable, they must be used immediately or preserved. So we prepare many of these luscious fig tarts for our customers. We also serve figs with prosciutto, and sometimes, for home use, we make batches of fig preserves. When the figs are very ripe, we can enjoy them just peeled and spread on toast. This is the best imaginable way to make natural fig preserves and the easiest recipe in our book.

Serves 8 to 10

Preheat the oven to 350°F.

Roll out the Pasta Frolla into a 10½-inch circle and fit it into a 9-inch cake pan that has been lightly greased with butter and coated with flour. Fit the Crema Pasticciera into the pastry shell and smooth the top evenly.

Bake in the preheated oven on a baking sheet for about 40 to 45 minutes, until the crust is golden brown. Cool for 30 minutes.

Set aside 2 whole figs, then cut the remaining figs in half crosswise. Arrange them, cut side up, on top of the *crema* in 2 concentric circles, pressing them down slightly, leaving the center area uncovered. Cut the reserved 2 figs into quarters from the top to the stem end, without cutting all the way through, like four-pointed

½ recipe Pasta Frolla (page 274)
½ recipe Crema Pasticciera (page 273), chilled
Butter and flour, for greasing and coating the pan
12–16 peeled fresh figs, depending on size
1 cup apricot preserves

stars. Place them in the center of the tart and refrigerate for a few minutes.

Boil the apricot preserves with 1 tablespoon of water for 5 minutes. Strain and cool for 10 minutes, stirring occasionally.

Remove the tart from the refrigerator and carefully spoon the apricot preserves over the figs, using a brush to evenly cover the tops of the figs. Serve immediately or refrigerate.

Torta di Mandorle

(Almond Tart with Chocolate Cream)

Serves 10

1½ cups blanched whole almonds, plus 12 extra whole almonds, set aside for topping
¼ teaspoon almond extract
¾ cup all-purpose flour
¾ cup sugar
1 large egg
½ cup sweet butter, melted
Sweet butter and flour, for greasing and coating the pan
½ recipe Crema di Cioccolato (page 273), warm, not hot

Grind the almonds in a food processor to a fine consistency. Remove to a large bowl and add the almond extract, flour, sugar, and egg. Mix very well. Stir in the melted butter. The dough should be semihard.

Butter and flour a 9-inch tart or cake pan. Roll two thirds of the dough into a 10½-inch circle and fit into the pan. Pour the warm Crema di Cioccolato into the shell. Chill the tart for 30 minutes, or until slightly set.

Roll about 16 little balls with the remaining pastry. Place the little dough balls and 16 whole almonds over the top of the chilled tart, like a mosaic.

Bake on a baking sheet on the middle shelf of the oven and bake at 350°F for 45 minutes, or until the crust is golden brown.

Torta di Gelo di Mellone

(Watermelon Tart)

1 large watermelon (about 10 pounds), with rind and seeds removed

Small watermelon jelly molds, flavored with cinnamon, are ancient Arabian sweets of Sicily. A purée of fresh watermelon is set in charming little ceramic molds called *formelle,* the inside centers of which are fashioned into all kinds of shapes, such as flowers, birds, hearts, or butterflies. The rosy-red unmolded shapes are presented garnished with jasmine blossoms and shaved chocolate. Although they are beautiful to the eye, so much cornstarch is used in the mixture that the result is a rubbery texture. Mamma transforms the delicious watermelon base using less cornstarch into a beautiful tart.

Serves 8

¾ cup sugar, or to taste
½ cup cornstarch, dissolved in
 ½ cup cool water
1 cinnamon stick, or ⅛ teaspoon powdered cinnamon
Sweet butter and flour, for
 greasing and coating the pan
½ recipe Pasta Frolla (page 274)
Confectioners' sugar

Purée the seedless watermelon pieces in a blender, in batches. You will need 1 quart of liquid watermelon. If you have more liquid than you need, reward yourself by drinking this delicious nectar.

Pour the liquid into a heavy-bottomed saucepan and stir in the sugar. Add the cornstarch and cinnamon stick. Slowly bring to a boil, stirring constantly for 3 minutes.

Remove from the heat. Taste for sweetness; you may need to add a little more sugar because the sweetness of watermelon is unpredictable.

Discard the cinnamon stick and pour the mixture into a bowl and let cool to room temperature.

Preheat the oven to 350°F.

Butter and flour the inside of a 9-inch tart or cake pan. Roll out three quarters of the Pasta Frolla into a 10½-inch circle and fit it into the pan with the sides coming up about 1½ inches.

Pour the cooled watermelon filling into the pastry shell. Make little ⅓-inch-wide ropes with the remaining dough and arrange in a lattice design as described in the recipe for Cassata al Forno di Ricotta on page 276, or just make a single row of ropes, about 1 inch apart.

Bake the watermelon tart on a baking sheet on the middle shelf of the preheated oven for about 45 minutes, or until the pastry is golden brown. Cool for 30 minutes, then dust with sifted confectioners' sugar and serve immediately or chill first.

Torta ai Frutti di Bosco di Betty

(Betty's Wild Berry Tart)   *Serves 9 to 10*

BETTY'S PASTA FROLLA

2¼ cups all-purpose flour
¾ cup sugar
1½ teaspoons baking powder
¾ cup sweet butter
Grated zest of 1 small lemon
2 large eggs, 1 separated
3 tablespoons heavy cream
½ teaspoon vanilla extract
Pinch of salt
Sweetened whipped cream
    (optional)

FILLING

4 cups mixed berries, such as
    blueberries, raspberries,
    small strawberries (or cubed
    large ones), blackberries,
    mulberries, or currants
½ cup sugar

Combine the dry ingredients for Betty's Pasta Frolla with the lemon zest in a large bowl. Work in the butter. Lightly beat together 1 whole egg and 1 yolk, and add the cream, vanilla, and salt. Little by little, add the egg-cream mixture to form a dough using a wooden spoon or pastry blender. Divide the dough in half. Wrap each half in plastic and refrigerate for 30 minutes.

In a bowl, gently toss berries with the sugar and set aside.

Preheat the oven to 350°F.

Roll the balls of pastry into 2 circles large enough to fit over the side of a 9-inch tart pan. Fit the bottom half of the pastry into the pan and trim off the overlapping edge. Turn the combined fruit and sugar into the pan.

Cut a 1-inch circle in the center of the remaining pastry. Fit it over the top of the berries and crimp the pastry edges together.

Brush the top of the dough with the reserved egg white.

Bake in the preheated oven on a baking sheet for 45 minutes, or until golden brown. Serve with sweetened whipped cream, if desired.

Cannoli

*C*annoli are perhaps the most famous dessert of Sicily. Every cook has his or her own special recipe for the pastry shell and *crema di ricotta* filling. I have tasted none better than my mother's. She is a purist where cannoli are concerned, and never adds candied citron to her creamy ricotta filling or uses those terrible cherries to garnish each end. We feel it is critical that the shells be deep-fried in lard. If you do not wish to use lard, or cannot find it, use sunflower oil or another seed or vegetable oil, but the cannoli won't be as good or taste the same as ours. Mamma believes that if you are going to the big trouble of making cannoli, why not prepare them right? (Read about lard on page 38.)

The most important thing to remember when preparing good cannoli is to fill the cooked shells just before they are served, so they are very crisp and crunchy. Mamma will never buy cannoli in a *pasticceria,* because they have been filled far too early. She says even 10 minutes is too long, and 1 minute is best. Luckily, the shells can be made in advance and stored in tin boxes with tight-fitting lids. When we are serving cannoli for a large wedding party or event, our kitchen and pantry are stacked like a supermarket with many, many tins of cannoli shells.

Makes about 24 cannoli

Put the flour and sugar into a large bowl. Make a well in the center and add the eggs and melted lard or sunflower or vegetable oil. Mix together the ingredients, adding enough vinegar, little by little, until you have a very smooth, soft dough. Knead the dough on a board for a few minutes and work into a ball. The dough should be soft and elastic. Let the dough rest, covered, at room temperature for 2 to 3 hours. It can be prepared a day in advance and kept in a plastic bag at room temperature.

Roll the dough into a very thin, large circle. You can also halve or quarter the dough, and roll each piece out into smaller circles. Cut the rolled dough into perfect 4-inch circles using the edge of a saucer or can. Pass the circles of dough through a manual pasta machine once, to make them slightly oval-shaped, or use a rolling

2 cups all-purpose flour

⅓ cup sugar

2 large eggs, at room temperature

⅓ cup lard, melted and cooled, or sunflower or vegetable oil, plus more for oiling forms and deep-frying

Red wine vinegar, as needed

1 egg white

1 recipe Crema di Ricotta (page 274—the ricotta must be made one to two days in advance; see page 39 for directions)

Confectioners' sugar

pin. Wrap each piece of dough around a lightly oiled cannoli tube form. Be sure the 2 shorter sides of the oval overlap at the middle. Dab a bit of egg white where the dough overlaps and press to secure it well. We suggest having at least 12 tube forms so that half the cannoli can be made in advance.

Heat about 3 inches of lard or sunflower or a vegetable oil in a

Canne per Cannoli
(Cannoli Forms)

The most commonly used cannoli-shell forms in Sicily and America are made of tinplate. At Gangivecchio, the cannoli-shell forms we use are natural ones made from *canna,* a bamboolike reed that grows wild here.

When we need to replace old *canna* forms, Peppe disappears into the woods with a sharp knife and returns with a basket of bright green *canne.* He selects perfect hollow reeds, about ⅞ of an inch in diameter, then cuts them into 5- to 6-inch lengths. For initiation as forms, *canne* are rubbed with oil, wrapped with dough, and baptized in boiling-hot lard. The color of the natural *canna* turns from green to various shades of brown during the frying process. The forms are used for up to a year or more.

We suggest having at least 12 forms to work with at a time, so all the shells can be made up in advance.

We keep a large supply of cannoli forms on hand because we sometimes must make over 250 cannoli shells at a time for the restaurant, at holiday time, or for special functions like weddings.

deep-sided frying pan until the lard is hot but not smoking. Fry 2 to 4 shells at a time, turning them with a slotted spoon, and watch them closely, until golden brown all over. Take care not to let them burn. This can happen if you look away for just 10 seconds, so don't. Drain the cooked cannoli on paper towels and immediately remove them from the hot metal tubes. This is easily done by holding one end of the tube with a pot holder and gently sliding the shell off with a wooden spoon. If preparing more than 12 shells at a time, allow the hot tubes to cool completely before wrapping more dough around them. (You do not need to re-oil them.)

You can let the shells rest for up to 1 hour before filling them. If you wish to fill them later or the next day, after they have completely cooled, store them in one or more tin boxes with tight-fitting lids.

To fill the cannoli, spoon a few tablespoonfuls of the Crema di Ricotta into the shell at each end with a teaspoon. Smooth the ends with the back of the spoon. Sprinkle sifted confectioners' sugar over the tops of the filled cannoli and serve at once.

NOTE: The recipe can easily be cut in half to make 12 cannoli.

Frittelle di Ricotta

(Ricotta Fritters)

Makes 30 fritters

Put the ricotta into a large bowl. Add the sugar and flour and mix well. Stir in the egg yolks and raisins and thoroughly combine.

Heat ¼ inch of sunflower or vegetable oil in the bottom of a large frying pan. Fry the batter in rounded tablespoonfuls, in batches, not allowing individual fritters to touch one another. Lightly press down the top of each fritter with the back of a spoon. Fry until golden brown on each side, then drain on paper towels. Let cool.

Sprinkle with confectioners' sugar and powdered cinnamon before serving.

2 pounds drained ricotta (see instructions on page 39)
1 cup granulated sugar
1 cup all-purpose flour
4 large egg yolks, at room temperature
¾ cup raisins, soaked in luke-warm water for 10 minutes and drained
Sunflower or vegetable oil, for frying
Confectioners' sugar
Powdered cinnamon

Sfince

*(Pastry Fritters Filled with
Sweetened Ricotta)*

1 cup water
¼ teaspoon salt
¼ cup lard or sweet butter
2 cups all-purpose flour
6 large eggs
1 teaspoon baking powder
1 tablespoon vodka
Sunflower or vegetable oil, for
    deep-frying
2 cups Crema di Ricotta (page
    274—the ricotta should be
    prepared one to two days in
    advance; see page 39 for
    directions)
Granulated sugar (optional)
Powdered cinnamon (optional)

*S*fince are small pieces of puffy fried dough filled with sweetened ricotta, traditionally served on Saint Joseph's Day, March 19, but nowadays we prepare them any time of the year.

Sometimes we make the fritters, roll them in granulated sugar, and forget about the filling. When filled, *sfince* normally are not rolled in sugar, but if you have an extrasweet tooth, there is no reason you can't coat the cream-filled *sfince* with sugar, adding a little cinnamon, if desired. Either way, they will disappear in a flash, as if a thief has been in the house.

I should mention that Sicilians like to dip *sfince* in honey, too. Although not customary, *sfince* can also be filled with marmalade or jelly.

Makes about 20 sfince

Put the water, salt, and lard or butter into a saucepan and bring it to a boil. Add the flour all at once, and vigorously stir it with a wooden spoon. Immediately remove from the heat. Stir the hard dough into a ball and turn into a large bowl. Let cool for 5 minutes.

One by one, beat the eggs into the mixture. The eggs resist joining the flour mixture, but pay no attention to this. Just keep adding the eggs, one at a time, until they are incorporated into the dough. Add the vodka. The consistency should be smooth and sticky. Stir in the baking powder.

Heat 3 inches of sunflower or vegetable oil in a deep-sided frying pan until the oil is hot but not smoking. Gently ease a few rounded tablespoonfuls of dough into the hot oil. Since the dough is sticky, you need to push it off the spoon with your finger. You can cook only about 6 *sfince* at a time because they triple in size. With a slotted spoon, constantly turn the fritters so they cook evenly to a golden brown. This takes only about 4 minutes. Very near the end of the cooking time, each *sfince* will burst and a little of the interior will be exposed. Keep turning the *sfince* for a few seconds, until this part is also golden brown. As the *sfince* are cooked, drain them on paper towels.

When the *sfince* are no longer hot to the touch, make a small incision with a small knife into the middle and wiggle the knife around a bit to make space for the filling. Spoon a little of the Crema di Ricotta into the center of each *sfince*. If you like, sprinkle with granulated sugar. You can mix a little cinnamon into the sugar, too.

La Torta di Nozze di Betty e Paolo

(Betty and Paolo's Wedding Cake)

$\mathscr{B}$etty and Paolo's beautiful wedding cake was actually six square, individually baked *pan di spagna* that were fitted snugly together in a rectangular shape. The cake was spread with a layer of *crema pasticciera* and topped with tiny wild strawberries, then sprinkled with confectioners' sugar. *Crème chantilly* was piped in rows along the sides of the cake. The finishing touch was a bouquet of roses placed in the center as the festive garnish.

The directions that follow are for 1 cake to serve 8 to 10. Double, triple, and quadruple the amounts for the cake, cream, and strawberries to make larger cakes, depending on the number of servings required.

The *pan di spagna* can be made up to a month in advance and frozen until needed and the *crema pasticciera* made a day ahead.

Serves 8 to 10

To make the Pan di Spagna, first preheat the oven to 350°F.

Butter the bottom and sides of a 10-inch square baking pan and set it aside.

Put the egg yolks and sugar into a large bowl, and beat with an electric mixer until very creamy and a pale yellow color. This will take about 10 minutes. Add the vanilla and lemon zest. Beat for another 30 seconds and set the bowl aside.

In another bowl, beat the egg whites until stiff but not dry. Fold half the egg whites into the batter. Add the remaining whites and fold them in thoroughly.

PAN DI SPAGNA

Softened sweet butter, for greasing the pan

6 large eggs, separated

1 cup granulated sugar

1 teaspoon vanilla extract

1 teaspoon freshly grated lemon zest

1 cup sifted all-purpose flour, plus extra for coating the pan

½ teaspoon baking powder

½ recipe Crema Pasticciera (page 273), at room temperature

1 pint small wild strawberries, or other small strawberries

Confectioners' sugar

CRÈME CHANTILLY

2 cups heavy cream

½ cup granulated sugar

1 teaspoon vanilla extract

La Torta di Nozze *(cont.)*

Combine the flour and baking powder and add about ¼ cup of the mixture at a time, folding each addition in gently.

Turn the batter into the pan and bake in the preheated oven for about 25 minutes, or until a toothpick inserted into the center comes out clean. Remove the cake from the oven and let it cool on a cake rack for 5 minutes. Then invert the cake onto a rack and allow it to cool fully. (At this point, you can wrap the cake in plastic wrap or aluminum foil and freeze it for up to a month.)

Spread the room temperature Crema Pasticciera over the top of the cake. Place the strawberries in a single layer over the entire surface of the cake and dust them with sifted confectioners' sugar. Refrigerate the cake until just before serving it.

Prepare the Crème Chantilly by whipping the heavy cream. Add the sugar and vanilla, and whip a few minutes more. Refrigerate if you are not ready to decorate the cake at this time.

Spoon the sweetened whipped cream into a pastry bag fitted with a small star tip. Pipe the cream in vertical rows along all sides of the cake and make a border with the final row along the top edge. Serve immediately. If you like, garnish the cake with a few baby roses in the center.

Dolce di Cioccolato

(Unbaked Chocolate Cake)

4 large eggs, at room temperature
1 cup sugar

*T*his is Grandmother Giovanna's recipe for a chocolate cake that my father loved so much, he learned to make it—the only dish he ever prepared. —G.T.

Serves 10

Beat the eggs and sugar together in a large bowl. Stir in the cocoa and blend well. Add the biscuit crumbs and mix, then add the melted butter.

Prepare a 9 × 4–inch loaf pan by coating it lightly with the extra butter. Cut pieces of parchment paper to fit the bottom and sides, and press them firmly in place. Turn the mixture into the pan and lightly press it down.

Cover the pan and refrigerate overnight.

When ready to serve the cake, invert it onto a work surface. Remove the paper. Heat a long, straight-edged knife and pass it over the top and sides of the cake to bring a shine. Serve slices of the cake with the Crème Chantilly, a sweetened whipped cream. (Don't refrigerate the cake again or it will dry out.)

¾ cup unsweetened cocoa powder

3 cups dry butter biscuits or cookies (not too sweet), chopped into fine crumbs

1¼ cups butter, melted, plus extra for coating the pan

1 recipe Crème Chantilly (sweetened whipped cream, page 284)

$\mathcal{B}$udini di Sicilia
(Sicilian Puddings)

We Sicilians have always had a great affinity for puddings. No one describes this esteem better than Giuseppe Tomasi di Lampedusa in his great novel, *The Leopard.*

At the end of the meal appeared a rum jelly. This was the Prince's favorite pudding, and the Princess had been careful to order it early that morning in gratitude for favors granted. It was rather threatening at first sight, shaped like a tower with bastions and battlements and smooth slippery walls impossible to scale, garrisoned by red and green cherries and pistachio nuts; but into its transparent and quivering flanks a spoon plunged with astounding ease. By the time the amber-colored fortress reached Francesco Paolo, the sixteen-year-old son, who was served last, it consisted only of shattered walls and hunks of wobbly rubble. Exhilarated by the aroma of rum and the delicate flavor of the multicolored garrison, the Prince enjoyed watching the rapid demolishing of the fortress beneath the assault of his family's appetites.

Dolce al Cucchiaio

(Cream and Fruit Pudding)

½ recipe Crema Pasticciera
    (page 273)
2 cups crumbled butter biscuits
    or cookies (not too sweet)—
    sometimes we use Pasta
    Frolla dough (page 274) to
    make little cookies if we
    have none in the house
1 cup canned crushed pineap-
    ple, very well drained
½ cup chopped mixed fruit or
    berries
2 tablespoons Cognac
¼ cup Amaretto
2 tablespoons gin (for the taste
    of the juniper)
2 tablespoons Cointreau
1 tablespoon white rum
½ cup semisweet chocolate
    pieces
½ cup chopped walnuts
Unsweetened cocoa powder

*M*amma invented this superb, liquor-laced pudding recipe a long time ago. She says it is my recipe now, because I am the only one who prepares it for the restaurant these days. Drinking our espresso together at 6:00 a.m., she issues my work instructions for the day, "Giovanna, you must prepare four of your double-sized Dolce al Cucchiaio this morning. Forty-five people are expected for lunch." Of course, it was I who had shopped for the ingredients for the puddings the day before, but I like the daily morning ritual of Mamma's commands.

This simple pudding is a wonderful dessert to serve for a dinner party of 10 to 12 people. Just double the recipe. The pudding can be conveniently cooked in the morning and kept refrigerated until just before it is served in the evening. It's good the following day, too.

Serves 6

Prepare the Crema Pasticciera according to the directions. When it has thickened, remove from the heat. Stir in the biscuits, fruit, and liquors. Cook, stirring constantly, for about 5 minutes.

Pour the pudding into a shallow bowl. Let it cool for 30 minutes. Refrigerate the pudding for several hours, until it is completely chilled.

Just before serving, sprinkle the top evenly with the chocolate pieces, walnuts, and cocoa powder—the surface should be completely covered with cocoa powder. Serve individual portions with a large spoon.

Budino di Ricotta

(Lemon and Ricotta Pudding)

Serves 6

Preheat the oven to 350°F.

Beat the drained ricotta vigorously in a large bowl with a wooden spoon. Stir in the egg yolks, almonds, cinnamon, sugar, and lemon rind.

Lightly grease a 3-cup mold with butter and coat with bread crumbs. Turn the pudding into the mold. Set the mold into a pan with hot water that comes halfway up the side of the mold like a bain-marie.

Bake in the preheated oven for 30 minutes, or until set. Remove from the oven and completely cool the pudding.

Invert onto a serving dish and unmold. Serve with whipped cream and cookies.

1¼ pounds drained ricotta (see instructions on page 39)
2 large egg yolks
½ cup chopped blanched almonds
¼ teaspoon cinnamon
¼ cup sugar
Finely grated rind of 1 lemon
Sweet butter and dried bread crumbs, for greasing and coating the pan
Whipped cream
Cookies

Crema di Bucce di Limone con Frutta

(Molded Lemon Peel Cream with Fruit)

*T*his is a delightfully refreshing lemon dessert to present at the end of a special dinner. We think the lemon mold surrounded by beautiful fresh fruit is enchanting. Preparation begins a day ahead.

Serves 8

Grate the zest of each lemon. Put the zest into a bowl with 1 quart of tepid water and leave at room temperature for 5 hours. (The recipe will require only 1 tablespoon of freshly squeezed lemon juice, so save the remaining lemons for another use.)

Pour the water through a very fine strainer—or one lined with a double thickness of cheesecloth—into a nonreactive saucepan. Stir in the sugar and vanilla.

Remove 1 cup of the lemon water and mix it with the cornstarch. Return the lemon water to the saucepan and slowly bring to

5 large lemons
¾ cup cornstarch
1¼ cups sugar, plus extra for the fruit
1 teaspoon vanilla extract
6 cups mixed fresh fruit—green and red grapes, blueberries, blackberries, raspberries, pitted cherries, sliced pineapple, peaches or plums, melon balls, raspberries. Any fruit you like can be used, but no apples or bananas, because they discolor.

Crema di Bucce di Limone con
Frutta (cont.)

1 tablespoon freshly squeezed
    lemon juice
Mint sprigs (optional)

a boil, whisking constantly. When thickened, remove it from the heat.

Pour into a 1-quart ring mold premoistened with water. Let rest for 1 hour, then refrigerate. The mold must be refrigerated overnight.

Just before serving the dessert, gently toss the mixed fruit in a large bowl with the remaining ½ cup of sugar. Sprinkle with the freshly squeezed lemon juice and toss again.

Dip the lemon mold, just up to the edge, in a larger bowl of hot water for 5 seconds. Put a large, round serving dish, several inches wider than the diameter of the mold, on top of the mold and, holding both securely, invert the dishes. Give the mold a good shake. It should release easily onto the dish.

Fill the hole in the center with a cup or so of the fruit. Spoon the remaining fruit around the mold. You can garnish the dish with mint sprigs, if you like. Serve at once.

Prugne Secche di Betty

(Betty's Dried Spiced Prunes
with Red Wine)

Serves 6

1¼ pounds pitted prunes
½ cup dry red wine
2 tablespoons sugar
Peel of ½ orange
1 clove
¼ teaspoon ground cinnamon
Vanilla ice cream

Heat all the ingredients with ½ cup of water in a small saucepan and bring to a boil. Reduce the heat and simmer for 10 minutes.

Turn into a bowl and let it cool completely.

Discard the orange peel and serve at room temperature. If you like, serve the prunes with vanilla ice cream.

Datteri con Pasta di Mandorle

(Dates Filled with Almond Paste)

Mamma loves these little date-stuffed confections. She says they are so delicious that they can sweeten the conversation during an argument.

The spinach in the recipe produces a green-colored cooking water that colors the almond paste.

Makes 30 to 40, depending on the size of the dates

Put the spinach in a saucepan with ½ cup of water and steam it for 10 minutes. Place the spinach in a clean dish cloth and wring out 1 tablespoon of green cooking water. If you used spinach, reserve it for another purpose.

Chop the almonds in a food processor to a very fine grain.

Put the almonds, sugar, Cognac or brandy, and green spinach water (or green food-coloring water) in a large, nonstick frying pan and cook over low heat about 10 minutes, stirring constantly.

Remove from the heat and turn onto marble that has been lightly sprinkled with water.

Make an incision along the side of each date from the stem to the opposite end. Fill each with about 1 rounded teaspoonful of the almond paste. After the dates are filled, roll them in enough granulated sugar to completely cover the date and the stuffing.

FILLING

¼ pound fresh spinach leaves, or 2 drops of green food coloring

3 cups whole blanched almonds

3 cups granulated sugar, plus more for covering the dates

2 teaspoons Cognac or brandy

30 large pitted dates

Bocconcini

(Coffee-Flavored Almond Balls)

*T*hese sweet coffee-flavored almond morsels are prepared in exactly the same manner and with the same ingredients as the previous recipe for Datteri con Pasta di Mandorle, except that no dates are used and the Cognac and spinach water are replaced in the recipe with 3 tablespoons of strong espresso.

Makes about 30 balls

After the coffee-flavored almond mixture has cooled enough to be handled, rounded teaspoonfuls of the mixture are rolled to form little balls and are then coated with granulated sugar.

Croccante di Mandorle

(Almond Brittle)

Sunflower or vegetable oil
4 cups sugar
1 pound whole almonds,
    skinned
2 tablespoons honey
1 lemon, cut in half and seeded
½ cup pistachio nuts, finely
    chopped

*A*lso known as *torrone,* Croccante di Mandorle is well loved in Sicily. Hazelnuts can be used instead of the almonds.

Makes about 2 pounds

Generously coat a jelly-roll sheet with sunflower or vegetable oil and set aside.

In a large, heavy-bottomed saucepan, melt the sugar over very low heat, stirring it often with a wooden spoon. When the sugar is half melted, stir in the almonds and honey. Increase the heat to medium and stir frequently, until all the sugar has melted and turned a caramel color. Take care not to allow it to burn.

Working very quickly, turn the mixture onto the oiled jelly-roll sheet and use the lemon halves to spread it evenly across the pan. (Don't squeeze the juice out of the lemons.)

Immediately sprinkle the top with the pistachio nuts and let cool completely.

Remove the large piece of brittle from the pan and place it onto a cutting board. Break it into 2- to 3-inch pieces with a cleaver or strong knife.

Store the brittle in a biscuit tin or a plastic container. It can be kept in the freezer.

Gelato di Ricotta

(Ricotta Ice Cream)

1½ cups drained ricotta (see instructions on page 39)
¾ cup sugar
Pinch of salt
½ cup heavy cream
½ teaspoon vanilla extract

*C*reamy and delicious Gelato di Ricotta is very popular in southern Sicily, especially in Siracusa. At the enormous Greek theater of this ancient city, where live performances of Greek tragedies are often given, there is a little stand at the entranceway that sells only Gelato di Ricotta. Before entering the theater, people traditionally buy some to take inside and enjoy before their predictable crying begins during the performance. We like to think that if you have gelato first, the tears will not be salty, but sweet.

Makes about 3 cups of gelato

Combine the ricotta, sugar, and salt well. Pass it through a sieve or food mill and put it into a large bowl. Stir it very well with a wooden spoon.

Fold in the cream and vanilla. Spoon this mixture into an ice-cream maker and follow manufacturer's directions for making ice cream. If you don't have an ice-cream maker, turn the mixture into a shallow bowl or dish and put it into the freezer. Stir the mixture every 30 minutes until it completely freezes.

Semifreddo di Caffè

(Frozen Coffee Cream)

3 large eggs, separated
1 cup sugar
2 tablespoons instant espresso
2 cups heavy cream
Sweet biscuits

*M*y father was especially fond of the flavor of coffee and loved this recipe. It's really very easy to make, but must be kept in the freezer and stirred every 30 minutes for about 3 hours. —G.T.

Serves 4 to 6

Beat the whites until stiff and set aside.

Put the egg yolks and sugar in the bowl of a food processor and let it run for 4 seconds. Add the instant espresso and process for 3 seconds, then pour the cream through the feed tube in a slow, steady stream.

Transfer to a large bowl.

Fold in the egg whites and turn the mixture into a 3-cup loaf pan. Put into the freezer. Stir the mixture every hour for about 3 hours, or until solid. When ready to serve, invert onto a plate. Cut into slices and serve with sweet biscuits.

Sofficini

(Fried Pastry Stuffed with Sweet Lemon Pastry Cream)

PASTRY

2 cups all-purpose flour
5 tablespoons granulated sugar
¼ cup lard, melted and cooled, or olive oil

FILLING

½ recipe Crema Pasticciera (page 273), well chilled and brought back to room temperature

*H*ere is Mamma's cherished recipe for *sofficini,* served at the end of every meal at Gangivecchio's restaurant. One or more special desserts of the day are always featured on the menu, but a plate of *sofficini* is never missing. Our guests would complain. The crisp little pastry squares, filled with lemon-flavored cream and sprinkled with confectioners' sugar, are devoured by both children and adults the minute they are served. There are never any *sofficini* left over.

As with many of our dishes, the recipe for *sofficini* is really a simple, basic one, but Mamma refused to give out the exact ingredients until the very last day of Michele's last stay here, when we were completing our work on this book. Mamma's mood became very dark when I told her that it was the only recipe missing. "We now must have it." She kept saying, "*Sofficini? Domani!*" Anyway, Mamma finally called me into the kitchen and dictated the recipe. She said, "Since I must give up my treasured recipe, be certain it is right. And place it last in the book." As you can see, we have obeyed her wishes.

Sunflower or vegetable oil, for deep-frying
Confectioners' sugar

Makes about 24 sofficini

To make the pastry, put the flour and granulated sugar into a large bowl and mix it together well with your fingers. Make a hole in the center of the mixture and add the lard or olive oil and 2 table-spoons of water. Work the flour mixture with your hands, adding a little water at a time, until a smooth dough is formed. You will use between ¾ to 1 cup of water. Cover the dough and let it rest for 1 hour.

Divide the dough into 2 pieces and roll each through a manual pasta machine, or use a rolling pin to form very long strips, about 4 inches wide and a little less than ⅛ inch thick.

Put a rounded teaspoonful of Crema Pasticciera in the center of the strips at 2-inch intervals. Fold the dough in half lengthwise, covering the lemon-cream-filled portion, as if you were folding a sheet of paper. Press the outer edges of the dough together, then press the dough down between each of the filled portions with your fingertips. Make 2-inch squares by cutting along the entire length of the pieces of dough with a serrated pastry cutter. Then cut between each filled portion. Three sides of each will have cut sides; the other, a folded-over side.

Heat 3 inches of sunflower or vegetable oil in a deep-sided frying pan until the oil is hot but not smoking. Using a slotted spoon, lower 4 to 6 *sofficini* into the hot oil and cook them until golden brown on both sides. This will take only a few minutes. Drain the cooked *sofficini* on paper towels. When all are cooked, let them cool for 2 minutes. Sprinkle with sifted confectioners' sugar and serve immediately.

NOTE: The recipe is easily doubled.

Quattro Menú di Gangivecchio

(Four Menus from Gangivecchio)

At Gangivecchio, whether in our home dining room or at the restaurant, menus for any occasion, from humble lunches to grand multicourse affairs, are chosen in harmony with the seasons.

The following menus represent each season, featuring meals for the family or for entertaining guests. We have included a typical menu from each of our restaurants: a spring dinner at home, an al fresco summer dinner at the *albergo* at Paolo and Betty's Tenuta Gangivecchio, an autumn Sunday lunch, and a Christmas dinner at the abbey at Gangivecchio.

Aside from these four menus, you will also find samples of special Sicilian menus in this book for the feast served throughout an old-fashioned breadmaking day in the Madonie Mountains (page 259), an elegant supper in Palermo (page 194), and the lunch we prepared for Prince Charles (page 182).

Buon appetito!

∞

Una Cena Primaverile a Casa
(A Spring Dinner at Home)

∞

Carciofi Ripieni
(Artichokes Stuffed with Garlic and Seasoned Bread Crumbs)

Pasta Trinacria
(Spaghetti with Swordfish, Eggplant, and Mint)

Insalata Mista con Pecorino di Betty
(Betty's Mixed Green Salad with Pecorino)

Torta di Mandorle
(Almond Tart with Chocolate Cream)

∞

Una Cena Estiva Fuori alla Tenuta Gangivecchio

(A Summer Outdoor Dinner at Tenuta Gangivecchio)

Frittelle di Fiori di Zucca
(Zucchini Flower Fritters)

Cuddura Patedda
(Fried Dough with Tomato, Anchovy, and Onion Topping)

Orecchiette alla Rucola e Salsa di Pomodoro di Betty
(Betty's Orecchiette with Arugula and Tomato Sauce)

Costate di Maiale con Rosmarino e Vino
(Sautéed Pork Chops with Rosemary and Wine)

Insalata Tricolore
(Green Bean, Potato, and Tomato Salad)

Torta ai Frutti di Bosco di Betty
(Betty's Wild Berry Tart)

Pranzo in una Domenica d'Autunno
a Gangivecchio
(An Autumn Sunday Lunch at Gangivecchio)

Antipasti Rustici:
Panelle *(Chick-Pea Fritters)* • Crostino con Patè di Olive Nere
(Black Olive Pâté on Grilled Bread) • Caponata *(Sweet and Sour Eggplant)*

Casareccia con la Frutta Secca
(Casareccia with Nut Pesto Sauce)

Penne con Agnello e Finocchielli in Salsa
(Penne with Lamb and Fennel in Tomato Sauce)

Involtini alla Benedettina
(Veal Rolls Stuffed with Ham, Provolone, and Pecorino)

Brasato di Sparacelli
(Braised Broccoli with Black Olives and Anchovies)

Sofficini
(Fried Pastry Stuffed with Sweet Lemon Pastry Cream)

Dolce al Cucchiaio
(Cream and Fruit Pudding)

Cena di Natale
(Christmas Dinner)

Arancinette
(Little Rice Croquettes)

Polpette di Sarde
(Sardine Balls)

Crêpes con Ricotta e Salsa di Finocchietto di Betty
(Betty's Crêpes with Ricotta and Fennel Sauce)

Anelletti al Forno
(Baked Timbale of Anelletti with Veal and Vegetables)

Filetto in Casseruola con Cognac
(Fillet of Veal Cooked in a Casserole with Cognac)

Broccoli Gratinati
(Au Gratin of Cauliflower)

Insalata di Natale II
(Christmas Salad with Oranges, Olives, and Capers)

Datteri con Pasta di Mandorle
(Dates Filled with Almond Paste)

Cassata al Forno di Ricotta
(Ricotta Cake)

Croccante di Mandorle
(Almond Brittle)

*L*a Prima Poesia a Gangivecchio

(The First Poem at Gangivecchio)

I had never written a poem before I came to Gangivecchio. The place awakened something in my soul—a mysterious desire to express my feelings in verse. I have written many poems since then, but this first one remains dearest to me.

W.T.

TI RICORDI 1949?
(Do You Remember 1949?)

And here I came when I was twenty-one.
I arrived late morning, at the beginning of the sweet season
When sunlight touched the heart and left the body mute and still,
Hands limp in lap, head lowered in contemplation.
Dreamlike thoughts, suspended in the wind by trickling water among
    the stones and grass,
By oaks and laurel and black cypress's crinkled leafy branches
Swirling out the green perfume of flowers from high above
Of beautiful nature speaking for God.
Each day since, nature molds my being, repetitious, yet faithfully
    revealing surprise.
I spy on nature when it wakes up.
I listen to it when it whispers at first dawn.
I listen to it when it sings through the voice of birds.
When it cries silent rain and whistles in angry wind,
When it falls asleep in shades of graying dusk—grayed by the vesper.
It awakens me with thoughts of pain and joy, the realities of my life.
When tranquil, I meld with nature.

Indice

(Index)

casserole
> potato
>> and fava bean, 239
>> with tomatoes and
>> anchovies, 228
> veal, with Cognac, 171

casseruola, filetto in, con cognac,
171

Castagna pasta mill, 130

cauliflower
> au gratin, 227
> pasta with currants, pine
> nuts, and, 105
> salad, with lemon juice, 255

cayenne pepper, 30

cazzili di patate, 46–7

ceci
> *minestra di*
>> *con pasta, 83*
>> *tuoni e fulmini, 87*
> *panelle, 48–9*

cernia al forno, 207

Charles, Prince of Wales, 182–4

cheese, 28
> baked potato pie with,
> 230
> caciocavallo
>> chicken breasts stuffed
>> with pancetta and, 187
>> sardines stuffed with fresh
>> bread and, 208
> local production of, 178–9
> mozzarella
>> pasta with, 118–20
>> rice croquettes stuffed
>> with béchamel, ham,
>> and, 146–7
>> veal stuffed with mor-
>> tadella and, 165
> Parmesan
>> eggplant Parmigiana, 223

cheese (*cont.*)
> gratin of mushrooms with
> ham, pecorino, and,
> 236
> rind, 82
> saffron risotto with,
> 143–4
> sardines stuffed with fresh
> bread and, 208
> pasta with eggplant, toasted
> bread crumbs, and,
> 119–20
> pecorino, 179
>> gratin of mushrooms with
>> ham, Parmesan, and,
>> 236
>> mixed green salad with,
>> 252
>> risotto with spinach and,
>> 154
> provolone
>> chicken breasts stuffed
>> with pancetta and, 187
>> risotto with spinach and,
>> 154
> ricotta, 39, 179
>> cake, 276
>> cream, 274
>> cannoli cream, 281–3
>> crêpes with fennel sauce
>> and, 64–5
>> fritters, 283, 284
>> gnocchi, lemon-flavored,
>> with sage butter, 63
>> and ham tart, 57
>> ice cream, 293
>> pasta with, with mint and
>> thyme, 107
>> ravioli stuffed with, 98–9
> ricotta salata, pasta with egg-
> plant and, 114

cheese (*cont.*)
> timbale of veal and vegeta-
> bles with, 132
> zucchini with ham and, au
> gratin, 225

chicken
> braised with potatoes,
> 186–7
> breasts
>> sautéed with spinach,
>> 186
>> stuffed with smoked
>> pancetta and basil,
>> 187
> legs and thighs, baked with
> tomatoes and onions,
> 185
> roast, with rosemary, 184–5
> salad, 267

chick-pea(s)
> flour, 27
> fritters, 48–9
> soup
>> with cabbage, 87
>> with pasta, 83

chicory, puréed fava beans
> with, 241–2

chiodi di garofano, 30

chocolate
> cake, unbaked, 286–7
> pastry cream, 273
>> almond tart with, 278

Christmas salad, 269
> with oranges, olives, and
> capers, 268

cicoria, purè di fave con,
241–2

cinnamon, 30

cioccolato
> *crema di, 273*
> *dolce di, 286–7*

meat (*cont.*)

  lamb

    fricassee au gratin, 180–1

    kidneys braised in red
      wine sauce, 181

    pasta with fennel and, in
      tomato sauce, 136

    stew, with rosemary and
      red wine, 180

  pasta with vegetables and,
    139

  pork

    braised in milk, 177

    casserole of turkey, veal,
      vegetables, and, 188

    with Marsala, garlic, and
      herbs, 175

    pasta with, 133, 135,
      137–8

    sausages, baked with
      potatoes and tomatoes,
      176

    sautéed with rosemary
      and wine, 175–6

    rice ball croquettes stuffed
      with, 145

  veal, 163–74

    baked chopped steaks,
      with pizza sauce, 174

    casserole, 171, 188

    cutlets with tomatoes and
      parsley, 166

    kebabs, 168

    medallions stuffed with
      mortadella and moz-
      zarella, 165

    pasta with, 132–5

    with pearl onions,
      173–4

    with puréed vegetable
      sauce, 169

meat (*cont.*)

    risotto timbale filled with,
      147–8

    rolls, stuffed with ham,
      163–4

    stew, 167, 173

    stuffed, 164–5

meatballs, veal and pork, 172

melanzane, 28, 51

  alla parmigiana, 223

  caponata, 44–5

  fricassea di, 221–2

  in agrodolce, 222

  involtini di, al forno, 50

  pasta con, e ricotta salata,
    114

  pasta con, e zucchine, 112

  polpette di, 41

  ripiene, 61–2

  sott' aceto, 71

mellone, torta di gelo di,
  278–9

melograni, 251

  rucola con pinoli e, 251

menta, 27

  pasta con ricotta, timo e, 107

menú

  cena di Natale, 301

  cena estiva fuori, 299

  cena primaverile a casa, 298

  *pranzo in domenica
    d'autunno*, 300

milk croquettes, 47

mezzaluna, 24

minestre, 72–87

  di ceci con pasta, 83

  di fagioli con pasta, 80

  di lenticchie e ditalini, 77

  *pasta con finocchietti in
    brodo*, 79

  di patate con pasta, 83

minestre (*cont.*)

  pesce in brodo con pasta, 86

  di riso in brodo, 84–5

  tuoni e fulmini, 87

  u'maccu, 75–8

  di verdure fresche, 81

  di zucchine con spaghetti, 78

mint, 27

  and garlic sauce, 200

  pasta with ricotta, thyme,
    and, 107

mollica, 121

  pasta con acciughe e, 129

Mollica, Vincenzo, 232,
  260–2

mortadella, veal stuffed with
  mozzarella and, 165

mozzarella

  pasta with

    with eggplant and toasted
      bread crumbs, 119–20

    with tomato cream sauce
      with basil, 118

  rice croquettes stuffed with
    béchamel, ham, and,
    146–7

  veal stuffed with mortadella
    and, 165

mushrooms

  ferla, 234–5

  gratin of, with ham, Parme-
    san, and pecorino
    cheeses, 236

  pasta with shrimp and, in
    béchamel sauce, 128

  preserved, 70

  risotto with, 149–50

  sautéed with garlic and
    onions, 234

mussels

  au gratin, 213

pasta (*cont.*)

   with lamb and fennel in
      tomato sauce, 136

   with meat and vegetables,
      139

   with mozzarella and tomato
      cream sauce with basil,
      118

   with nut pesto sauce, 102–3

   with pancetta

      and fresh fava bean
         cream sauce, 108

      and tomato and hot pep-
         per sauce, 115–16

   with *picchio pacchio* sauce,
      122

   with pork

      sauce, 135

      and peas in tomato sauce
         au gratin, 137–8

   with prosciutto, spinach, and
      peas, 138

   ravioli stuffed with ricotta,
      98–9

   with ricotta, mint, and
      thyme, 107

   salad

      with tuna, peppers, and
         mint, 257–8

      with tuna and black
         olives, 259

   with sardines, 124

   with scallions, 110

   with seafood, 127–8

      baked in foil, 126–7

   with shrimp and onions,
      126

   soup with

      fava bean and fennel,
         75–6

      fennel in broth, 79

pasta (*cont.*)

   lentil, 77

   zucchini, 78

   with spinach

      and escarole, 110–11

      and pancetta, 123

   with swordfish, eggplant,
      and mint, 125

   timbale

      with veal and vegetables,
         132

      with veal, pork, and fen-
         nel, 133

   with tomatoes, black olives,
      and capers, 117

   with tuna roe, 131

   with veal sauce, 135

   with yellow and red pepper
      cream sauce, 106

   with zucchini

      and eggplant with herb
         sauce, 112

      and tomatoes and pine
         nuts, 114–15

pasta frolla, 274–5

   piccante, 275

pasta reale, 5

pasticcerie, 272

pastry

   cream, 273

      sweet lemon, 294-5

   dough, 274–5

   fritters, filled with sweetened
      ricotta, 284–5

   lard in, 38

patate

   cazzili o crocchè di, 46–7

   gatto' di, 230–1

   ad insalata, 254

   minestra di, con pasta, 83

   novelle in umido, 231

patate (*cont.*)

   orribili, di Vincenzo, 232

   *pasticcio di, con cinque for-
      maggi*, 230

   di Peppe, 229

   salsiccia con pomodori e,
      176

   a sfincione, 228

pâté

   black olive, 66

   green olive, 65

   tuna, 66

patè

   di olive bianche, 65

   di olive nere, 66

   di tonno, 66

peas

   pasta with

      with artichokes, 111

      with pork and tomato
         sauce, au gratin, 137–8

      with prosciutto and
         spinach, 138

      timbale of veal and, 132

   risotto ring covered with
      ham and, 148

pecorino

   insalata mista con, 252

   risotto con spinaci e, 154

pecorino, 179

   gratin of mushrooms with
      ham, Parmesan, and,
      236

   mixed green salad with,
      252

   risotto with spinach and,
      154

pepe nero, 30

peperoni

   *con capperi e olive nere al
      forno*, 237

A NOTE ABOUT THE AUTHORS

Wanda Tornabene and her daughter, Giovanna, live in the interior Madonie Mountains in Gangivecchio, Sicily, in a restored fourteenth-century Benedictine monastery, where they have operated a restaurant since 1978. The Tornabenes opened a nine-room albergo with a second restaurant, called Tenuta Gangivecchio, on the property in 1992. Tenuta Gangivecchio is run by Wanda's son, Paolo, and daughter-in-law, Betty.

Michele Evans is the author of thirteen previous cookbooks, and is also a travel writer. Her *Caribbean Connoisseur: An Insider's Guide to the Islands' Best Hotels, Resorts, and Inns* is in its third edition. She and her husband, Tully Plesser, are residents of St. Thomas, Virgin Islands.

A NOTE ON THE TYPE

This book was set in Adobe Garamond. Designed for the Adobe Corporation by Robert Slimbach, the fonts are based on types first cut by Claude Garamond (c. 1480–1561). Garamond was a pupil of Geoffroy Tory and is believed to have followed the Venetian models, although he introduced a number of important differences, and it is to him that we owe the letter we now know as "old style." He gave to his letters a certain elegance and feeling of movement that won their creator an immediate reputation and the patronage of Francis I of France.

Composition and color separations by
North Market Street Graphics,
Lancaster, Pennsylvania
Printed and bound by
Quebecor Printing, Martinsburg, West Virginia
Designed by Virginia Tan